WHITE DIASPORA

CATHERINE JURCA

White Diaspora

THE SUBURB AND
THE TWENTIETH-CENTURY
AMERICAN NOVEL

PRINCETON UNIVERSITY PRESS

PRINCETON AND OXFORD

Library of Congress Cataloging-in-Publication Data

Jurca, Catherine, 1964–

White Diaspora : the suburb and the twentieth-century American
novel / Catherine Jurca.

p. cm.

Includes bibliographical references and index.

ISBN 0-691-05734-6 (cl.)

ISBN-0-691-05735-4 (pbk.)

1. American fiction—20th century—History and criticism.

2. Suburban life in literature. 3. Whites in literature. I. Title.

PS374.S82 J87 2001

813'.509321733—dc21   00-058881

This book has been composed in Sabon

The paper used in this publication meets
the minimum requirements of
ANSI/NISO Z39.48-1992 (R1997)
(*Permanence of Paper*)

www.pup.princeton.edu

Printed in the United States of America

10   9   8   7   6   5   4   3   2   1

10   9   8   7   6   5   4   3   2   1
(pbk.)

CONTENTS

ACKNOWLEDGMENTS

MANY PEOPLE have, in various ways, helped me in the writing of this book. First, I would like to thank my teachers at Johns Hopkins, especially Walter Benn Michaels, Neil Hertz, and Ron Walters, and readers and friends from graduate school: Mark Cañuel, Tim Dean, Graham Finlay, Jared Gardner, Claudia Klaver, JoAnne Mancini, Sandra Macpherson, Sharon Marcus, Jim Sidbury, and Mike Szalay. At Caltech, through their shrewdness as scholars and generosity as colleagues, Kevin Gilmartin and Stacey Margolis in literature, and Bill Deverell, Dan Kevles, and Robert Rosenstone in history sharpened the book manuscript and taught me the advantages of working in an interdisciplinary humanities program. I am grateful as well to other colleagues here and elsewhere who read the manuscript in part or in its entirety or conversed with me about it, and whose questions, criticisms, and encouragement improved it and energized me: Sara Blair, Bill Brown, Frances Ferguson, Jonathan Freedman, Dori Hale, Andrew Hoberek, Howard Horwitz, Amy King, Jeff Knapp, Mac Pigman, Ross Posnock, Gabi Starr, Cecelia Tichi, Jen Travis, and Chris Wilson. I also wish to thank Bill Sharpe and Peggy Ellsberg, the instructors of a 1998 National Endowment for the Humanities Summer Seminar on ethnicity and identity in New York at Barnard, and participants Gabrielle Ibieta, Stephen Knadler, and Amitava Kumar, who persuaded me to keep the title. At Princeton University Press, Mary Murrell made the publication process straightforward and surprisingly pleasant, and I also thank Deborah Malmud for her enthusiastic efforts on my behalf. Friends provided me with much-needed distractions and support—Meg and Paddy Kearns, Christiane Orcel, Jay Polk, Hilbert Shin, Elizabeth Shipley, Tom Turnbull, and Youlee You—as did my family: Sonja Cave and Joe Jurca, Merrill and Victoria Berkley, Chris, Jennifer, Heather, Benjamin, Tori, Justin, and Zachary.

There are three people without whom this book would not have been written. Cindy Weinstein, my compatriot in American literature at Caltech, read the manuscript in all its incarnations and gave me crucial comments, advice, and reassurance at every point. Joanne Wood, my Long Island doppelgänger, saw me and the project through from dissertation to book and kept me going as my best reader and friend. To Mark Rigstad, who was always as eager to hear me babble about the suburbs as to contrive ways to make me forget them, my warmest thanks.

While researching and writing this book I received financial support from the Newberry Library, the National Endowment for the Humanities, and Caltech. I am grateful for permission to reprint here previously published material. Portions of chapter 1 appeared as "Tarzan, Lord of the Suburbs," in *Modern Language Quarterly* 57 (copyright 1996 by University of Washington), and chapter 5 as "The Sanctimonious Suburbanite: Sloan Wilson's *The Man in the Gray Flannel Suit*," in *American Literary History* 11 (copyright 1999 by Oxford University Press).

WHITE DIASPORA

INTRODUCTION

THE WHITE DIASPORA

EDITH WHARTON'S "The Great American Novel," a review essay published in 1925, lauds the expansive "scenes and settings" of nineteenth-century American literature while it denounces the "narrow" "social and geographical limitations" of its modern counterpart.[1] Where, for example, the tropics had afforded Melville "the freest range to [his] invention" (653), twentieth-century novelists were imaginatively fettered by what she called the "Main Street" (647) phenomenon. For Wharton, "Main Street" signified American provincialism in general rather than the village ethos per se; that is, it expressed the literary privileging of "the common mean of American life anywhere" (649) in the United States, at the expense of more differentiated, international, and urbane sites of experience. But Wharton reserved harshest judgment for an environment that she initially excluded from her inventory of conventional literary settings: "its million cities and towns, its countless villages and immeasurable wildernesses" (649). She suggested that in seeking to create a "typical" (646) portrait of modern American life, novelists had developed a deplorable obsession with "the little suburban house at number one million and ten Volstead Avenue" (655), the essay's most pronounced icon of literary failure:

> Inheriting an old social organization which provided for nicely shaded degrees of culture and conduct, modern America has simplified and Taylorized it out of existence. . . . [S]he has reduced relations between human beings to a dead level of vapid benevolence, and the whole of life to a small house with modern plumbing and heating, a garage, a motor, a telephone, and a lawn undivided from one's neighbor's.
>
> Great as may be the material advantages of these diffused conveniences, the safe and uniform life resulting from them offers to the artist's imagination a surface as flat and monotonous as our own prairies. (650)

Wharton complained that "the whole of [American] life" had been reduced to the material artifacts of the good life; she further indicated that novelists who represented that diminishment were in fact participating in it. Contemporary writers had so confined their attention to national "baseness in the midst of plenty" (648) that they reproduced the very sterility they sought to critique and combat. The Main Street "theme" (648) had become "a canon, a first principle in the laws of American fiction" (649), and the American novel would never be great so long as it explored, and thus ensured, the absence of "*nuances*" (650), of "nicely shaded degrees" and differences, a lack that is constitutive of a "middling," "middle class" (651) existence as embodied in the mundane machinery of the small suburban house.

This book takes as its subject the suburban literary tradition that Edith Wharton identified here and tried to thwart. Her failure to dislodge "the little suburban house" from the twentieth-century American novel is evident from even a cursory glance at some of the writers who have turned it to account: Sinclair Lewis, James M. Cain, Sloan Wilson, Richard Yates, John Updike, Frederick Barthelme, and Richard Ford. The suburb has remained uncharted literary territory only among critics, while for decades the city has enjoyed, in Wharton's own novels among others, significant scholarly favor as the complex generative location of realism, modernism, and, more recently, ethnic and African American literatures.[2] By contrast, "The Great American Novel" identified an emergent suburban "canon," established its preoccupations as insuperable deficiencies, and so undermined the possibility of canonical consideration by setting the terms on which it could be ignored: its dedication to analysis and critique over aesthetics, its tropes of typicality and "mediocrity" (651), its focus on the "safe, shallow, and shadowless" (650). My aim is less to refute or prove the charges against this literature than to analyze the assumptions that sustain them and the kind of novels Wharton repudiates: the suburb is the exemplary location, not only of middle-class advantages, but of middle-class abasement; moreover, its abasement is a function of its advantages. The material benefits, however "great," are cultural and spiritual handicaps. For Wharton, the fully loaded suburban house is intrinsically inimical to meaningful literature because it precludes a meaningful life.

More generally, this study examines the tendency in twentieth-century literary treatments of the American suburb to convert the rights and privileges of living there into spiritual, cultural, and political problems of displacement, in which being white and middle class is imagined to have as much or more to do with subjugation as with social dominance. I trace two distinct but contingent narrative patterns. The first marks the systematic erosion of the suburban house as a privileged site of emotional connection and stability. It undoes the colloquial substitution of the word *home* for *house*, as though only one kind of residence possesses intrinsic affective value, and presumes an almost automatic discrepancy between material and spiritual shelter, structure and sentiment, suburban house and home.[3] In a paradox that is fundamental to novels about the suburb, white middle-class characters are homeowners, as the expression goes, who are plagued by the problem of "homelessness." *Babbitt* (1922) begins by comparing the protagonist's standardized bedroom to a room in a good hotel and Babbitt to a guest, as Sinclair Lewis laments that "there was but one thing wrong with the Babbitt house: It was not a home";[4] in *Mildred Pierce* (1941), James M. Cain furnishes his protagonists with a department-store living room that they use only for funerals; the first thing we learn about Tom and Betsy Rath in the opening sentence of Sloan Wilson's *The Man in the Gray Flannel Suit* (1955) is that they detest their development house that looks just like all the others; Peter Jernigan claims that he is "into the degradation" of his "God damn tract house" in David Gate's Pulitzer Prize–nominated *Jernigan* (1991).[5] Central to the logic of homelessness is the premise that as the suburban house becomes the primary locus and object of consumption for the white middle class, the artifacts and habits of domestic culture are seen to jeopardize or to destroy the home's emotional texture. Thus, even as an "indigenous ideal of suburban residence and home ownership" has become crucial to and equated with the achievement of the "American dream" in this century, an ongoing strain of the American novel has insisted instead that the suburb and suburban house cheat characters out of the very thing that is supposed to be their white, middle-class, property-owning due.[6]

Like the rise of great industrial cities in the nineteenth century, the dispersal of population to the suburbs in the twentieth century has been one of the most significant social and political facts of modern American life. The novel's intervention into the cultural meanings of this transformation is worth examining, not as it records the experience of actual suburban Americans, but, on the contrary, because it seems to diverge so palpably from that experience, as it has been documented and interpreted by social and cultural historians of American suburbs, housing, and the white middle class. Whether discussing transportation technologies, construction and real estate practices, architecture, or family and social life, these historians have tended to emphasize the traditional role of the suburb in *placing* its residents, physically and emotionally, within changing social and economic orders. According to feminist historians, in the last decades of the industrializing nineteenth century "the cult of home and motherhood . . . reached its pinnacle" in the freestanding, single-family suburban house, which fostered an ideal of the home as private, family-oriented, and nurturing as "an essential aspect of the identity and self-definition of the middle class."[7] The "suburban ideal" described a model of white middle-class community as well as of private domestic life. From the 1880s through World War I, planned suburbs for the affluent, which incorporated technological advances and the health and moral benefits of natural settings, enabled a newly consolidating professional and managerial class (the PMC) to "formalize its life-style and position in society in a suitable residential environment" of single-family houses inhabited by "socially equal, like-minded" neighbors.[8] With the proliferation of attractive sub-urban houses and communities, comfortably removed from the city where the residents' wealth was produced and much of it spent, the PMC ac-tively constructed a confident, prosperous "social identity" based on "consumption, location, homogeneity of family presentation, auton-omy"; in short, the suburb expressed the idea that "a new class" was literally and figuratively "at home with itself."[9]

By the 1920s the suburban home emerged as a crucial symbol of con-sumer prosperity and fulfillment in popular periodical articles, modern advertising, and a national "Own Your Own Home" campaign, spon-sored by the government and business interests. For the first time, popula-tion at the periphery of American cities grew at a faster rate than in the central core, as more middle-class families sought and found in the bur-geoning suburbs what came to be known as "the good life."[10] After the severe abatement of single-family house construction during the Depres-sion and war, mass-produced housing developments exploded in the fif-ties, and the suburban home life of housewives and commuter husbands has generally been regarded as the approximation of a Victorian ideal of domesticity, a "haven in a heartless world," to cite Christopher Lasch's famous and favorable title, or alternatively, an anachronistic "source of meaning and security in a world run amok."[11] In addition, suburban house ownership has provided white residents with substantial material benefits that have continued to place them at an economic and social advantage over nonwhites, whose participation in the housing market has been constrained by racist laws and practices.[12] Current scholarship and opinion polls discover both individual satisfaction and community ties in contemporary American suburbs. As John Stilgoe writes in the introduc-tion to a splendid landscape history of the farthest "borderland" suburbs, for those who live in them or who aspire to, suburbs in general "represent the good life, the life of the dream, the dream of happiness in a single-family house in an attractive, congenial community."[13]

And yet, beginning with *Babbitt*, American novels typically point to the downfall of that dream. Twentieth-century novelists who have written about the suburb present their work as a critique of its culture, and this oppositional gesture, much like Wharton's own attack, is predicated on their disavowal of the very real privileges that the suburb has offered those who live there. One effect of ubiquitous complaints about mass production, standardization, dullness, and conformity, which novelists have developed and refined in the context of a broad-based intellectual resistance to the suburb, is to generate a twentieth-century model of white middle-classness based counterintuitively and, indeed, incredibly on the experience of victimization. The suburban house and its contents are not associated in this literature with the consolations of ownership, with the productive or scandalous function of property to mark, even constitute, identity that has been labeled *possessive individualism* and identified in this century with the ascendance of modern advertising and consumer culture; they signify instead what we might call, by way of reworking Gillian Brown's term for Harriet Beecher Stowe's sense of the proper emotional investment in property, "sentimental dispossession."[14] *Sentimental dispossession* refers to the affective dislocation by which white middle-class suburbanites begin to see themselves as spiritually and culturally impoverished by prosperity. Wharton's scorn for the suburban house came from a position of class and cultural authority far above that domestic establishment, but novels such as *Babbitt*, *The Man in the Gray Flannel Suit*, Barthelme's *Natural Selection* (1990), and Gates's *Jernigan* and *Preston Falls* (1998) consider a similar sort of resistance and contempt to be the inescapable outcome of the residents' self-reflection. Literary representations of the suburb propose that white middle-class identity is not grounded in safe havens or homes but in its alienation from the very environments, artifacts, and institutions that have generally been regarded as central to its affect and identity.

To this point my discussion of the novel has assumed the residential suburb's homogeneity, its achievement of racial and class uniformity. But obviously no story of the suburb would be complete without examining the processes by which such homogeneity is established and enforced. Contests over suburban space provide an important exception to the narrative of alienation. When the focus is on the separation of white suburbanites from people of different races and lower classes, the literary suburb is indeed identified with the placement and prerogatives attendant upon property ownership, the freedom to live where and how one pleases. The practice of self-segregation is not represented as unmotivated exclusion, however, but as a necessary retreat from and defense against a colonizing presence that is metonymically figured as the city. By seeking their own residential freedom, these invaders are imagined to interfere with the inhabitant's basic right to self-determination. Thus I read *Tarzan of the Apes* (1912), by future real estate subdivider Edgar Rice Burroughs, as deeply invested in the racial and class logic of the suburb insofar as the virtually aboriginal white hero is obsessed both with protecting the free-standing beach house that harbors the secret of his Anglo-Saxon heritage from aggressive African savages, and with finding a community of "other white people like himself."[15] In a chapter on *Native Son* (1940) I suggest that the principal site of racial contestation is less the white body of the landlord's daughter than the "quiet and spacious white neighborhood" of Hyde Park–Kenwood, an isolated, affluent suburban enclave on Chicago's South Side, which is, by the novel's publication, just one block from a porous "color line" that Bigger Thomas is driven to cross.[16] Whereas

Tarzan justified the racial and class restrictions of burgeoning suburbs as a defense of residential freedom on the part of besieged white inhabitants, *Native Son* brilliantly dramatized the relation of white flight and freedom to black homelessness and incarceration within the city. I include *Native Son* in this study, furthermore, as a kind of reality check, to gauge through Wright the real injuries inflicted on those who are denied the opportunity to become upwardly mobile in the suburbs.

As the relative eccentricity of this pairing suggests, to talk most explicitly about the dynamics of racial exclusion I have had to turn to novels that deal obliquely, but nonetheless quite powerfully, with the suburb. Most literature written before the 1960s and set in suburbs engages the topic of race only indirectly. The suburb's racial composition is so unremarkable to most white novelists that in general it is indistinguishable from the suburb's middle-classness. In the absence of direct threats to property from those who are kept out, especially through racist covenants and customs, the suburb is not experienced as the freedom to live how and where one pleases, nor is the suburban house considered a thing of value; the racial and class uniformity of the suburb functions instead as the condition of community in which questions about the alienation and insecurity of the white middle class can be safely raised. When suburban characters articulate their freedom, it is because they perceive that freedom to have come under assault. When that freedom seems assured, it is evacuated in favor of emotional and spiritual dispossession.

In describing a population of "homeless" suburbanites as *diasporic*, I invoke the term in an ironic sense and with the intention of exposing the cognitive and rhetorical chicanery by which the privileged come to be seen and to see themselves as the disadvantaged and dispossessed. The diaspora signifies a spatial and sometimes even a temporal disparity between the place one inhabits and that place somewhere else where one imagines one's real home or homeland to be. Displacement is dependent upon a prior fact of physical dispersal, of one's self or one's ancestors. If the psychical dimension of the geopolitical diaspora is about imagining and forging spiritual and cultural connections to the place that you are not, the white diaspora of the suburb is instead about the failure to produce such connections to the place that you are.[17] And given that the places of the white middle class are houses filled with comforts and conveniences, in communities of their own making and choosing, I draw from this literature its conviction that the white middle class is the preeminent casualty of the suburb's affluence and advantages. To put it crudely, this study highlights the ways in which Babbitts begin to think of themselves as Biggers, and suburban novelists come to regard such perceptions as reasonable points of view. The term *white diaspora* is designed to emphasize and lay bare the role of the novel in promoting a fantasy of victimization that reinvents white flight as the persecution of those who flee, turns material advantages into artifacts of spiritual and cultural oppression, and sympathetically treats affluent house owners as the emotionally dispossessed. Such fraudulent identifications are treated as the birthright of the suburbanite and are the hallmark of the suburb's luxury and privilege.

SENTIMENTAL DISPOSSESSION

The suburb is a valuable thematic framework for analyzing the novel because it requires us to revise our current understanding of the home as a gendered fixture in American literature and literary criticism and to rethink the cultural phenomenon of whiteness, particularly as it relates to class; more generally, it affords an opportunity to expand the conventional ways of organizing studies of twentieth-century American literature. Literary scholarship on the home has continued to be confined almost exclusively to nineteenth-century texts and contexts and to the experience of women. Brown's *Domestic Individualism*, to which I have already alluded, represents an important shift in the analysis of the home in the nineteenth-century American novel, from an alternative value system and separate sphere of women's culture within a rapidly industrializing society to an integral site in the development and triumph of an industrial-commercial economy. Brown attends to the role of the home in securing a stable identity for men that enabled them to participate in the market and retain an interiorized or "domesticated" self that was withdrawn from it, but the relation of men to the domestic in her account is more intimately connected with this model of selfhood than with the interior space and routines of the home as such. And Brown's study, like Nina Baym's earlier examination of women's sentimental literature, ends with the late-nineteenth-century transformation of private women into public women, as though the home ceased immediately to be a primary site of either feminine influence and identity or of masculine selfhood.[18]

Further challenges to the spatial and social binaries implied by the concept of separate spheres, which include essays in *The Culture of Sentiment* and a September 1998 special issue of *American Literature*, have focused on the explanatory inadequacy of distinct gendered domains for the complex identifications and experiences of women, who may be divided, even as they are aligned with men, by a host of other factors such as race, class, sexuality, and region. This work has complicated the relation between public and private identities for women of all classes and colors, especially, once again, in the nineteenth century, while it still generally neglects to remap the social and affective geographies of men. The interesting exception that proves the rule is recent literary scholarship on the nine-

teenth-century domestic culture of bachelors. The relation of men to the
emotional and material space of the home is worth considering only when
middle-class wives and mothers are gone from it, when, that is, women
have in effect been replaced by men who occupy an implicitly feminized,
sexually problematic position by virtue of their anomalous domesticity.[19]

My project demonstrates the durability of the home in the twentieth
century as an idealized, because also frequently unactualized, refuge of
security and fulfillment, whose attractions cut across race and class as
well as gender. The home continues to be an insistent object of literary
attention, but more often for its regrettable absence than its proximity or
plenitude, not only for those who are denied its comforts, but even and
most strikingly for those who have always had readiest access to and been
most protected by it. It is not surprising that the facts of racism and class
injustice have inspired a body of novels that address the literal dispossession of male and female immigrants, African Americans, and poor white
migrants: think of *The Jungle* (1906) and the wrenching seizure of the
Rudkus family's small house and equity, into which members have poured
their "souls"; the Joads' expulsion from their land and futile pursuit of
one of "the little white houses among the orange trees" in California; the
temporary thrill of house ownership enjoyed by the Italian family of
Christ in Concrete (1939), just before the breadwinner Geremio is killed
in a construction accident and the house is lost; Lutie Johnson's desire to
move off "the street," that is, out of a tiny, dingy, and insufficiently private
Harlem apartment and into a house like the one she once shared with
her husband, before financial hardship forced her into another family's
domestic service.[20] Where contemporary critics are at pains to emphasize
the differences between representations of the conventional domestic desires of the white middle class and the community-oriented as well as
kinship-focused values of people of other races and classes, these examples invoke correspondences rather than sheer contrasts. The protagonists
of these novels have access to a vision of house ownership as a vehicle of
Americanization and social mobility, a marker of stability, independence,
and respectability, a source of emotional as well as material shelter, even
as the novelists take pains to establish how difficult ownership and its
outcomes are to achieve for the variously outcast. Simply to label these
ways of conceptualizing house and home as *bourgeois* is both to miss how
pervasive these values have become across twentieth-century American
cultures and to ignore as well the ways in which some middle-class attitudes toward houses and homes may be thought to have changed.[21]

My interest in narratives about suburbs and white middle-class homelessness arises in part from their denial of the values and benefits that
powerfully sustain such novels of disenfranchisement. The suburban
house is not merely the setting for dramatic encounters and the resolution

of conflicts; rather, the home itself is the topic, the problem around which many of the novels I focus on revolve. In the context of the suburb, one encounters a male-authored and frequently male-focused body of litera-ture that is obsessed with the meaning and value of home and community, with reassessing the boundaries that separate domestic life from other activities and places, and with exploring the limits and opportunities of a so-called displacement. As a tradition of popular writing about the home, the suburban novel provides a useful lens through which to view an emergent version of a domestically oriented male identity that is at odds with the usual rituals, defensive strategies, and compensatory proj-ects of masculine refurbishing. At its center are men who desperately want the promises of home fulfilled. Thus, in contrast with standard accounts of canonical nineteenth-century and modern literature that rely, as Baym and Lora Romero have argued, on a gendered aesthetic of male alienation from "a feminized realm of domestic familiarity," the alienation of men from the suburban home in the popular novel expresses the *desire for* domestic familiarity.[22] This desire obtains among characters, who seek to reestablish the emotional connection of home, and among novelists, who invoke the home as the measure of the characters' loss. In discovering the deep domestic attachments of a range of literary texts by and about men, including those within genres such as hard-boiled fiction and naturalism, which have traditionally been conceived in opposition to emotional work of any sort, this project indicates how we might begin to reevaluate the arc of the sentimental tradition in the twentieth century.[23] My primary emphasis, though, is not on arguing for the existence or tracing the impli-cations of male sentimentality, but rather on explicating what it means for affect so readily to fail disgruntled men as well as women who live in circumstances for which the Rudkuses, the Joads, Geremio, and Lutie Johnson fight and in some cases die. If living in a suburb means feeling dispossessed, the white middle-class home is reconfigured in the twenti-eth-century novel not only as a desirable site of male affect and identifica-tion, but as an institution that delivers far more in the way of self-pity than gratification.

Before I turn to the significance of self-pity for cultural studies of racial and class identity, it is worth examining the differences between the con-tours of sentimental dispossession and the potential violation associated with the influx of mass-produced commodities into the mid-nineteenth-century home, to clarify the profound inadequacy of the prevailing para-digms for the twentieth century. In Stowe's *House and Home Papers*, for example, when the wife and daughter of the narrator flood the house with sterile commodities in a corrupt redecorating effort, he differentiates between a home filled with well-used, well-loved, and comfortable fur-nishings and a house of formal, fashionable goods that is for looking at, not living in. At stake is the right affective relation of persons to meaningful objects as against the impersonal transactions of the market, and it is telling that Stowe announces through a man's voice that the house ceases to provide sanctuary from the commercial world when it becomes women's conduit to it. But for Stowe's narrator, there is nothing wrong with wanting the house "to appear a little as other people['s] do."[24] Sixty years later the idea that one's house resembles those of "other people" is exactly the concern with mass production in and of the house and the processes of standardization with which it is associated by the 1920s. Once the home has begun to be staked out as the inevitable, indeed natural, territory of consumer culture in advertising, feature articles, and household advice columns, disapproval over commodification per se becomes increasingly irrelevant; the massification of both the home and the middle class is the salient issue.[25]

In other words, houses that contain mass-produced and -consumed goods and department-store living rooms or that are built en masse in post–World War II developments are associated with homelessness not because they have been improperly penetrated by an abstraction called the market. Rather, the association comes through the undesirable multiplication of such houses and furnishings, interiors and exteriors, that look exactly alike. The twentieth-century home is under siege, not from any conventional notion of the public or commercial sphere, but as it has been opened up to other private homes. Warren Susman influentially described the preoccupation with developing and projecting a self that is different from "the crowd" as one of the most significant cultural shifts in twentieth-century American mass society.[26] In objecting to the indignity of having a house that looks like others, the suburban novel suggests that the individuated home is the place where individuated selves are formed and sustained, its role in this process expanding as the economic base of white middle-class men shifts further toward managerial and white-collar employment for others and away from entrepreneurship. Labor historian Gary Cross has argued that suburban house ownership and the independence it seemed to promise became "part of a trade-off" after World War I for the employee's increasing dependence in a bureaucratizing workplace; the American Dream became more closely associated with the chance to "own your own home," rather than "your own" business or the means of production.[27] While *Mildred Pierce* and *The Man in the Gray Flannel Suit* protest against a proliferation of identical houses as impediments to this dream, they also propose a beneficial fluidity between homes and businesses—the home as a commodity that restaurants can produce more effectively than lone housewives can, white-collar values as a model for domestic life. The affinity between middle-class homes and workplaces seems utterly unimaginable if one's primary frame of reference is an outworn tension between home and market.

The representation of the suburb in the American novel points to men's and women's participation in consumer and work cultures; it articulates the relations between individuals and a dense network of local and national affiliations that mass production, standardization, and, by the fifties, the specter of conformity served to clarify and reinforce. Indeed, the literary figure for the exemplary consumer in the 1920s is not a woman, as we would expect, but Lewis's beleaguered businessman, Babbitt, and one result of his consumption practices is the erosion of all boundaries between his Floral Heights house and the houses of his neighbors, who come to be defined in terms of their similarity rather than their proximity to him.[28] Historians of the suburb have tended to emphasize the radical break between the building boom of the 1920s and, following a sharp decline in suburban construction during the Depression and World War II, the national proliferation of large-scale subdivisions in the late forties and the fifties and, again, in the last twenty years or so, the rise of modern, uniform "edge cities" or "technoburbs" of decentralized labor and commercial leisure, as well as living, spaces.[29] I do not want to minimize the tremendous demographic and topographical differences between eras, even decades, of development, but Lewis's vision of a national neighborhood in the early twenties anticipates the unprecedented homogeneity associated with the paths of suburbanization since World War II. "How to tell if one is in suburban Atlanta or Denver or Houston?" Richard Rodriguez wondered in December 1999, as a television camera panned over bland strip malls.[30] Rodriguez's "Where am I?" is an emblematic expression of what we often think of as a definitively postmodern dislocation. Examining its antecedents in the work of Lewis and others allows us to consider important continuities, and not just changes, in ways of thinking about and representing the twentieth-century suburb and suburban house, which is the primary object of my analysis—the suburb as created in and through various discourses, rather than the suburb itself.

Obviously the kinds of suburbs whose depictions I discuss, which include upper-middle- and upper-class East Coast and midwestern garden suburbs, small-scale lower-middle-class subdivisions in southern California, postwar developments modeled after Levittown, and contemporary gated communities, differ significantly from one another. One of my reasons for examining representations of a variety of residential environments is to draw meaningful connections between them in order to understand how and why such a generic term as "the suburb" might have come to stand in for them all. The boundaries between suburbs as well as between houses are long seen to be in flux. Beginning with Lewis, to write about the suburb is to express a constitutive tension between the locally specific and the uniformly unlocatable, in which regions are routinely represented through domestic architecture, artifacts, and landscape to be in the process of absorption into a national suburban totality. The powerful affiliation of writers with particular regions—Lewis and the Midwest; Cain and southern California; Wilson, Updike, and Rick Moody, the Northeast; Barthelme, the South—is necessarily complicated by their contributions to a literary tradition that has by the nature of its preoccupations gone so much against the grain of regional writing.

In covering so much ground, temporally and spatially, this book seeks not only to analyze and synthesize the literature of different regions and genres, but also to move beyond the typical ways of periodizing American literature. If, as I would argue, it is impossible to understand the range and complexity of the suburb's cultural meaning without taking into account the literature that has explored and interpreted white middle-class suburban experience, the suburb also can shape our ideas about twentieth-century literary production by presenting a fuller picture of novelistic convergence and coherence than is available in literary studies set in some more or less discrete portion of the twentieth century. Critics regularly categorize twentieth-century American literature according to fairly rigid periods that promote rupture: turn of the century ending just before or after World War I; the interwar years; postwar; contemporary or postmodern. There is also the momentous decade phenomenon: the prosperous 1920s, the traumatic 1930s, the complacent 1950s, and so on. With the exception of the 1890s, gateway to the modern, only the twentieth century is divided up in this fashion. My study concentrates on the 1890s through 1960; by confining my discussion of post-1960s novels to the epilogue, I may seem to give them unduly short shrift, especially to readers who assume that a study of the suburban novel begins with Updike and Cheever. But I read these novelists and their later incarnations as heirs rather than inaugurators of a tradition; what impresses me are the relative modesty of formal shifts in literary treatments of the suburb and the conspicuous continuities of thematic preoccupation and representational strategy.

EMPTY WHITE PEOPLE

This study also reveals how these representations of suburban life have produced the suburbanite as a kind of sociological label within literature whose contours remain consistent in important ways. In attending to the sociological dimension of this literature, I follow the example of Christopher P. Wilson in *White Collar Fictions*. Wilson not only brings class to the forefront of popular American literature during the early decades of bureaucratization, but he also demonstrates the significance of the "normative," "paradigmatic," and "typical" to literary representations of white middle-class life, to the extent that individuals within an unrepresentative occupational class were regularly made to stand in for the "average" American and their social life for that of the "mass."[31] My recourse to the sociological does not, of course, imply any claims about the statistical pervasiveness of real aggrieved suburbanites, nor about the novel's accuracy in modeling the feelings and habits of actual residents of the suburb. Like Wilson, however, I am interested in the power of cultural representations, specifically, in this case, best-selling novels, to enter into the popular consciousness, to construct imaginative and yet influential worlds to which they frequently claim to be referring.

This power is evident from the way in which suburban novels have been discussed by critics and readers. I am hardly the first to read suburban novels as sociologically important; in reviews and popular references, the significance of *Babbitt*, *The Man in the Gray Flannel Suit*, and the Rabbit novels, among others, has been cast in terms of the truth and utility of their insights into and assessments of American society rather more often than in terms of aesthetics. And in contrast with Wharton, this has been by way of praise as frequently as blame. Between the years when allusions to Babbitts and gray flannel suits took on a life of their own in commentaries about the middle class, *Native Son* was controversially embraced and disputed as a signal contribution to the study of African American urban experience. Even Cain, whose fiction might at first glance seem resistant or irrelevant to this framework, was acclaimed by a reviewer for possessing an "anthropologist's tenacity" in his treatment of suburban culture, and *Mildred Pierce* was cited as a potentially "invaluable gloss on Middletown," the setting for two celebrated sociologies of middle-American life in the 1920s and 1930s.[32] Burroughs had no such intentions for *Tarzan*, at least, that is, until he began to promote the Tarzana subdivision in Los Angeles. Then he drew upon the superiority of community-minded yet self-sufficient white people like Tarzan to conceptualize the ideal suburbanite and neighbor. The novelists as well as many reviewers and other cultural critics understood these novels to be documents freighted with social import, with the exception of *Tarzan*, and to participate in describing, mapping, and molding the cultural meaning of places and people, and here *Tarzan* is relevant, if only after the fact. To read these novels in an informed way, as interventions in the production of a distinctly suburban identity, and thus to retrieve a sense of their currency requires one to attend to the ways in which they reworked and reinvented the ideas and issues that invigorated their historical moment.

To varying degrees, each of the texts I examine directly engages popular and professional discourses about the suburb and frequently the city, which include sociology, architecture and architectural criticism, interior decoration, urban planning, and real estate advertising. Although my chapters are variously structured around individual literary texts, clusters of novels by several authors, and in one instance, the authorial career, I employ a contextualist approach throughout the book in order to explicate and relate diverse cultural representations of the suburb. For me the most interesting feature of the suburban siege mentality in literature lies in its discontinuities with the accounts of suburban habits and habitats offered by other intellectuals, particularly the image of the self-satisfied, even haughty, suburbanite. Harlan Paul Douglass, author of the first full-length sociology of suburbanization as a national trend, observed without prejudice in 1925 that "the suburbanite cherishes a characteristic sense of superiority," just as the suburb was becoming a favorite target among hostile intellectuals who, as Stilgoe has argued, "hated most what they saw as smug satisfaction in 'American ways' " enshrined there.[33] And widespread attacks on the complacency of postwar suburbanites are well known. But the characteristic suburban affect in *Babbitt* and *The Man in the Gray Flannel Suit* involves extremes of discontent rather than satisfaction, pathos not complacency. This substitution may seem self-evident to us now; if so, it is a further tribute to the potential "power" of literature to "becom[e] axiomatic."[34] With *Babbitt*, the dissatisfied suburbanite is basically a literary invention as an American icon, which emerged at a time when stereotypes of the suburb had not yet hardened and its meaning was up for grabs. It continues to sustain contemporary novels of white middle-class dispossession such as Joyce Carol Oates's *Expensive People* (1968), Moody's *The Ice Storm* (1994), and Gates's *Preston Falls*. The enduring popularity of this narrative, with readers as well as writers, and the difficulty of telling other kinds of stories about an environment that has historically been a bastion of racial and class privilege reveal the importance of laments about the suburban house and way of life—of a deeply fraught self-pity—to the meaning of white middle-classness in this century.

The prerogatives and pitfalls of white identity have generated a good deal of commentary in recent years, but to a surprising degree critics have downplayed or ignored the centrality of self-pity to it. Studies of whiteness have been concerned with exposing its invisibility as a racial identity, with demonstrating the centrality of other races to so-called white identity and culture, and with imagining the social and political consequences of making the actual content of a culturally situated whiteness manifest. Richard Dyer, who analyzes cultural representations of whiteness, and Ruth Frankenberg, who studies its sociological construction, have argued with others that to itself whiteness appears to be unmarked, the presumptuous baseline against which the racial presence and hence marginality of others are established. The paradox of whiteness is that its very amorphousness as an identity is understood simultaneously to situate its social privilege and to describe an embarrassing cultural and spiritual banality. It is often experienced as a distressing lack of hipness among people who see themselves as "cultureless": "to be really, absolutely white is to be nothing," to relinquish "fun, 'life.' "[35] Frankenberg observes in passing "white women's mourning over whiteness" (200) as deficiency, and Dyer notes, and is fearful of seeming to contribute to, a "Poor us" (10) refrain, but their interest in describing the signification of whiteness as "apparently empty cultural space" (Frankenberg 192) is primarily to expose it as further evidence of the white normativity and entitlement that prevent whiteness from seeing or naming itself.

By contrast, David Roediger insists unequivocally that in the absence of specific ethnic affiliations, whiteness really is an "empty culture."[36] *Nothing* is its proper name and content. He points hopefully to the popularity of hip-hop music and style among younger white people as both a spontaneous and rebellious alternative to "what passes as white culture" (15) and "an explicit, often harsh, critique of whiteness" (16). Eric Lott develops the relation of African American culture to the construction of white culture and identity to make a different point about their emptiness. Describing "the (b)lack on which whiteness depends," Lott rhetorically mimics the synchronism of white lack and black plenitude that reinforces whiteness as an enduring, constitutive absence even in the process of its creation.[37] Nonetheless, white male working-class appropriations of black cultural forms, whether in the case of nineteenth-century minstrelsy or of Elvis and his impersonators, are retrieved from mere vacancy. They are treated as richly textured and complex white/(b)lack subcultures, in which "racial ambivalence" may also in some instances, according to Lott, hold out the "possibility of radicalism."[38]

It is in the historical and cultural study of the white working class that whiteness studies has been especially influential.[39] Whiteness as an identity and a culture is complicated in ways not yet fully explored when the middle class comes into focus. As the cultural mainstream, the white middle class is unamenable to recuperation through the concept of subcultures.[40] If we recall Wharton's criticisms of a "middling," "middle class" American life, and consider similar rebukes offered in different contexts and periods by intellectuals ranging from Van Wyck Brooks and Lewis Mumford to David Riesman and William H. Whyte, along with various suburban novelists across the century, we see that there is an illustrious tradition of associating the middle class with cultural emptiness and spiritual poverty. It is most apparent in relation to white people and characters, those who have constituted the majority of the middle classes in and out of fiction; indeed, the virtual invisibility of race in *Babbitt*, *Mildred*

Pierce, The Man in the Gray Flannel Suit, and other novels of the suburb, which I do not otherwise belabor in my readings of them, signals not only, obviously, the real absence of African Americans from white suburbs, but also the inclination to see middle-class culture and status as the unique prerogatives, or rather, the unique drawbacks, of nonethnic white people. More than twenty years after *Babbitt*, Lewis devoted a whole novel, *Kingsblood Royal* (1947), to discovering the existence of a black middle class, which he associated with deep cultural reserves and spiritual integrity. But among African American intellectuals the black middle class has of course received its share of scorn as well, most famously in sociologist E. Franklin Frazier's study of the "black bourgeoisie" in the 1950s, but also in the work of such writers as Langston Hughes, Chester Himes, and Gloria Naylor. Only in Naylor's *Linden Hills* (1985), as we shall see, is black middle-classness confident enough in itself to be structured around the feeling, rather than the fear, of dispossession. In contrast with a monolithic idea of empty white culture, then, culturelessness is an evolving concept and complaint that is crucial to the construction and representation of the middle class and flexible with respect to race.

The factor of class further prompts us to reexamine the significance of culturelessness as potentially radical self-critique. Frankenberg mentions briefly that the criticisms of white culture she heard during her fieldwork were often indistinguishable from critiques of the basic features of middle-class life, the privileged but boring class identity and the privileged but boring racial identity essentially fusing in some women's minds.[41] Rather than simply viewing these feelings as further evidence of the invisibility of race or even class, it is worth considering how and why white middle-class self-representations have come to be associated with such excesses of self-pity, as though this population is prostrated by privilege. Novels such as *Babbitt, The Man in the Gray Flannel Suit*, and *Jernigan* pose problems for the assumption that if white people could be made to see how vacuous they are, their identity and affiliations would reorient in progressive ways. In these novels, white middle-class identity is premised on the recognition of its vacuity. Even as protocritiques of the national scale and costs of suburbanization, by emphasizing the fate of the white middle-class home they work to constrain potentially progressive intentions or effects.

George Lipsitz and Lott have observed that the folk cultures of the disenfranchised have provided a resource for combating "the alienation and isolation of bourgeois life, as well as . . . the relentless materialism of capitalist societies."[42] The legitimacy of this point is clear, but I want also to consider instances when the experience of white middle-class alienation has had more to do with self-pity than profound or even trite resistance to capitalist culture. The consumer is easily demonized or pitied as someone for whom mass-produced goods are "sympathetic extensions of self," but perhaps it ought to be more difficult either to extol or commiserate with the affluent consumer for whom mass-produced houses and furnishings reflexively become evidence of and opportunities for alienation.[43] Other scholars have described the place of alienation and victimization in white middle-class self-perception; perhaps most influentially, Jackson Lears has noted the disillusionment that fueled antimodernism at the turn of the century, when "many beneficiaries of modern culture began to feel they were its secret victims."[44] Lears's work explores the emergence of a therapeutic culture that accommodated, rather than challenged, the sources of the middle class's disaffection. David Savran has more recently analyzed the ascendance in contemporary American literature, film, and politics of the angry white male "as victim."[45] On different grounds, Lears and Savran legitimate the experiences of victimization. Savran's text is framed by the concerns of lower-middle- and working-class white men in a downwardly mobile world. The problem is not with their anger but with its misdirection; they mistake women and minorities for the real oppressors. For Lears, a sense of "weightlessness" (32) is the appropriate, if hopelessly inadequate, response among "beneficiaries" of the transformations associated with modern commodity culture and bureaucratization. My own work seeks to supplement rather than supersede these analyses. It suggests, with novelists like Lewis, Wilson, Updike, Ford, and Gates, that perhaps nothing comes more naturally to the affluent white middle class than feeling bad—maltreated, rather than angry or guilty—about being the white middle class.

The mentality of the suburbanite has recently been described by Homi Bhabha in terms of an almost global "fear and loathing," a description that is clearly on the mark as contemporary suburbs evolve toward ever greater insulation, by developing as magic corporate kingdoms (Disney's refuge at Celebration, Florida) and gated communities, where residents are willing to lock themselves in to shut the world out.[46] These long-standing feelings have played an important role in the literary suburbanite's retreat from the city and in the steps taken by white characters to justify their hostility to encroachment in *Tarzan, Native Son,* and Lewis's *Kingsblood Royal.* But I also seek to demonstrate the centrality of an independent *self*-loathing to suburban experience and identity. *White Diaspora* probes the "wounds" (Lipsitz 123) of white middle-class characters and asks whether it makes sense to think of the homelessness represented in popular novels about the suburb, the ground floor of bourgeois alienation as well as affluence, as evidence of empowering rhetorics of victimization, which somehow only seldom manage to be anything but rhetorical.

CHAPTER ONE

Tarzan, Lord of the Suburbs

WHITE SKIN, WHITE HOME

IT IS ONLY NATURAL that Edgar Rice Burroughs's *Tarzan of the Apes*, a novel that so openly endorses imperialist assumptions, has become a bête noire of postcolonial studies. Eric Cheyfitz has argued that *Tarzan* enacts the willful displacement characteristic of American foreign policy in the twentieth century. Imperial violence and the dispossession of colonial subjects are obscured and superseded by the hero's personal identity crisis over the transition from savage ape-man to Lord Greystoke. The triumph of biology, which is figured as linguistic and hence cultural primacy, confirms Tarzan's superiority to blacks, women, and apes and naturalizes the imperialism of Anglo-Saxon men.[1] Marianna Torgovnick emphasizes the novel's "potentially utopian uses of the primitive" to demonstrate the cultural determination of so-called natural identities but also finds that *Tarzan* ultimately affirms racial and gender hierarchies.[2] The answer to Tarzan's possibly liberating question "What does a man do?" is the ominous "[Men] control and subordinate others" (68). For Torgovnick, Tarzan's touching but temporary insecurity initially negates the traditional Western hierarchies that enable and justify the imperialist project, but his eventual "fall into humanity" "implies a permanent fall into the need to master human Others" (72). Tarzan of the apes is readily transformed into Tarzan, lord of the jungle.

But if we are to take *Tarzan* seriously, as Cheyfitz and Torgovnick urge us to do, it should not be as a conventional exemplar of white imperial domination. Tarzan's father is an agent for the British Colonial Office, who sails to Africa with his wife in order to investigate "the unfair treatment of black British subjects" (2) by Belgian officers. John Clayton, Lord Greystoke, never accomplishes his official mission, however; mutineers seize the ship and abandon the couple on an uninhabited section of the West African coast, where "as yet . . . no hardy pioneer from the human beasts" (64) has set foot. Prevented from acting in their colonial capacity, Tarzan's parents are cast instead as originary human residents who inhabit a natively white section of the African coast. *Tarzan* banishes the British imperial context; rather than depict the struggle between white imperial agent and black colonial subject, it insists that the pivotal confrontation is between the son of the rightful white inhabitants and a tribe of unruly newcomers, "savage natives of the *interior*" (64, my emphasis), who threaten to displace and eat him.

Tarzan's enabling myth of settlement, a myth available at least since Robinson Crusoe arrived upon an uninhabited island only to be besieged by outsiders, posits the white European as the target of imperial aggression. The age of empire produced many such narratives, but in *Tarzan* the plot of reverse colonization operates within a distinctively twentieth-century and American context.[3] Domestic troubles erase global imperialist concerns as Lord and Lady Greystoke build, decorate, and leave their son to defend a small cabin on the beach, the real center of the novel's racial friction. Tarzan is ultimately more interested in keeping his black neighbors at bay than in mastering them; he is not driven in this novel by the typical imperialist ambition to control Africa. Uncompromising in its support for the geographic separation of the races, and viewing their integration as a particular danger to the sanctity of the Anglo-Saxon home, *Tarzan of the Apes* begins to look more like a novel of white flight than white rule.

The racial and political issues that *Tarzan* raises are more plausibly understood as domestic, in both senses of the word.[4] In what follows I examine Tarzan's peculiar obsession with the freestanding, single-family house, which harbors the secret of his noble Anglo-Saxon birthright, and his fierce commitment to protecting the home that literally civilizes him from a displaced tribe of savage Africans. Through the violent conflicts between the Africans and Tarzan, whose name means "White-Skin" in the ape language, Burroughs dramatized the perils to which alien expansion and interracial contact were imagined to expose the domestic property and persons of whites. In its commitment to linking discourses about house and home, class and white supremacy, *Tarzan* more specifically reproduces and justifies the emerging exclusionary logic of the twentieth-century American suburb, anticipating in particular the moment when generic fears about the dark-skinned city would become the prospect of black invasion. For this Englishman's home to be his castle, racial and class exclusivity eventually become the better part of domestic solitude.

However counterintuitive a reading of *Tarzan* as a suburban novel may seem, it becomes far more plausible when considered in light of Burroughs's dedication to reproducing the early-twentieth-century suburb's physical as well as logical structure. He converted the early profits from the *Tarzan* series into a southern California estate, which he subdivided and marketed exclusively to white homeowners in the early 1920s. As a literalized community of "White-Skins," the suburb of Tarzana, like the character it was named for, embodied an American commitment to isolat-

ing white skin by isolating white homes. I address the relationship between the novel and the author's subdivision more fully in the final section
of the chapter, but the way into *Tarzan of the Apes* is not through the
African coast or Tarzana; instead, its suburban imperatives are best ap-
proached by way of the American city—its residents, the housing stock,
and their putative savagery—at the turn of the century.

"Suburban or Savage"

While Tarzan was busy making the African jungle safe for civilized white
people, native-born white Americans watched with dismay as a flood of
foreign-looking immigrants from southern and eastern Europe and the
beginnings of black migration cityward created an urban jungle within
the United States. John Higham, a historian of American urban immigration and nativism, has identified the period from 1890 through World
War I with "a new feeling of defilement through contact with what was
dark and unclean."[5] In a monumental quantitative history of nineteenth-
century urbanization, Adna Ferrin Weber argued in 1899 that among immigrants to the United States, the most recent and, according to many
Americans, the "least desirable" were as yet those "most prone to remain
in the great cities."[6] Although Weber pointed to the low mortality rates
and general healthfulness of affluent urban residential areas, rejecting the
idea of "race suicide" among native-born white city dwellers, eugenicists
nonetheless foretold the extinction of the older American stock, alleged to
be subjected in the nation's cities to "an eliminating agency of enormous
efficiency, a present condition that sterilizes and exterminates individuals and lines of descent."[7] Anti-immigrant, antiurban attitudes among
eugenicists treated the American city as a bastion of racial and economic
undesirables, a refuge of the uncivilized; solving its problems meant relocating "the superior elements (not the slum dwellers)" that had already
settled there.[8]

Civilization's battle against savagery during the age of imperialism has
been addressed primarily as a war waged on distant shores, as the white
Western world's justification for the economic exploitation of other people and cultures. Recent studies of the literature and culture of empire
tend to equate the Western metropolitan subject with the imperial subject.
In seeking to uncover what Edward Said calls the "colonial actuality existing at the heart of metropolitan life," they treat the interests and aspirations of the city as indistinguishable from those of the dominant national
culture.[9] When the domestic aspects of urban imperialism are addressed,
the city is still identified with the ruling elite and the forces of national
incorporation. Alan Trachtenberg, for instance, discusses how by the

1890s American cities had "colonized" both the countryside, where they exported goods and imported labor, and suburbs and neighboring industrial towns, which cities held "within their orbit" with "electrified mass transit."[10] According to Amy Kaplan, "[j]ournalists, reformers, and pulp novelists depicted the city as a new frontier or foreign territory to settle and explore and regarded its inhabitants—usually immigrants—as natives to civilize and control."[11] Colonization also took place within the American city and was directed against recent immigrants by native-born whites.

But classifying the urban immigrant working class as uncivilized "natives" obscures some of the objections to the immigrants, namely, that they were not natives at all but rather "foreign elements" who were themselves accused of colonizing and displacing a "native" population.[12] Jacob Riis, a Danish immigrant who nonetheless identified with the native-born middle class for whom he wrote, foregrounded the processes of colonization he believed to be at work in New York City. He complained in *How the Other Half Lives* that less racially desirable immigrants had overrun "the decorous homes of the old Knickerbockers" and the gardens of "the stolid Dutch burgher," a figure that captures in particular Riis's nostalgia for a departed, dislodged, middle-class way of life. Observing a row house of less illustrious lineage that had been converted into a tenement, Riis wondered "what glowing firesides, what happy children may it once have owned? Heavy feet, too often with unsteady step, for the pot-house is next door . . . have worn away the brown-stone steps since; the broken columns at the door have rotted away at the base. Of the handsome cornice barely a trace is left." Here the reformer reserved his primary sympathies for the old house and family rather than the "heavy feet" that had dislocated the previous residents and accelerated the building's decay. Purpose-built and conversion tenements had colonized and virtually crowded the middle-class house out of New York City: "In fifty years [the tenements] have crept up from the Fourth Ward slums and the Five Points the whole length of the island, and have polluted the Annexed District to the Westchester line. . . . The one thing you shall vainly ask for in the chief city of America is a distinctively American community."[13] In Boston, Philadelphia, and Chicago, social workers, reformers, and sociologists similarly noted the transformation of the single-family houses and neighborhoods of the affluent into tenement and lodging-house accommodations for poor urban newcomers.[14] Even as the American city intensified white authority and domination in the national context of industrial capitalism, as Trachtenberg argues, white middle-class Americans and their single-family houses and communities were routinely depicted as endangered urban species.

Houseless white urban middle-class people could either move outward from the city or upward within it. A mode of urban housing imported from Paris, apartment buildings flourished in the United States at the turn of the century, most notably in New York, but also in such cities as Chicago, San Francisco, and Boston, where the first American example, the Hotel Pelham, had been built in 1855. The earliest American apartment buildings catered exclusively to the rich, but those designed for the middle classes had already become a fixture in the urban landscape by the 1880s. Both advocates and critics of apartment life agreed that it signaled a "domestic revolution," which one commentator described as a vaguely sinister, indeed colonizing, trend, "quietly, quickly, permanently extending its influence through all the cities in the United States."[15] For apartment enthusiasts, however, revolution implied "evolution."[16] Bringing multiple families together under a single roof, where they shared public spaces such as entrances, hallways, and lobbies but had separate living quarters, the vertically oriented apartment building marked the productive adaptation of private domestic space and family life to the special exigencies of urban crowding and expense. One particularly favorable response, in the *Architect and Building News*, argued that apartment life also marked the adaptation of human nature to the new urban environment. It attacked "the old and barbarous custom" of inhabiting far-flung private houses; in the "savage state" people could not live "cooperative[ly]," but as "civilization advanced," close proximity to others became no obstacle to enjoying the basic requisites of a private home life: "peace of mind and rest of body."[17] The most recent technological innovations—elevators, gas, electric lighting, fully equipped bathrooms, and vacuum-cleaning systems—were incorporated into building plans and further fueled the equation between apartment life and the progress of American civilization. In 1903 Charlotte Perkins Gilman touted the amenities of the apartment hotel—a variation of the multioccupancy building that offered residents communal services such as a public dining room and centralized laundry—precisely because it heralded the "passing of the home in great American cities," at least in its most oppressive, isolated, and outdated form. An "architecture of independence" would potentially grant women more freedom from so-called *housework* to take part in the cultural and commercial life of the city.[18] Apartment life, Gilman argued, embodied the basic principle of American progress: "throwing aside good for better, and better for best" (138).

On one level, the apartment's detractors agreed with her. It did indeed imply "the passing of the home," and they attacked the apartment in all guises for abjuring the basic requirements of middle-class home life as instantiated in the single-family house: not simply the domestic attentions of the wife and mother, but also family privacy, respectability, permanence, and independence. An article in the *Architectural Record* suggested that the apartment hotel exhibited an architecture of *dependence*. It promoted not freedom but "domestic irresponsibility," especially among women; however, the apartment also undermined the autonomy of all tenants: it "reduces the trouble of living to a minimum. . . . Once a week they sign a check, thereby pressing a button. The manager does the rest."[19] An anonymous writer for *Harper's* had earlier described the impotence of New York's apartment dwellers in general; they lacked "independence [and] freedom" and were by definition "homeless." Although house ownership at the turn of the century was not the white middle-class norm it would become, apartment life was singled out for its intrinsic transiency: "[A]partments at best cannot be, in any accurate import, homes. They are abodes where persons stay until they can find an opportunity or the means to go somewhere else." As housing "for Anglo-Saxons," apartments were "totally inadequate."[20] A short story, "Their Experience in a Flat," vividly describes the apartment's assaults on the independence and privacy of a middle-class couple who have sought in vain for a single-family house in the city. The manager is not a convenience, but a person who establishes rules that the "Goodenoughs" must live by or risk eviction. They find themselves constrained as well by communal living, with people not of their own choosing or subject to their control. Filled with the sounds of arguing from below and music from above, and with the smells of someone else's food, their apartment never feels like a home because they are forced to share it with unseen others, whom the scent of onions unmistakably codes as immigrants and inferiors. Immediate proximity to random strangers destroys their peace of mind, effectively turning even their private quarters into public space; the apartment is figuratively, as the tenement was literally, overcrowded.[21]

As Gwendolyn Wright has observed, unflattering comparisons between slum and apartment housing were commonplace once exposés of tenement conditions became standard fare in the American press.[22] In fact, the line between the apartment and the home was relatively clear-cut for critics, in part because the line between the apartment building and the tenement was not. The *Harper's* writer called the apartment building "a genteel tenement" (920), while another traced at length the etymology of the words *apartment* and *tenement* in order to clarify the "hazy" distinction between them. He concluded that they differed only in degree and dollars, rather than in kind: "Economy . . . is the purpose of the tenement—comfort, that of the apartment" (Blanke 355). Elsewhere, differences in comfort and income did not prevent more direct analogies between residents as well as their housing: "The middle classes, including a large majority of business and professional men, have been forced into apartment houses, as the wage-earning classes long since were forced into tenements."[23] Although apartments attracted middle-class residents who appreciated their amenities and the pleasures of urban life, single-family houses are treated here as expressions of the residential choice of self-determining individuals, apartments as housing by necessity. Riis speculated that "the gap that separates the man with the patched coat from his wealthy neighbor is, after all, perhaps but a tenement." He then closed the gap when he noticed workmen "putting the finishing touches to the brown-stone front of a tall new tenement. This one will probably be called an apartment house" (32). Riis's reversal suggests that whether the urban middle class was dislodged from the single-family house *by* immigrants and the urban poor or lodged within the apartment house *like* immigrants and the urban poor, it was physically and conceptually difficult to make tenement dwellers keep their distance.

Turn-of-the-century American novelists were likewise preoccupied with the homelessness of apartment dwellers, the lack of privacy and independence, and the muddling of differences between immigrants and the white middle class. While apartment hunting in New York, the protagonist of William Dean Howells's *A Hazard of New Fortunes* meditates on the differences between the flat and the tenement after he and his wife wander into an impoverished but picturesque immigrant district. Basil March declares the apartment to be "the negation of motherhood" and "family consciousness." With "marble halls and idiotic decorations," the apartment is designed for "artificial" show, breeding social competition and "the pretence [sic] of social life." It sacrifices both the natural relations of the family and true social intercourse, privacy, and community. What begins as a discussion of the tenement's inability to produce "any conception of home" among "poor people" ends with the melancholy proposition that tenement dwellers are virtually the only New Yorkers to know what a home is like: "Why, those tenements are better and humaner than those flats! There the whole family lives in the kitchen, and has consciousness of being. . . . No: the Anglo-Saxon home, as we know it in the Anglo-Saxon house, is simply impossible in the Franco-American flat."[24] With characteristic semi-irony, Basil credits the tenement and the cozy proximity of poverty with enabling family life among immigrants. Rather less facetiously, the urban apartment is also depicted as an immigrant, a hyphenated American that is destroying the home life of the natives.

Amy Kaplan has influentially identified *Hazard* and the turn-of-the-century realist project in general with the attempt to make middle-class "readers . . . feel at home" in the "rented spaces" of an "unreal" metropolitan landscape.[25] *Hazard* does not establish or embrace the apartment as a home but does make it habitable, a *genteel* tenement, because of the gentility and good sense of Basil and Isabel March, who continue to recognize the features of a proper home, even if they cannot afford one in New York. For those who truly lack "any conception of home," in Henry Blake Fuller's *The Cliff-Dwellers* and Frank Norris's *Vandover and the Brute*, the apartment not only eliminates the "Anglo-Saxon home" but also exterminates the Anglo-Saxon. Jessie Ogden persuades her husband to give up their single-family house and move into a Chicago apartment hotel by telling him that "[l]ots of nice people live that way now," an argument that underscores even while protesting the tenuous distinction between communal housing arrangements for different classes.[26] But "cliff-dwelling" marks a reversion to a "tribal" (5) way of life that is anathema to middle-class domesticity. She abandons the duties of the housewife and her family in favor of ceaseless socializing: "life to her had now come merely to mean receiving and being received" (271). As a general result of maternal neglect, Jessie's daughter dies, and so, finally, does she, but not from grief or remorse. Jessie simply wastes away from the inadequate sustenance of public meals and the nervous excitement of too much meaningless sociability.

Female residents are particularly susceptible to the fatal attractions of apartment life in *The Cliff-Dwellers*, while *Vandover* explores its degenerative force even for an upper-middle-class bachelor. As in Fuller's references to the uncivilized predecessors of modern cliff-dwellers, Norris likewise associates the apartment with atavism rather than evolution. Upon his father's death, Vandover moves from their uptown house to an expensive apartment building in midtown San Francisco, where he leads, just like Jessie, "a life of luxury and aimlessness . . . [with] no duties, no cares, no responsibilities."[27] The apartment militates against Vandover's autonomy; unanchored, he free-falls into increasingly shabby and destructive versions of it, such as the Lick House, once one of the finest hotels in the city, now a grim flophouse. He degenerates in tandem with a fast deteriorating urban environment, and each stop hastens his bizarre transformation into a wolf. His last semipermanent residence is the Reno House, "a sort of hotel," where his neighbors are poor, transient immigrants. In this environment he literally "*become[s] the brute*" (316), the final step in his devolution from a property-owning man-about-town to a homeless beast of the slums.

These novelists proposed that in turn-of-the-century New York, Chicago, and San Francisco, how the middle class lived might become how the other half lived. Critics of the apartment lectured, in narrative as well as in treatise, about the indiscriminate threat of the city's housing stock to the middle-class home, whether from the conversion of single-family houses into tenements or the apartment's conversion of the white middle class into functional tenement dwellers. From their perspective, the apartment abolished domestic comforts, privacy, and independence—the home—for men as well as women, and eroded the very civilization proponents claimed it advanced. The logical focus of Norris's first experiment with the naturalist novel, multioccupancy dwellings were implicated in the general deterioration of the city's physical landscape and its domestic interiors, the degeneration of the urban middle-class topography and population.[28] By the 1920s Harlan Paul Douglass, a self-styled "suburban evangel," gave sociological weight to the fictional theses of Howells, Fuller, and Norris in his conclusion to the first full-length sociology of the American suburb. Douglass argued that the modern American city had reduced its inhabitants to hopeless barbarism: "the city [is] the final expression of a discrepancy between human nature and environment which is wrecking the race. The caveman . . . is trying to live in modern New York, Chicago, and San Francisco." Similarly disastrous was a return to rural life, "the cave of the primitive man." Caught between the prehistoric and the merely primitive, Americans could salvage their civilization only by submitting to the civilizing forces of the "little home, surrounded by land" in the suburbs.[29]

At the turn of the century detractors measured the apartment, either implicitly or explicitly, against the familiar domestic virtues of the single-family house. Often they alluded directly to the detached suburban residence. At the end of "Their Experience in a Flat," for example, the Goodenoughs decide that a flat is not good enough, and they move to a suburban area, where they escape shared walls as well as tyrannical managers and secure the "freedom of their own cottage" (31). The issue of domestic privacy prompted a 1907 editorial in the *Independent* that asserted "[t]he middle classes especially desire less publicity and more retreat" than city flats afforded: "Suburbanism is growing in popularity . . . from the Atlantic to the Pacific," and wherever "the trolley" extended, "people are pushing out for homes."[30] Transportation was not the only technological development to foster suburbanization. But although the comforts increasingly matched the attractions of "freedom" and privacy, late-nineteenth-century fictional commentaries often treated the residential suburb humorously, as about a half step from "the wilderness," where skeptical visitors from the city wondered "how much further from civilization" they would have to travel to locate their "exile[d]" friends.[31] The suburb provided writers with a new literary and residential "frontier," as described by the bemused narrator of William Dean Howells's *Suburban Sketches* (published in 1871; reprinted in 1898). The narrator refers early to the "conveniences and luxuries" of life on the Boston periphery, but nowhere are they in evidence.[32] Instead we read all about the inconveniences of the suburbs: the undrained and unlighted streets, the lack of adequate fire and police protection, the uncomfortable journey to and from the city on the horse cars, the difficulty of finding and keeping servants. Likewise, the inhabitants of the New Jersey neighborhood described in Henry Cuyler Bunner's comic stories, *The Suburban Sage* (1896), struggle to conquer the furnace and tame the wilderness of the front lawn; newcomers are so terrified by the quiet and darkness that they treat a surprise visit by the narrator "as if my coming had saved the house from an attack of Apache Indians."[33] Bunner notes that the suburbanite is defensive about his primitive lifestyle, "just a little bit pitying himself," but he takes comfort in the "pleasant individuality" credited to him by sophisticated city-dwelling friends for living in an uncharted outpost of civilization, where eventually he comes to "feel . . . quite at home" in spite of the material hardships.[34]

Early-twentieth-century articles, editorials, and advertisements more routinely bypassed references to the frontier and instead commended the suburb for "the innumerable modern conveniences" once found only in the city and "city home."[35] The improvements that developers made to the land and amenities available within the single-family house meant that to enjoy wholesome contact with nature in a suburb such as Park Hill, just outside Manhattan, "a man of moderate means" did not need to forgo all "the requirements of civilization."[36] Advertisements for suburban lots sought to emphasize "[a]ll the latest and modern improvements," luring prospective house builders with such features as gas, electricity, telephone service, sewers, the "purest water," even sidewalk cement of "the choicest grade."[37] By the first decade of the twentieth century, designs and plans for modern suburban houses in a range of middle-class incomes, featuring the latest domestic technology, were regularly offered to the readership of *Ladies' Home Journal, House Beautiful,* and *American Homes and Gardens,* as well as Gustav Stickley's *Craftsman,* an influential organ of the American Arts and Crafts movement. The *Craftsman,* published from 1901 to 1916, spoke constantly to the natural, material, and spiritual advantages of suburban life. Stickley set out, under the influence of William Morris and John Ruskin, to restore the craftsman's autonomy in an age of dehumanizing industrial work. He also tirelessly promoted the independence of the American suburban house owner in an age of hobbling urban life and labor: "The man who was once 'cabined and confined' in the city, and daily led by that sternest of all jailers, custom, from the brick or brown stone prison of his residence to the granite fortress of his offices, has now taken 'the keys of the fields.' The trolley has provided him with the means of escape."[38] The city is defined in terms of confinement and constraints; while he must still submit to the demands of the urban office, the male suburbanite seizes at least one set of "keys" and breaks free from the prisons of both his city residence and the custom of living near his work.

Escaping city for suburb, the restricted urban residence for the detached house, did not, however, guarantee independence and asylum. When Jane

Addams decided in 1889 to locate the Hull-House settlement "in a fine old house standing well back from the street," she observed that it had been "the homestead of one of Chicago's pioneer citizens." The house "once stood in the suburb," but "its site now has corners on three or four foreign colonies," the suburb having been overtaken by a multiply alien city.[39] Riis's previous reference to the "Westchester line" as the boundary of tenement expansion in New York suggests that immigrants were pursuing previous residents who moved toward the edges of the city, while his reference to the "Annexed District" reveals the slippery and transitory status of the political boundaries between the city and what lay beyond.[40] The term *annexation* referred not only to the nation's efforts to expand its empire overseas but also, and sometimes more controversially, to the process by which American cities extended their local borders. As in the forcible annexation of foreign territories (Hawaii, for instance), the city could seize adjacent inhabited land over the protests of its newly "colonized" population. The rhetoric of Theodore Roosevelt, who warned against international isolationism as the evading of "duties to the nation," infused a Maryland judge's 1917 ruling on the city of Baltimore's campaign to increase its territory and its tax base:

> In my judgment it is not only *right* for the legislature to extend the limits of Baltimore City without any referendum—if in its judgment, the public welfare demands the extension—but it is its duty to do so. The duty rests upon the legislature to determine when the progress of the city and the welfare of the state demand an extension of the city limits, and it would be shirking its duty for the legislature to submit the decision of that question to a majority of the voters in the territory to be annexed.[41]

The emphasis on public duty and public welfare, the gesture toward progress, the indifference to the people's will in the "territory," the sermon against shirking obligations—here, in brief, is a domestic version of Roosevelt's international imperialist platform.

The American city did seem to harbor imperial ambitions, but the alleged targets were white domestic citizens and not dark-skinned foreign subjects. For some white inhabitants of the suburb, then, the unpleasant realities of empire seemed to begin at home. By referring proudly and earnestly to "this distant, darkened, unmapped country of the Commuter," in protest against the coming city, one writer rhetorically converted the farthest suburban reaches into a space of colonial encounter, evacuation, and domination.[42] Such rhetoric was not exceptional, even in more developed suburban areas. During the Baltimore annexation crisis, affluent residents of the city's oldest garden suburb chose to present themselves as the victims of urban imperial aggression. The community newspaper adopted the language of the colonized to plead their case: given the "intelligence, wealth, [and] . . . activity" of Roland Park residents, "[h]ome rule, actual beneficial home rule is, indeed, the ultimate and most desirable end."[43] The political principle of home rule has a special resonance in this context, because the suburb sought political autonomy precisely to protect the sovereignty of the suburban home. White inhabitants of the suburbs sometimes found themselves under political and economic attack from a place they identified with social, economic, and racial inferiority, almost as though England had suddenly been invaded by India. The developers of Shaker Heights, Ohio, demonstrated their commitment to excluding "all that disturbs home welfare" from their elite planned residential community by advertising its "change from a colony to a village," which was realized not only by the departure of the original Shakers but also by the incorporation of the suburb, intended to preempt the advances of nearby Cleveland.[44]

For Douglass, the city "reaches at and takes over" (16) land at the periphery. It is an "upstart . . . master" that has to "be reduced to his proper place as servant" (312), an analogy that confirmed and denounced the city's imperialist agenda. *The Suburban Trend* described various aspects of decentralization in the United States, which included production and consumption as well as poor industrial "suburbs" where workers lived near their factories, but it actively promoted the middle-class residential areas that the word *suburb* more frequently invokes.[45] Douglass's frequent recourse to images of the primitive and the ferocity of his conclusion—"A crowded world must be either suburban or savage" (327)— underscores the tensions that underlay the conflict between the residential suburb and the city by the 1920s. Well-to-do garden suburbs such as Roland Park and Shaker Heights, as well as more modest developments, proliferated as an American city of apartment buildings and tenements, overrun by dark-skinned inhabitants, came increasingly to be seen as inimical to the home environment. The movement of white people to these suburbs and the steps residents took to ensure racial and class segregation attest to the pervasiveness of the belief that Anglo-American civilization and home life could flourish only in isolation.

Although few novels seem more geographically and narratively remote from the suburb than *Tarzan*, perhaps no other American novel is quite so conspicuously driven by the very tensions—between savagery and civilization, colonization and home rule—that were evident in the nation's urban-suburban conflict in the early twentieth century. In the decade preceding the "suburban or savage" ultimatum, Burroughs inverted and tacitly sanctioned the naturalist trajectory that reduces Vandover to an indigent urban wolf-man, by celebrating the power of the single-family, freestanding house and its contents to develop a noble Anglo-Saxon out of a savage ape-man. For Burroughs, no white man's house is so primitive that it fails to fulfill its civilizing mission, but savagery is understood to be intrinsically expansionist; a civilized white home is thus also predicated on the ability to segregate and defend it. The suburb offered civilizing homes for the white middle class, insofar as the suburban house would foster independence and segregate its families from one another and from families of other races, which the city and its apartment houses did not seem adequately to do. And yet as one defender of apartments indicated, proximity to other people could also be desirable. In *Tarzan* the house that provides unlimited possibilities for self- and race-advancement is instrumental to his transformation, but as in the suburb, domestic isolation must also be supplemented by the right kind of community, that is, people of one's own kind and choosing.

THE ANGLO-SAXON HOME

Tarzan demonstrates its sensitivity to the finer requirements of turn-of-the-century home life as soon as his parents lay claim to their strip of West African real estate. Their first order of business is to build a house, and although a premium is placed on security—"They could hope for no safety and no peace of mind at night until four strong walls effectually barred the jungle life from them" (20)—"heavily barred windows" that keep out intruders also supply the "air and proper ventilation" that any healthful contemporary residence had to have. Greystoke likewise takes great pains to "beautify the interior of the cabin" (24) with bookcases for the volumes they brought from England, "grass and bamboo" curtains, "[o]dd vases made by his own hand from the clay of the region" (24), and animal-skin rugs. He creates a perfectly personal artifact, a radical embodiment of the Arts and Crafts ideal of simplicity, regionalism, and honest, unalienated hand-workmanship that presupposed, if often only in theory, some identity between maker, place, and object, as endlessly promoted in the pages of the *Craftsman* and its catalogs. The one-room house protects them from a hostile environment, but it also achieves a certain aesthetic integrity. The primitive form and features of the cabin and its furnishings are determined by the exigencies of location and materials, but they enable rather than constrain the artistic sensibilities and cultural refinement of the Anglo-Saxon inhabitants. Hardly the rude shelter one might otherwise expect, their little beach house is a home.

Devoted to the home-making activities of a marooned aristocrat, *Tarzan* picks up where Jack London's *The Sea-Wolf* (1904) leaves off. Like Humphrey "Sissy" Van Weyden, a pampered American "gentleman" whose virtual enslavement aboard a seal-hunting vessel teaches him the meaning of work, Lord Greystoke is forced by circumstances to "turn his hands" to "unaccustomed labor" (24). In *The Sea-Wolf*, however, the point is that Sissy can be neither a real man nor a fit mate for his beloved Maud Brewster until he has learned the virtues of hard work and self-reliance. Urban civilization has made him weak, but after extensive apprenticeships in navigation, carpentry, engineering, and seal hunting culminate in the arduous construction of a "snug little habitation" on a deserted island (appropriately christened Endeavor Island), his callused hands finally earn him the right to Maud's love and respect.[46]

Tarzan, on the other hand, establishes a causal relation between Greystoke's nobility and the facility and good taste that he brings to the process of house construction, and it downplays the masculine identity that such experiments in craftsmanship might make available to him. Van Weyden's initial weakness is precisely Greystoke's strength; the latter's innate superiority to labor, as a gentleman, enables him to labor with remarkable grace and to exhibit "the same indifferent ease" (8) no matter what trial he faces. Greystoke speaks to his wife of the need to work, both to shelter them from the jungle and to preserve their sanity, "as quietly as though they were sitting in their snug living room at home" (16). The innate ability that underlies his unflappable manner allows him to reproduce the Anglo-Saxon home even in the African house. In *Tarzan*, so utterly natural is the home-building instinct of the Anglo-Saxon aristocrat that with no training and few tools he miraculously constructs a structurally sound, well-ventilated, and beautiful cabin. For London, labor must be learned and homes earned; for Burroughs, both are the natural prerogatives of civilized white men.

The blue blood of the Greystokes flows in Tarzan's veins, but following the death of his parents Tarzan is brought up by apes, which takes a predictable but by no means permanent toll on his behavior. The handsome, distinguished gentleman that Tarzan becomes is Burroughs's tribute to the indomitable blood of Anglo-Saxon aristocrats, but it is not the case that heredity simply triumphs over environment.[47] Rather, Tarzan's inherent nobility must be cultivated in the right environment. The house that one gentleman has naturally built becomes the site where another gentleman is naturally constructed, where the primitive virility produced by Tarzan's jungle training is refined by the recuperative influence of his Anglo-Saxon heritage. Tarzan's contact with the beach house and its contents allows him to realize the potential of his noble birth; the house, in other words, teaches him his place.

The savage young aristocrat is inexplicably drawn to his birthplace. Ignorant of its relation to his true identity as well as its generic function, Tarzan nevertheless finds the house "a source of never-ending mystery and pleasure," peopling it in his imagination with "wonderful creatures" (41). Even in the absence of any people to teach him about himself, the house and the treasures it safeguards are imagined as transcendent agents of cultural transmission. Most usefully, he effects the evolution from Tarzan of the apes to Tarzan, Lord Greystoke by teaching himself to read from the picture books his parents brought to Africa:

> By the time he was seventeen he had learned to read the simple, child's primer and fully realized the true and wonderful purpose of the little bugs [the letters].
>
> No longer did he feel shame for his hairless body or his human features, for now his reason told him that he was of a different race from his wild and hairy companions. He was a M-A-N, they were A-P-E-S. (50)

For Tarzan, learning to read is valuable because he reads about himself. The purpose of writing is to enlighten Tarzan about the differences between apes and men, which are discernible because the signifiers differ. Apprising him of his "true and wonderful" identity, writing teaches men who they are and makes them proud of their distinguishing characteristics.

Perhaps because the lesson of writing is the lesson of superiority, Tarzan believes that he differs racially from the apes. Eventually, he learns the meaning of early-twentieth-century race relations when he meets and kills his first black man, but his initial experience of race pride precedes actual knowledge of other human races. Before skin color can have a determinate meaning for him, learning that he is a man is already to have learned that he is a white man. The civilizing influence of the beach house cements his racial self-definition. That a sense of his own whiteness is fundamental to Tarzan's identity is made clear in the note he affixes to the cabin door for a group of white people who have landed on his beach: "THIS IS THE HOUSE OF TARZAN, THE KILLER OF BEASTS AND MANY BLACK MEN. DO NOT HARM THE THINGS WHICH ARE TARZAN'S. TARZAN WATCHES" (103). However unlikely it is that Tarzan could teach himself to read and write English with no prior knowledge of written language, it would of course be impossible for him to translate phonemes from the spoken language of the apes into writing. He could never spell or write his own name. But the miraculous intuition that enables him to write *Tarzan* is more than a gaffe on Burroughs's part. It naturalizes Tarzan's identity and makes it innately representable. And because *Tarzan* means "White-Skin," his ability to write his name and the insistent repetition of that name suggest above all an intrinsically white identity. The novel describes the absolute legibility of Tarzan's whiteness by the immanent transcription of his white name.

It is important that the note's assertion of Tarzan's white skin both serves as a notification of house ownership and a warning not to damage his personal effects, and identifies him as a killer of black men. In the novel, white skin, property rights, and violence against Africans are fundamentally connected. "As Tarzan of the Apes sat one day in the cabin of his father delving into the mysteries of a new book, the ancient security of his jungle was broken forever" (64). Thus Burroughs announces the arrival of "fifty black warriors" and their families into Tarzan's territory, which the passage elevates to a kind of ancestral property. Their presence seems to violate time-honored rights, and the juxtaposition of their activities—Tarzan's quiet enjoyment of a good book at home versus the military advance of the cannibal tribe—not only betrays the violent nature of the disruption but points to the exact risk. Trespassing against Tarzan's "ancient security," the homeless African tribe represents an explicit threat to his home and land.

Tarzan is now presented as the target of imperial violence and not a perpetrator of it. Decimated by the Belgian military, the tribe has unwittingly entered his territory while escaping from their own genocidal rulers, yet the novel translates their act of colonial self-defense into colonial aggression: "That which meant freedom and the pursuit of happiness to these savage blacks meant consternation and death to many of the wild denizens of their new home" (65). Burroughs draws on the language of the Declaration of Independence to call into question the Africans' right to a "new home." For them to exercise the right not to be enslaved and murdered by white Europeans infringes on the rights of prior residents not to be murdered and devoured. The dangers occasioned by the free mobility of Africans are immediately realized when a warrior kills Tarzan's adoptive mother, Kala. Liberty and the pursuit of happiness for blacks thwart the rightful occupants' right to life.

The overtones of American democratic rhetoric convey Burroughs's sense of the national relevance and even urgency of an African adventure story that dramatizes the awful consequences of bringing black skin and white skin together in the same neighborhood. As American cities grew more crowded and more heterogeneous, city officials, planners, developers, and house owners sought to preserve home environments. Zoning legislation, which rationalized the growth of urban areas, was also used to prohibit or restrict certain uses—industrial, commercial—and eventually even types of buildings, such as apartment houses, within particular residential areas in order to "guarantee to the home owner that the area in which his home is located shall not be subjected to uses which might have a tendency to destroy the area for home purposes."[48] But the belief that to maintain "the purity of the two races . . . they cannot continue to live side by side" found expression in another kind of restrictive housing legislation.[49] Acting in 1910 to "preserv[e] order, secur[e] property values and promot[e] the great interests . . . of Baltimore," the Baltimore City Council passed the first municipal ordinance in the United States to establish separate blocks for black and white occupancy.[50] Cities in Georgia, South Carolina, Virginia, North Carolina, and Kentucky followed Baltimore's lead, adding provisions that neither race could own or tenant residences in zones designated for the other race. The Supreme Court invalidated the practice in 1917; although its opinion expressed concern about unfair treatment based on race, the constitutional issue on which the court was asked to rule in *Buchanan v. Warley* was not equal protection but the right of owners to dispose freely of their property. Unanimously upholding the rights of Americans to buy and sell buildings without undue restraint, the Court sustained "long established Anglo-Saxon legal principles protecting the free alienation of property."[51]

The desire of Anglo-Saxon Americans—or Americans who wished to think of themselves as Anglo-Saxon—to segregate their families and property into all-white neighborhoods came into conflict with equally Anglo-Saxon notions of property rights: "The old English idea that every man's house is his castle is so deeply rooted in every Anglo-Saxon mind that it is a difficult matter to look with impartial eyes at any curtailment of personal liberty upon one's own special plat of ground."[52] The connection between American houses and English castles assumed particular force in the garden suburb. Robert Fishman has persuasively argued that this type of suburb originated in the opulent country villas of London's bourgeoisie, who first were "aristocrat[s] on weekends" (41) before relocating permanently from a city that was perceived as dangerous, dirty, and immoral. One architect defined the effect the American house owner sought to achieve in terms that acknowledged these lofty origins:

> The home one builds must mean something besides artistic and engineering skill. It must presuppose, by subtle architectonic expression, both in itself and in its surroundings, that its owner possessed, once upon a time, two good parents, four grandparents, eight great-grandparents, and so on; had, likely brothers and sisters, uncles and aunts, all eminently respectable and endeared to him; that *bienséance* and family order have flourished in his line from time immemorial—there were no black sheep to make him ashamed—and that he has inherited heirlooms, plate, portraits, miniatures, pictures, rare volumes, diaries, letters and state archives to link him up properly in historical succession and progression.[53]

The house was designed to manufacture one's credentials for inhabiting it. For those not actually descended from William the Conqueror, Palladian windows or a tasteful cornice produced the atmosphere of family antiquity and propriety. Jay Gatsby's mansion at West Egg, a hybrid upper- and middle-class "commuting town," is the clearest example in American literature of the house as aspiring and failed Anglo-Saxon manor: "A brewer had built it early in the 'period' craze . . . and there was a story that he'd agreed to pay five years' taxes on all the neighboring cottages if the owners would have their roofs thatched with straw. Perhaps their refusal took the heart out of his plan to Found a Family—he went into an immediate decline." The brewer and Gatsby, no heirs to "the staid nobility" of East Egg, learn the same lesson, that families, unlike houses, cannot simply be constructed.[54]

The developers of the prestigious Shaker Heights subdivision recognized the same Anglo-Saxon affiliations when they boasted about the costs of improvements and then promptly disclaimed their crassness: "The dollar sign does not appear on the Shaker Village coat of arms" (Van Sweringen Co. 41). The only titles American homeowners might possess were those to their land and houses, but they conferred a certain nobility when linked to an elite subdivision. A writer for the *Architectural Record*, for example, identified the male homeowners in the small upper-middle-class community of Brentwood Park, outside St. Louis, with the title *Esquire*.[55] The rhetoric of the time converted ordinary suburban Americans into Anglo-Saxon lords of the manor.

It seemed as though one's property could feel most like an estate when development of it was regulated. In the early twentieth century, planned residential communities sought to overcome the visual disorder and social haphazardness that had characterized much suburban development, past and present, and to sell "a stable future."[56] Property owners were frequently compelled by the original developers to obey minimum expenditure and lot-size requirements when building their houses, to exclude the riffraff, and were encouraged to create a residential landscape of attractive, harmonious houses and properties. Deed restrictions or covenants prevented property owners from doing anything perceived to undermine the character and value of the neighborhood. In the Atlanta development of Druid Hills, one of many suburban place names that suggest ancient British affiliations, Frederick Law Olmsted's firm argued for necessary basic restrictions: only single-family dwellings with a minimum cost of $6,000, no subdividing of lots, no hogs or poultry, and no placards or advertising signs. The aesthetic of the estate was enforced by preserving the natural contours and features of the land as much as possible and by a covenant requiring the main wall of every house to be set back one hundred feet from the road. Imagining "how damaging it would be to persons who have erected handsome residences on adjoining lots to be annoyed by the erection of tenement houses and such like," he called for the restrictions to remain binding until 1999.[57] Such restrictions were also a feature of less-imposing middle-class suburbs; for example, Shawnee Place, in Fort Wayne, Indiana, where houses cost between $3,000 and $5,000, advertised its restrictions on the use of property and number of residences per lot, as well as minimum front set-back requirements of twenty feet. Residents built or bought a house, but they also bought into a community, and only by coming together under its restrictions could they protect themselves and their houses from "the whims of the few," those who would either agree to submit to the preferences of "the many" or buy elsewhere.[58] The principle that a man's house is his castle implied not only the right to defend against immediate threats, but also the desirability of preempting them. The desire to protect property values, establish an agreeable home environment, and prevent deterioration of the community could take precedence over some property rights of individual owners.

John Stilgoe has described "the overriding effort to create a totally homogeneous place" (230) at Forest Hills in Queens, a tightly restricted, Gothic-Tudor-style development, planned by the Russell Sage Foundation to offer rental and owner-occupied housing primarily to skilled workers "of moderate income and good taste."[59] What began as an attempt to control the community aesthetic and set new and more attractive standards for future developments for all classes resulted in an upper-middle-class environment that the intended inhabitants could not afford.[60] The pursuit of homogeneity in suburban areas assumed explicitly racial dimensions as well. The narrator of Howells's *Suburban Sketches* notes the proximity of "Dublin," a picturesque but rundown Irish settlement that disconcerts the residents of suburban Charlesbridge. "Values tremble" when the Irish build near the Yankees, who prepare to abandon their houses; the residents also fear the construction of houses below a certain cost in their own neighborhood as "portending a possible advent of . . . the calamitous race."[61] To protect property values and fend off the calamitous races of the twentieth century, white house owners began to restrict their personal freedom of alienation by purchasing property covered by racially restrictive covenants, which prevented them from selling or renting property to African Americans, Jews, and, depending on the region, other minorities. There were no communitywide race restrictions when the development of Roland Park was begun in 1891, or even after it had begun to assume its character as a garden suburb with the involvement of Olmsted Associates in 1897, but when the same company began to sell lots in the neighboring garden suburb of Guilford in 1913, racial covenants covered all properties there.[62] A white man's subdivision was becoming his fortress.

The same racial and class allegiances are displayed in Tarzan's different responses to his new African neighbors and to a group of English and Americans who land on his beach. He is initially fascinated by the African newcomers, the first humans he has ever seen. His experience of aversion and attraction in the encounter with the African warrior Kulonga—"this sleek thing of ebony, pulsing with life" (68)—is at first consistent with the interracial ambivalence that Eric Lott and Michael Rogin have analyzed in relation to working-class and ethnic whites.[63] After Tarzan comes upon the Africans' "poor little village" and witnesses their cruelty to a prisoner, he begins "to hold his own kind in low esteem" (80); finally, however, he ceases to think of them as "his own kind" at all. Tarzan loses all interest in the Africans, except as their proximity makes him keenly anxious for his house and personal effects: "The blacks had not as yet come upon Tarzan's cabin on the distant beach, but the ape-man lived in constant dread that, while he was away with the tribe, they would discover and despoil his treasure. So it came that he spent more and more time in the vicinity of his father's last home, and less and less with the tribe" (90). The need to guard his property from the Africans alienates him from the apes that raised him and that he now rules. But the ape-man's allegiances are redirected rather than dissolved, because concern over his black neighbors returns him to his racial heritage. Before he can claim his rightful lordship, Tarzan must renounce the kingship of the apes: "Tarzan is going back to the lair of his own kind by the waters of the great lake which has no further shore. . . . Tarzan will not return" (95). The decision to reside in his father's cabin is evidence of greater ambitions: "Thus young Lord Greystoke took the first step toward the goal which he had set—the finding of other white men like himself" (95). The Africans galvanize Tarzan's commitment to his kind, that is, to his own race; the white man's defense and enjoyment of the home are indistinguishable from the desire to live with white people.

Tarzan never has to seek them out, because his beach cabin is a magnet for them. On returning to his father's house, he discovers "a number of white men like himself" already there. Stifling his "first impulse to rush forward and greet these white men as brothers" (100), Tarzan sees them argue and witnesses a cowardly murder. Tarzan promptly learns that all white men are not just "like himself," that, in fact, these "villainous-looking," foul-tempered sailors are "evidently no different from the black men" (100). Cheyfitz has rightly observed that the repetition of the word *black* to describe the uniformly uncivilized and murderous British sailors in the novel merges racial and class categories. The overlapping of these working-class white men and blacks is further confirmed when Tarzan finds the cabin ransacked and his "little store of treasures . . . littered about" (101), the very act of vandalism that he had anticipated from the Africans.

Clearly, racial similarity is not enough to transform working-class white men into Tarzan's "brothers." If the sailors' barbarity virtually turns them into Africans—significantly, they later engage in cannibalism when they become stranded at sea—the inherent blackness of their natures throws into relief the nobility of their passengers, including Jane Porter and her father, an old but impoverished Baltimore family, and Tarzan's cousin, William Clayton. As Tarzan watches the sailors approach the cabin with them, "who were of so different a class" (102), his sympathies are drawn to the "fine-looking young man" who tries to compel courteous treatment from "the little rat-faced sailor" (104). In particular, Tarzan's attention is arrested by "the face of the beautiful white girl. . . . Here at last was one of his own kind; of that he was positive. And the young man and the two old men; they, too, were much as he had pictured his own people to be" (109). Tarzan's intuitive kinship with these white strangers is actualized through his blood tie to Clayton and his social tie to Jane, whom he marries in the next book of the series. In *Tarzan*, upperclass whites are literally members of the same family.

Tarzan's catalog excludes Jane's servant, Esmeralda, "a huge Negress" whose "great eyes roll . . . in evident terror" (102) at the slightest danger, and whose fits, faints, and malapropisms provide stock comic relief. She is by no means villainous, but the novel deliberately contrasts her cowardice and superstitions, which align her with the sailors, Africans, and apes, to the quiet dignity of her white companions. While Tarzan is kindly disposed to Esmeralda, he does not commit the gross social error of classifying a servant with her employers, nor does he misidentify a black woman, even a Westerner, as "one of his own kind."

In marking the difference between himself and both the white sailors and the black servant, Tarzan cleverly positions himself at the top of the novel's racial and class hierarchies. His immediate and lasting identification with Clayton naturalizes their familial connection, of which Tarzan is unaware. Class is as transparent as race, and Tarzan embraces the obvious civilization of Clayton and the Porters by opening his father's home to them.[64] He not only feeds and houses the stranded party but repeatedly saves them from grisly deaths and prevents the rape of Jane. By treating them as a surrogate family, Tarzan is "uniformly consistent in his role of protector and provider" (199). On the other hand, only by lynching the Africans can "THE KILLER OF . . . MANY BLACK MEN" defuse the threat that they pose to the Anglo-Saxon home. Later, when Jane's father and a companion wander away, Tarzan "seized and securely bound [them] by the neck with the same rope" (130), not to hang them from the nearest tree, however, but to lead them back to the safety of the beach house.

Tarzan's role as "protector and provider" is tellingly confirmed after he rescues Jane from an ape. His class is also clearly legible; Jane reads the "chivalry" proclaimed by his "noble face" and "fine features" (163). He nonetheless wonders what to do with the grateful woman panting before him, miles from the beach house. "Was not Tarzan a man? But what did men do?" (163). Men, which is to say, civilized white men, do not bestially rape the women they love. So Tarzan fashions her a "little shelter" over a bed of "soft grasses and ferns" (166), transforming the "savage African jungle" (169) into a "sylvan paradise" (170) for Jane.

Overwhelmed by feelings of "peaceful security" (169), she never wants to leave. The mark of Tarzan's civilization, as of his father's before him, is his natural grace as a homemaker.

Tarzan's domestic moment with Jane has been read by Gail Bederman as his rejection of a turn-of-the-century ideal of primitive masculinity for an outdated and unsustainable notion of civilized white manhood. Tarzan loses Jane, at least until the sequel, because he does not claim her violently in the jungle and later refuses to kill her white suitors, including Clayton. It makes more sense, I think, to attribute his self-control less to the absolute sacrifice or loss of masculinity, with Jane as the uncollected prize, than to a domestic masculine project that is linked to the achievement of racial and class solidarity.[65] This interpretation is validated by Tarzan's response to Lieutenant D'Arnot, a white "officer and a gentleman" (176) whom he saves from cannibals and treats as kindly as he did Jane. Brought into the family through the chapter title "Brother Men," the Frenchman awakes "upon a bed of soft ferns and grasses beneath a little 'A' shaped shelter of boughs" (189). Tarzan once considers abandoning him to his fate because he correctly fears that Jane will depart Africa in his absence, but condemns the apelike selfishness of the impulse: "if you are a man, you will return to protect your kind" (196). His treatment of D'Arnot indicates that Burroughs's point is not simply that white women exercise a civilizing influence over white men, or that the response of the civilized man is to build a shelter solely for the woman he loves. Although Tarzan's sexual desire for Jane distinguishes her from the other white people he encounters, his ambition to carve a domestic haven out of the jungle is more convincingly attributed to his recognition of Jane, like D'Arnot, as "one of his own kind," connected to him by race and class, and meriting his protection, rather than differentiated from him by gender. The domestic impulse is not here directed primarily toward the preservation of the nuclear family, as it was for Tarzan's father. Rather, it is identified with the well-bred white man's ability to tame the wilderness and with his desire to house and provide a community for the extended elite white family. Only then do the "instincts" of the "polished gentleman" finally overshadow the training of the "savage ape-man" (169).

THE BIG BWANA OF TARZANA

Given that the novel makes the same case for racial separation that shaped the twentieth-century suburb, it is not strange that Burroughs's effort to house "his own kind" doubled as a tribute to his fictional hero. Moving like Tarzan from individual isolation to white community, Burroughs planned to preserve intact the 540-acre estate he had purchased in the

San Fernando Valley in 1919, but escalating property values tempted him to persuade aspiring white house owners to join him in 1922. Tarzana was not a planned suburb with endless restrictions, but Burroughs actively encouraged "the sort of folks to come here whom I want for neighbors."[66] All property sold in the community that became Tarzana was subject to the following restriction: "That said premises or any part thereof shall not be leased, sold, or conveyed to or occupied by any person not of the Caucasian race."[67] Tarzan's inflexible views on Africans relax somewhat later in the series—even by the end of the first novel D'Arnot has taught him to "wait until the blacks spring upon you . . . then you may kill them" (213)—but Burroughs's own conviction that they made undesirable neighbors endured.[68]

In advertisements for Tarzana, Burroughs promoted himself as the center of the community he was trying to establish, an unusual marketing strategy, to say the least: "Let me tell you the sort of colony I hope to see grow up around my home—a colony of self-respecting people who wish to live and let live—who will respect the rights and privileges of their neighbors, and mind each his own affairs."[69] The advertisement mitigates the threatening potential of the "colony" references by constructing a unique colonial subject still in possession of his or her privacy and independence. Burroughs, the benign ruler, would enforce the rights of his people, who were also his peers. As a community, Tarzana would guarantee the property rights and home life of its residents. Whites could enjoy the "privileges" of suburban house ownership in his peaceful domain without undue constraints upon their liberty, because they were really masters of themselves.

Tarzan and the Golden Lion, serialized in the same year that Burroughs began to subdivide his estate, suggests why he refused to place black residents in Tarzana's colonial scheme. Tarzan enlists the aid of an enslaved African tribe in a plot against their cruel masters, a "dominant and intelligent race" of gorillas.[70] He promises the Africans their freedom but is thwarted by their colonial mentality. Unable to imagine independence, the tribe cannot act to secure it. Tarzan concludes that "an attitude of mind . . . keeps the Gomangani in perpetual slavery" (113). His arguments and threats finally penetrate their "stupid minds" (122), but when the gorillas have been slaughtered and liberty is won, Tarzan decides that slavery has unfitted the Africans for self-rule and that they "must select a ruler from another race than [their] own" (141)—so he hands them over to a white former member of Stanley's expedition. For these Africans, independence is but a moment between two forms of colonial rule, because they are thought to be incapable of mastering themselves. Their failed quest for independence suggests that slavery is inescapable, and, according to Burroughs, slaves just don't make good neighbors.

On the other hand, working-class whites in the novel are no longer versions of blacks but demonstrate a clear will to self-determination. Racial identity supersedes class difference; even the white villains express a desire for independence, which they imagine as a kind of residential opportunity. The explicit motivation for stealing a fortune in gold, an ignoble means to a noble end, is their anticipation of the moment when, as Tarzan's British maid puts it, "we are free to live where and how we like" (23), a moment that is unimaginable for the African tribe that Tarzan liberates. Burroughs conceived of his subdivision as a place where such freedom could be achieved by those who preferred to "live our own life in our own way . . . free from [the] conventionalities and restrictions of cities."[71] What the suburb offered white Americans like Burroughs was the chance to become like Tarzan, who constantly feels "hemmed in by restrictions and conventionalities" (*Tarzan of the Apes* 218), and he finds himself drawn back to Africa from the great European capitals, "more dangerous than my savage jungles" (*The Return of Tarzan* 31). *Tarzan*'s portrait of the white home under siege helps to make sense of Burroughs's desire to guarantee residents that a home in Tarzana meant peaceful security, far from "the dangers or temptations" of the city, and would permit independence in a place where a man's home was indeed his castle.[72] True to the namesake who personifies "White-Skin," Tarzana was modeled along the lines of other twentieth-century suburbs, as a place intended to ensure that white American civilization could thrive in isolation and where ordinary middle-class people could think of themselves as extraordinary Anglo-Saxons.

CHAPTER TWO

Sinclair Lewis and the Revolt from the Suburb

THE SUBURBAN SAGE

IN 1922, the same year that Burroughs offered Tarzana to white middle-class homeowners as a civilized refuge from the urban jungle, Sinclair Lewis redescribed the suburb as the failed sanctuary of the businessman-barbarian. *Babbitt* begins with an enthusiastic description of Zenith's downtown skyscrapers, "austere towers of steel and cement and limestone, sturdy as cliffs and delicate as silver rods. They were neither citadels nor churches, but frankly and beautifully office buildings" (5). The passage has rightly been cited as evidence of Lewis's sincere admiration for some of the technological masterworks of modernity.[1] He soon distinguishes, however, between the candid beauty of its most celebrated architectural and civic artifact, the skyscraper, and the deceptively attractive single-family residences on "the farther hills" of Zenith, "shining new houses, homes—they seemed—for laughter and tranquillity" (5). The "seemed" disrupts the equation of suburban house and home and marks instead the disjuncture between appealing physical structure and inadequate metaphysical shelter. When Zenith is dismissed at the end of the first section as "a city built—it seemed—for giants" (6), the echoing "it seemed" implies that the deflation of the city has something to do with the shining houses at its periphery, a conclusion that is supported with the immediate introduction of the puny protagonist: "There was nothing of the giant in the aspect of the man who was beginning to awaken on the sleeping-porch of a Dutch Colonial house in that residential district of Zenith known as Floral Heights" (6).

Lewis knew his suburban trends. Both the Colonial style of residential architecture and the sleeping porch, a popular amenity that took advantage of the privacy and fresh air afforded by spacious lots, associate Babbitt's house and lifestyle with the typical aspirations and achievements of the middle class in the 1920s.[2] With *Babbitt* Lewis sought to portray the "Tired Business Man" in a city of three or four hundred thousand people, but as we meet Babbitt the novel reveals that to accomplish this project was also, already, to produce an anatomy of suburban life.[3] Historians have viewed the 1920s as a watershed in the development and promotion of the suburb: the "road-building revolution" opened up outlying areas to automobiles and new residential development; from 1922 to 1929 the pace of new construction, at 883,000 housing starts per year, more than doubled that of any previous seven-year period. In the 1920s, rates of population growth at the periphery of American cities outstripped those in the central core, 33.2 percent to 24.2 percent. Meanwhile, according to Mary Corbin Sies, the prewar "suburban ideal" of a single-family house on its own lot, within a homogeneous community, did not evolve further but was subject to "commodification and mass production" during this decade, as small-scale builders who worked from standardized plans gained control of the single-family housing market from architects. The suburban house was also treated as a commodity that housed other commodities; advertisements and feature articles in popular periodicals and home-management literature, and a government- and business-sponsored "Own Your Own Home" campaign, marketed the suburban home as the natural site of white middle-class family life and the proficient consumption of mass-produced goods of all kinds.[4] Lewis conducted his analysis of the suburb as an attack on the modern consumer culture from which it soon could not be disentangled. In contrast with the handcrafted cabin and furnishings of *Tarzan*, which are treated as an impressive individual accomplishment that also expresses and reproduces a refining Anglo-Saxon culture, Babbitt's suburban house is identified with the proliferation of mass-produced commodities, the evisceration of culture, and the debilitating uniformity of middle-class dwellings and residents. The disparity between the "giant figure" (*Tarzan of the Apes* 233) of Tarzan and the diminished figure on the sleeping porch underscores a conceptual shift from the autonomy of the suburbanite, articulated in the Tarzanian ideal of freely living how and where one pleases, to his weak conformity.

The absolute centrality of racial difference and conflict to Burroughs's thinking about the home generates a vision of community in *Tarzan of the Apes* and Tarzana that is dedicated to enforcing and defending the residential freedom of one's own white kind. In *Babbitt* the assault on his well-being is not from a city of dark-skinned people from without, but from the self-destructive excesses of the suburbanite within. *Babbitt* is almost exclusively preoccupied with the intricacies of middle-class identity and affiliations in a literary environment where suburban homogeneity along racial and class lines is basically established; *standardized* is, after all, the word Lewis uses in its broadest sense to define and critique Babbitt and his milieu. In the absence of a territory that needs immediate defending, Babbitt perceives himself as requiring protection from it. The central tension in the novel is thus between Babbitt's allegiance to the safe, standardized middle-class world he inhabits and his resistance to it. Until recently literary critics have tended to treat this tension as a trajectory: moving from devotion to disavowal, Babbitt rebels against the conventions of his peers, at last going so far as to speak on behalf of striking workers and refusing to join his friends' reactionary political organization. In the end, however, he returns to the fold because he lacks the values that might sustain his opposition. Babbitt's unsuccessful revolt has signified Lewis's own failure to propose adequate solutions to the problems of a mass society that he so wittily diagnosed, but critics have also usually perceived it to be more or less a step in the direction of enlightenment, as Lewis himself struggled toward the terms and values through which a more radical rebellion could be successfully articulated and achieved.[5]

It seems to me that solutions are beside the novel's point. The "desire to escape" does not "challenge middle-class society in America," but rather expresses the tensions between affluence and diffidence, self-appreciation and self-loathing, complacency and revolt, which Lewis understood to be the structural underpinnings of white male middle-class identity in and after *Babbitt*.[6] Thus the shift from his first spectacular best-seller, *Main Street* (1920), to the equally successful *Babbitt* not only registered geographical changes in modern middle-class experience, from the small town and its frontier values to the metropolitan environment and suburban way of life, but it also insisted on significant differences in middle-class consciousness. In *Main Street*, outsider and frustrated reformer Carol Kennicott is annoyed by the "grayness" and "dullness" of Gopher Prairie, but she is particularly tormented by the residents' "complacent" attitude toward their mediocrity: "She could, she asserted, endure a shabby but modest town; the town shabby and egomaniac she could not endure."[7] *Main Street* focuses on how repulsive the self-satisfied small-town bourgeoisie is to an outsider, a woman from the big city whose gender and geographical differences motivate her to resist and transform her environment. In a letter to Lewis, Edith Wharton praised the novel for situating the critique "in the consciousness of a woman who suffered from it because she had points of comparison." She was more qualified in her regard for *Babbitt* because it lacked the estranged internal viewpoint to enrich its critique: "Babbitt is in and of Zenith up to his chin and over."[8] Wharton's reservation about *Babbitt* is, in fact, its achievement. It shows how unsatisfactory the middle-class suburbanite is to *himself*, as the pleasure he takes in his standardized house, furnishings, car, and life is undercut by his growing perception of their hollowness as rewards. The point of situating the critique, and the suffering, with an insider—white, male, house owner, businessman—is to establish alienation as the authentic voice of that culture. *Main Street*'s "revolt from the village" describes the experience of one who doesn't belong; through its association with the representative middle-class consciousness of *Babbitt*, the revolt from the suburb is instead characteristic of someone who does.[9]

My reading of middle-class ambivalence is obviously indebted to Christopher P. Wilson's insights into Lewis's early white-collar fiction to *Babbitt*, and in particular to his observation that Lewis sought to create "a paradigmatic character who internalized the faith, doubt, and dissent of white collar justifications in his soul."[10] Wilson's interest in the white-collar dissenter has more to do with Lewis than with Babbitt; drawing on extensive archival research that includes the author's early work in publicity and advertising, Wilson emphasizes Lewis's enmeshment in the language and culture of the promotional world that he sought futilely and rather ambivalently, like Babbitt, to escape. Lewis found it "difficult to reconceive 'freedom' in anything but publicity culture's terms" (248), and *Babbitt* exemplifies the processes by which white-collar protest is, almost playfully, contained and conscripted by that culture. My account places *Babbitt* at the beginning of a different moment in Lewis's career. Looking briefly back to *The Job* (1917) and ahead to such novels as *Dodsworth* (1929), *It Can't Happen Here* (1934), and *Kingsblood Royal*, I want to suggest that *Babbitt*'s contribution may be less to the final staging of a critique of middle-class culture that either subverts or is subsumed by that culture than in generating a model of white male middle-classness that is defined in terms of a perpetual and perpetually unprogressive critique of itself.

Babbitt's "rebellion" (223) embodies the unrevolutionary expression of a prototypically middle-class discontent, because it is so thoroughly domestic. Manifested in the protagonist's flight from his fully loaded house and the novel's own sentimental nostalgia for "home," it is a quest for emotional refuge and consolation, which ought to be characterized as specifically suburban as well as generically middle class. One of the most modern aspects of the novel is its refusal to distinguish between these identities; as a realtor who specializes in "suburban real-estate" (72) and sometime developer of suburban properties, Lewis's typical middle-class man is professionally as well as domestically saturated by this environment, his significance determinable only within its context. Another modern feature is its assumption that opulent suburban houses are impoverished places from which to escape, that the white middle-class home is inevitably elsewhere. Never is Babbitt more representative of his kind than when he is desperately trying to be someplace and something else. The materiality of suburban life matters most in *Babbitt* as it generates a definitively white middle-class affect—the feeling of homelessness—that is characterized by an irresolvable psychic split between the material delights of affluence and its corresponding spiritual horrors.

Babbitt has recently been described by Jackson Lears as "one victim" of "the wave of life-worship" that spread "across the coasts of bohemia and into suburban living rooms" in the 1920s, when disillusioned members of the middle class sought "authentic" and "intense" experiences that "advertised commodities" could not provide.[11] His account of the novel sets it firmly within the pattern of modern bourgeois dissatisfaction, therapeutic response, and accommodation that he elaborated in *No Place of Grace*. More revealing, I think, in relation to Lewis is the novel's insistence that middle-class discontent is not only impervious to but also stimulated by one's therapeutic reactions to it. Babbitt's discontent does not merely "*lead* to circularity and self-absorption"; it is an accommodation, an end, and even an intense experience in itself.[12] This chapter redirects the meaning of his discontent from the well-intentioned but hopeless revolt of the justly disgruntled consumer and businessman toward the suburban dynamics of an empowering and unmerited white middle-class self-pity. To anticipate the terms Lewis uses to bring the contradictions of Babbitt's identity into focus, one of the *master* narratives of his career as a best-selling novelist is largely a *martyr* narrative that chronicles how tough it is to be a white middle-class male.

The Satisfied Suburbanite

From the first, commentators have shared Lewis's understanding of himself as a writer with "that sociological itch."[13] Reviewers proclaimed the significance of *Babbitt* to be broadly cultural and sociological rather than essentially literary. H. L. Mencken's enthusiastic review, tellingly entitled "Portrait of an American Citizen," called the novel "fiction only by a sort of courtesy"; for Lewis Mumford, the brilliant architectural and cultural critic, Babbitt was less a character than a "flesh and blood" commentary on American life.[14] As "a contribution to the prevailing mood, among intellectuals," however, *Babbitt* did not inaugurate a critique, polemic, or debate; rather, it further explored the discrepancy between material sustenance and spiritual malnourishment that had already framed objections to the American middle class since before World War I.[15] Such cultural critics as Van Wyck Brooks, Waldo Frank, and Mumford had traced and were continuing to elaborate a natively American lineage that bound American icons—the Puritan, the pioneer, and the "tired businessman"—together in their "crass material endeavor[s]" and resultant "starved inner life."[16] Writing in 1908, Brooks argued that whatever logic of material necessity might once have driven the Puritan and the pioneer, industrial commercialism had become "a habit" for the "well-fuelled and well-fed" modern businessman, who in his prosperity "loves the machine for itself."

Brooks sought not to banish the machine but to reduce its affective power. The businessman would cease to fetishize it only when he had "learned to accept the machinery of life as a premise." Once the machine and its products were normalized, their hold on the middle-class psyche released, Brooks hoped that "the arts of life" might then also be embraced as "normal, natural elements of civilized life."[17]

A "civilized life" signified the spiritual and cultural fulfillment of the individual; historian Casey Blake has clarified, however, that for these "young intellectuals," the personal did not preclude, but was ideally predicated on, the reciprocal rejuvenation of a democratic community.[18] In the early postwar period, the suburb emerged, albeit in a tentative, exploratory fashion, as an index of the failures of American civilization on both levels. In *Our America* (1919), a study of national letters and landscapes, Waldo Frank considered the material and symbolic value of built environments, sites at once aesthetic and inescapably social, shaped by particular uses and answerable to the requirements of human communities. His portrait of Los Angeles anticipates, or perhaps calls into being, the categorical association of southern California with the worst excesses of suburban banality and monotony. "Los Angeles is not a city" (103), he protested, with reference to "[e]ndless avenues strewn with prim bungalows" (102), "the flat tidiness of little houses, little flowerpots, and little palms," and the "swarms of bleached men and women" (103). This bland sub-urban landscape is juxtaposed with the regenerative regional and ethnic residential spaces of the Indians and Mexicans, the rich "buried cultures" (93) of the Southwest. Hovering somewhere between "actual locales and speculative spaces of possibility," as Susan Hegeman recently puts it, their housing satisfies the spiritual needs of individuals and cultures, in contrast with the "ugly houses" (96) of the Anglo-Americans.[19] Prehistoric Indians, for example, built "great community houses, sometimes of more than twelve hundred chambers" (110) into the cliffs. Unlike the white inhabitants of Los Angeles—homogeneous and yet atomized, a mass that never coalesces into community—and the apartment-loving primitives of *The Cliff-Dwellers*, who choose a "tribal" existence at their peril, the highrise "communities" of the Indians ingeniously adapted their structures to the purposes of civilized living. Special rooms were devoted to sacred rituals of "meditation"; wall paintings and "gorgeous pottery" (111) exhibit keen aesthetic sensibilities. Frank also admired the single-family adobe houses of the Mexicans, which necessarily achieved an organic relation to "the earth" and the region and symbolized the "inner life" of "a man . . . in harmony with his surroundings" (94–95). Hegeman emphasizes the recuperative symbolic function of such "autonomous cultural sites" (94) for Frank, who also wrote from a weary conviction that the only civilizations worth preserving in the West were already gone or going. In Los Angeles, the "crumbling 'dobe houses" were arrogantly "being swept away by the broom of progress" (102), in time, one imagines, to "the march of the bungalow" (103). Indifferent to the Mexicans' "spiritual wealth" (97) and their own spiritual poverty, decentralizing white Angelenos reincarnated the pioneer's destructive "spirit," "sterile," "complacent," "in repose" (104).

In "The Wilderness of Suburbia," published the year before *Babbitt,* Mumford located a spiritual wasteland within a broader, but equally bleached, national topography. He drew on the etymology of *civilization* to denounce "[t]he commuter" as "a man without a city—in short, a barbarian." Both the old humorous association of the American suburb with material hardship and its ongoing affiliation with the ways of civilized white people have given way in Mumford's account to a degraded backwoods of "bathtubs and heating systems," a material bonanza that reveals "the incapacity of our civilization to foster concrete ways and means for living well."[20] Mumford returned to the constitutive tension between "living well" and the suburban "good life" a year later in his contribution to *Civilization in the United States,* an essay collection that disparaged the nation's "emotional and aesthetic starvation."[21] In "The City" Mumford invoked *suburbia* as a metaphor for the generic contrast between desirable artifacts of affluence—"bathtubs and heating systems" again—and the atrophied "art of living," which pointed to spiritual gratification within an egalitarian communal framework: "[c]ivic life, in fine, the life of intelligent association and common action."[22] The sprawling, undisciplined suburb dehumanized the landscape and replaced community with mere proximity, democratic purpose with "social stability" and "security" (6). "Suburbia" stood for an "inferior" (15) life; "suburbanite" was another way of saying "idiot" (16).

By the time *Babbitt* appeared, Mumford had made explicit that the problem of the suburb was also the problem of the suburbanite, who put up with an inhumane environment that had more respect for machinery as such than for the people it was meant to serve. Harold Stearns, the editor of *Civilization,* echoed this assessment: "That the life of the mind might have an emotional drive, a sting or vibrancy of its own, constituting as valuable a contribution to human happiness as, say, the satisfied marital felicity of the bacteria-less suburbanite in his concrete villa has been incomprehensible."[23] The suburbanite does not simply tolerate the hygienic environment but also relishes its sterility. Like Mumford, Stearns emphasized the spiritual bleakness of the suburb as well as the suburbanite's infuriating indifference to it.

For Stearns, Mumford, and, more obliquely and prototypically, Frank, the suburb represented the antithesis of the attributes required to make "real civilization possible" in the United States. The narrowness of the suburban mind, but also its self-satisfaction and complacency, were at odds with one of their chief ambitions: to foster a "self-conscious, deliberately critical examination of ourselves, without sentimentality and without fear."[24] As these criticisms of the suburb were taking shape, however, more powerful voices promoted homeownership on the basis that it fostered exactly the kind of satisfied citizenry condemned by the intellectuals. In the suburban "Own Your Own Home" movement of the 1920s, which has been labeled "Building for Babbitt," government and business leaders "looked to the home as a symbol which would build consensus" and strategically linked the ownership of a house and other consumption practices to family well-being, social stability, and good citizenship.[25] Much has recently and rightly been made of the racial construction of citizenship in the period, but the "Own Your Own Home" movement reminds us how often one's capacities as an American are also associated with the attainment of what suburban historian Margaret Marsh has called, with reference to the twenties, "the hallmark of middle-class 'arrival' in society."[26]

"Own Your Own *Home*" was advocated on political and economic grounds, activated by the force of affective appeal. As Commerce secretary between 1921 and 1928 and then president, Herbert Hoover was the leading figure in government associated with the movement. William Leach has described Hoover as a "managerial statist," who "watched and guided" market forces and intervened freely in the economy.[27] In the same year that *Babbitt* and *Civilization in the United States* were published, Hoover created a division of Building and Housing to coordinate the activities of builders, real estate developers, social workers, and homemakers. Throughout the 1920s the division nationally publicized the virtues of homeownership in speeches, posters, and pamphlets. Beginning in 1922 Hoover also headed the "Better Homes for America" campaign, launched by the *Delineator*, a mass-circulation women's magazine designed for a middle-class readership. His article in the inaugural issue, "The Home as an Investment," associated ownership with "security, independence and freedom" for the individual, while warning readers against "that unrest which inevitably results from inhibition of the primal instinct in us all for home ownership. It makes for nomads and vagrants."[28] *Unrest* suggests both the domestic disequilibrium and mobility that result from the thwarted property-owning "instinct" and Hoover's sense of their broader political implications. The "home" is sold as a sentimental stake in one's own financial security and personal independence as well as the stability and freedom of the nation.

A year later Hoover drew a stronger connection between personal and national interests in the foreword to John Gries's *How to Own Your Own Home*: "The home owner has a constructive aim in life. He works harder outside his home; he spends his leisure more profitably, and he and his family live a finer life and enjoy more of the comforts and cultivating influences of our modern civilization. A husband and wife who own their home are more apt to save. They have an interest in the advancement of a social system that permits the individual to store up the fruits of his labor. Above all, the love of home is one of the finest instincts and the greatest of inspirations of our people."[29] Hoover defines Americans in terms of a native love of home that can be expressed only by the ownership of a house. Ownership increases the productivity of the husband and, paradoxically, both the consumer pleasures and saving habits of the family. The house as home intrinsically unites material comforts and civilizing influences and is constitutive of family happiness. The home as house ensures the family's loyalty to a capitalist system that protects its economic as well as emotional investments.

On one level, Hoover and the intellectuals agreed about what might be at stake in the American suburb and its housing. Hoover's happy homeowners, the tools and beneficiaries of a thriving industrial consumer culture, were Mumford's idiots and Stearns's mindless, soulless suburbanites, satisfied in absolute ignorance of their own and society's best interests against the narrow, sterile preoccupations of that culture. Like Hoover, Mumford and Stearns believed in, but they deplored, the suburb's self-protective enforcement of the status quo. *Babbitt* struggles uneasily between the intellectuals' critique and the politician's endorsement. That is, Lewis attacked the spiritual, aesthetic, and cultural deficiencies of the suburb and suburban house, but his criterion for judging their inadequacies aligns him with Hoover's sentiment rather more insistently than with the intellectuals' humane social order. Lewis refuted Mumford's and Stearns's notions of the satisfied suburbanite; the word that he contributed to the critique was Hoover's own talisman of *home*. If Americans had to examine themselves and their environment critically and fearlessly, but also "without sentimentality," as Stearns demanded, asserting Babbitt's homelessness hardly carried the point. The political "unrest" that Hoover associated with renting and the stability he associated with ownership are replaced in *Babbitt* by the dislocated suburbanite's "restlessness" (49), the most important and utterly ineffectual symptom of his discontent.

HOUSE AND HOMELESSNESS

For the man on the sleeping porch, the first stirrings of consciousness produce an overwhelming desire to avoid consciousness; realizing "that there was no more escape," Babbitt reflects more fully on awakening that he "detested the grind of the real-estate business, and disliked his family, and disliked himself for disliking them" (7). The alarm clock that ends his dreams of escape is "the best of nationally advertised and quantitatively produced alarm-clocks," and he is "proud of being awakened by such a rich device" (7). His pride in the alarm clock temporarily awakens him, as it were, to his self-satisfaction, but his earliest, uncensored thoughts express his discontent and self-loathing.

Although Babbitt wakes up detesting real estate, revealing the home as a place where the worries of business freely penetrate, work is not the primary source of the "mysterious malaise" (29) that afflicts him. A name partner in the Babbitt-Thompson Real Estate Company, the self-employed businessman has tedious responsibilities that he dislikes, such as looking over the "details of leases, appraisals, mortgages" (44), and duties that he enjoys, such as writing newspaper advertisements and negotiating a delicate transaction in which a small businessman is forced to pay twice the value of a property. Lewis takes a transparent poke at the dubious ethics of standard business practice, but the workplace scenes seem also designed to suggest that all jobs are sometimes boring, a premise whose obviousness has been easy to overlook amid our sense of the profound changes that characterized the bureaucratization of early-twentieth-century white-collar work. Babbitt is the middle-class man as middleman, a marketer rather than a producer, but he is not personally caught in the shift from an entrepreneurial to a salaried middle class, nor is Babbitt an especially powerful expression within Lewis's fiction of its attendant crises of agency, alienation, and security, which haunt his best early novel, *The Job*.[30] In that novel, the malaise of protagonist Una Golden is not mysterious; she performs assembly-line secretarial labor as part of a dehumanizing "office system" (44), and her discontent is linked at every point to ceaselessly tedious work and financial worry and to escape from them both. But Una is not "satisfied easily" (77) with an ignominious place. She finally leaves the dead-end routine for a job she finds wonderfully challenging: selling suburban lots on Long Island. She theorizes about the failure of other office workers to find satisfying work: they "weren't discontented enough; they were too patient with lives insecure and tedious" (236). In the financially ruinous and socially inconspicuous white-collar world of *The Job*, discontent motivates the ambitious working woman to improve her economic and social fortunes, by becoming more like Babbitt.

Babbitt's discontent expresses economic and social success rather than failure. He is not so much alienated from his labor as from his house, which is to say, that while he never stops working, he does run away from home. Lewis emphasizes the house owner's degradation in the description of the Babbitts' bedroom, which displayed a modest and pleasant color-scheme, after one of the best standard designs of the decorator who "did the interiors" for most of the speculative-builders' houses in Zenith. The walls were gray, the woodwork white, the rug a serene blue; and very much like mahogany was the furniture—the bureau with its great clear mirror, Mrs. Babbitt's dressing-table with toilet-articles of almost solid silver, the plain twin beds, between them a small table holding a standard electric bedside lamp, a glass for water, and a standard bedside book with colored illustrations—what particular book it was cannot be ascertained, since no one had ever opened it. The mattresses were firm but not hard, triumphant modern mattresses which had cost a great deal of money; the hot-water radiator was of exactly the proper scientific surface for the cubic contents of the room. The windows were large and easily opened, with the best catches and cords, and Holland roller-shades guaranteed not to crack. It was a masterpiece among bedrooms, right out of Cheerful Modern Houses for Medium Incomes. Only it had nothing to do with the Babbitts, nor with anyone else. . . . It had the air of being a very good room in a very good hotel. One expected the chambermaid to come in and make it ready for people who would stay but one night, go without looking back, and never think of it again.

Every second house in Floral Heights had a bedroom precisely like this. (15–16)

The distinction between "shining new houses" and "homes" in the novel's opening section has prepared us for the meaning of this onslaught: "There was but one thing wrong with the Babbitt house: It was not a home" (16).

The bedroom exemplifies what Jean-Christophe Agnew has called the "commodity aesthetic," a view of the world—and implicit in his essay, of the domestic interior especially—"as so much raw space to be furnished with mobile, detachable, and transactionable goods." With the emergence of an "aesthetic" triggered by a proliferation of commodities, the boundaries between "the self and the commodified world" frequently "collapse," an erosion that becomes crucial to the affective economies of advertising and consumption.[31] In the description of the bedroom, the commodity aesthetic is linked in particular to the dissolution of a different boundary, that which distinguishes one thing from another. The passage presents a tableau of standardization, in which each object and detail signifies only in relation to the total portrait. Thus while it acknowledges the excellence of equipment whose purpose is primarily utilitarian, the benefits of modern mattresses and radiators are surrounded by and subordinated to its attack on the inauthenticity and impersonality of the decor. The indictment of the bedroom standardizes standardization, as Lewis refuses even to contemplate the possible differences between technology, furniture, and ideas, between the unarguable advantages of scientifically

designed radiators, the venial sin of a poorly chosen lamp, and the potential disadvantages of an object such as the standardized book.

In an exacting analysis of the debates over standardization in the 1920s,
Janice Radway documents an analogous conflation among those who
were opposed to the mass distribution of literature and the standardization of books, as well as of appliances, cars, and clothing. Appalled by
the prospect of "millions of Ford-driving, silk-shirted Babbitts," critics
of standardization were inspired, according to Radway, largely by the
conservative desire to preserve "the man of letters," that is, "the white,
male, middle-class citizen of the bourgeois republic."[32] Babbitt and his
unread book indeed register Lewis's resistance to the potential oblitera-
tion of the free-thinking and -reading subject, but Babbitt does not stand
for the possible disintegration of the white middle-class male's status and
privilege, which Radway further suggests were thought to be imperiled by
the standardized commodities that "threatened to erase the distinctions"
(244) whereby this citizen ruled. On the contrary, the things available to
him as an affluent consumer attest to his privileged position in the social
order. They secure him and his family a literal place reserved for the "Medium Incomes."

Radway's analysis establishes an important context for understanding
that there is nothing intrinsically subversive about a sweeping attack on
suburban houses and heaters and toiletries, on "altogether royal bathroom[s] of porcelain and glazed tile and metal sleek as silver" (8), on
standardization as such. Lewis's attack, however, is less politically reactionary, in the strong way Radway indicates it may have been for some
of his contemporaries, than politically disabled. That is, standardization
is associated with the erosion of Babbitt's advantages; at stake, however,
is affect rather than power. The totalizing critique of standardization is
motivated by the sentimental requirements of the middle-class home. Cecelia Tichi has observed of *Babbitt* that Lewis disdained the machine and
its aesthetic possibilities, in contrast with his modernist contemporaries,
who found formal as well as thematic inspiration in the new technology.
While this reading does not account for his brief praise of the skyscrapers'
beauty, it is entirely pertinent with regard to ordinary household machinery.[33] In a subsequent passage that is seldom addressed by critics, Seneca
Doane, Zenith's "radical lawyer" (85), argues to a cranky European that
"[s]tandardization is excellent, *per se*," that quality "tool[s]" such as In-
gersoll watches and Fords and, one might presume, radiators and mattresses leave "more time and money to be individual in" (86). He even
speaks favorably of new architectural standards for American houses.
Unlike recent arguments for the consonance between individuality and
standardization in the Progressive era, Doane's claim is not that standardization provides opportunities for newly thinking of oneself as an individ-

ual—a size "8," someone who likes Fords—in the process of becoming "the statistical person."[34] It is instead a version of the far more commonplace twenties defense of the "right kind of standardization," of things not "thought" (86), which is imagined to help preserve the boundary between commodities and self; in this account, one's personal individuality could never be effaced by using a name-brand watch nor yet established by using a handmade sundial, because what matters is how one spends time, not how one keeps it.[35]

My point is not that *Babbitt* is inconsistent, nor that Lewis is ambivalent. Doane's instrumental endorsement of standardization does not undercut the earlier, hysterical denunciation, so much as explains it. Inside the house, standardized radiators, lamps, and books are equally culpable, insofar as they contribute to a uniform and interchangeable effect or aesthetic that eliminates the personal traces of the inhabitants and thus just those differences between a house and a home (it seemed). The reference to the hotel resonates with the disproportionate emphasis placed on Babbitt's surreptitious use of a bathroom guest towel in the opening pages of the novel, underscoring the author's point that Babbitt is merely a homeless guest in his own house. Homes, for Lewis, have something "to do with" the people who live in them; they are predicated on intimate ties between people, places, and things. Although Babbitt represents the "Standardized American Citizen" (154), Lewis is less committed here to his standardization than to the house's; in fact, the passage asserts the Babbitts' individuality as the surprising measure of the bedroom's inadequacy, *its* failure of personal expression and intimacy, the commodity anaesthetic. Lewis seems to want us to read the bedroom passage as a denunciation of the Babbitts' misguided middle-classness, but it is impossible to take it entirely in that way. The house fails because it is so full of the goodies that form middle-class standards of taste, comfort, and culture that they are prevented from reaping their middle-class reward. It is Lewis who uses the word *home* to evaluate their loss. The terms of his critique affiliate it with the values he claims to be repudiating.

Hoover's unconditional, unwarranted identification of homes with house ownership linked emotional satisfaction to the consumer and construction engines that drove the capitalist economy he oversaw, but the reflexive disunion of house and home is suspect too. Hoover at least treated the ownership of a single-family house in the twenties as a tangible benefit for those who could afford it, an economic investment in property, as he also exploited the sentimental payoffs. *Babbitt*'s appeal to the home is marshaled in the service of representing suburban house owners as emotional casualties of the proliferating comforts and conveniences achieved and represented by standardization. To possess these commodities is to be dispossessed by them. Babbitt comes around to Lewis's understanding of what can only be called his plight; his crisis is nothing more than the recognition of his homelessness. Babbitt's resistance to standardization, to having a bedroom like his neighbors and to being just like them, is supposed to be the most redeeming thing about him. But the basic premise, which is established through periodic, richly detailed inventories of the house's amenities, has remained uninterrogated: that such things as comfortable mattresses, window shades that don't crack, and standard lamps are somehow understood to be intrinsically alienating for the consumer and legitimate sources of middle-class dissatisfaction, as though living in "a very good hotel" were some kind of terrible penalty.

Neither Mumford, Stearns, nor Frank excoriated the suburb to expose its inadequacy as an emotional sanctuary for the middle class. Stearns's point was just the opposite: he pitched the "emotional" "sting" of intellectual life as a substitute for insulated domestic happiness at the expense of critical social engagement. Mumford, who would argue in the thirties against sentimental ideas about the house, as we shall see in the next chapter, insisted that Americans needed instead to live up to their marvelous mechanical environment, to master the machine for the creation of humane lives in humane communities, to meet the material and spiritual needs of all. Hating the machine for itself made no more sense than loving it for the same reason. *Babbitt*'s assault on the suburban house replaced the businessman's conceit of progress with the novelist's fetish of degeneration. Babbitt is both an agent and principal beneficiary of suburbanization, but we are to understand that the kind of person most responsible for the texture of modern civilization and who most enjoys its material pleasures is simultaneously the one most dispossessed and dehumanized by them.

MIDDLE-CLASS MALAISE

Babbitt's discontent and restlessness are crucial but still barely acknowledged features of his archetypal figuration; indeed, as the novel unfolds, they almost replace standardization as the standard marker of his middle-classness. In the Real Estate Board address, Babbitt publicly delights in all the material advantages of his class. He boasts that "it's the fellow with four to ten thousand a year, say, and an automobile and a nice little family in a bungalow on the edge of town, that make the wheels of progress go round!" (152). He further comments on his self-satisfaction: "we like ourselves first-rate" (154). During a private lunch at the Athletic Club, however, Babbitt confesses to his friend, Paul Riesling, that his complacency has been disturbed by the very things that make him a "Solid American Citizen," "the type of fellow that's ruling America today" (152):

Kind of comes over me: here I've pretty much done the things I ought to; supported my family, and got a good house and a six-cylinder car, and built up a
nice little business, and I haven't any vices 'specially, except smoking—and I'm
practically cutting that out, by the way. And I belong to the church, and play
enough golf to keep in trim, and I only associate with good decent fellows. And
yet, even so, I don't know that I'm entirely satisfied! (53)

Like the enthusiastic speech, Babbitt's protest expresses an accurate sense
of his advantages and the prerogatives of his social position, but they are
now invoked as the conditions of his dissatisfaction. Babbitt is "discontented about nothing and everything" (34) because he has achieved everything that comes to be associated with the good life. The nature of his
discontent differentiates him from the stereotype of the perpetually un-
gratified consumer, who could be soothed only by further acquisitions,
according to modern advertisers and their critics, as well as from Daniel
Horowitz's illuminating account of the deeply gratified consumer, for
whom a higher standard of living also involved "the pursuit of 'higher'
goals."[36] Babbitt disclaims the spiritual rewards of consumption. Discontent is the final register and, one might say, the advertisement of his affluence. Even his attempt at self-improvement—to quit smoking cigars—
involves sacrificing something.

Discontent is represented as endemic rather than unique among the
men of Babbitt's set, a function of, rather than traitorous to, his class.
Thus Paul, a closet musician who sells tar-roofing, responds to Babbitt's
confession: "Good Lord, George, you don't suppose it's any novelty to
me to find that we hustlers, that think we're so all-fired successful, aren't
getting much out of it? You look as if you expected me to report you as
seditious?" (53). Paul is a spokesman for a central insight of the novel:
nothing comes more naturally to the white middle class than feeling unful-
filled. For Lewis, being middle class is indistinguishable from feeling bad
about, impoverished by, the markers and material rewards of middle-
classness.

Middle-class women are discontented too. With "gas stoves, electric
ranges and dish-washers and vacuum cleaners and tiled kitchen walls,"
forbidden to labor for money outside the home, many women in "Floral
Heights, and other prosperous sections of Zenith" "worked perhaps two
hours a day, and the rest of the time they ate chocolates, went to the
motion-pictures, went window-shopping . . . and accumulated a splendid
restlessness that they got rid of by nagging at their husbands" (104). The
novel parodies the assumptions of the domestic science movement, which
promoted labor-saving technology and a rationalized housekeeping system in part to give housewives more time with their families and to make
their work seem more fulfilling. Lewis blithely underestimated women's

work in the home but he also justified their alienation from the "splendid" privileges of the suburb, and from their husbands, by emphasizing rightful boredom with the limited role permitted them.[37] Myra Babbitt exemplifies the different decentralization of women; Babbitt's work and car take him downtown, where he meets "all sorts of interesting people," while she labors in isolation. "I get so bored with ordering three meals a day, three hundred and sixty-five days a year, and ruining my eyes over that horrid sewing-machine, and looking after your clothes and Rone's and Ted's and Tinka's and everybody's, and the laundry, and darning socks" (288), she complains, during "a small, determined rebellion of her own" (286). Middle-class women feel bad insofar as their status limits their aspirations, while with men, the satisfaction of aspirations deadens into discontent.

In *Main Street* as well, Carol Kennicott's gender militates against her efforts to reform Gopher Prairie, but it also inspires them: "She was a woman with a working brain and no work" (89). And for years Una Golden could find only mindless work for her working brain. For Lewis, women's discontent has a particular content. I am not claiming that white middle-class women in *Babbitt* are the real casualties of suburban affluence, either absolutely speaking or in comparison, say, with the Babbitts' servant, who gets to clean the "royal bathroom" but not bathe in it. But at moments the novel apprehends a difference between the pleasure of buying one's wife a sewing machine and the tedium of having to use it, even as it ultimately disrespects that difference by emphasizing the husband's ambivalence toward such purchases. Although Myra has the chance to articulate her discontent with a busy and boring routine, her "small" protest isn't taken seriously. It culminates when she attends Mrs. Opal Emerson Mudge's lecture, " 'Cultivating the Sun Spirit' before the League of the Higher Illumination" (289), her idea of revolting against the dull, uncultured life of the suburban housewife.

Not surprisingly, Myra is less important as a discontented being in her own right than as a force for Babbitt's conformity. At several points he turns her into the easy scapegoat for his disaffection, believing her to be "so darn satisfied with just settling down" (246). When she goes to care for a sick relative, he yields to his restlessness and, predictably, has an affair, which draws him temporarily into Zenith's Bohemian set. But Babbitt has no interest in a counterculture. His paramount desire as a swinger is to be settled, to "fe[el] utterly at home" (269). The first evening he spends with Tanis Judique she sings "My Creole Queen" while preparing tea: "In an intolerable sweetness, a contentment so deep that he was wistfully discontented, he saw magnolias by moonlight and heard plantation darkies crooning to the banjo" (264). Domestic intimacy can be figured and enhanced by the proximity of these black people because they are the property of others, not property owners, and are content to remain out-side and in their place, rather than clamoring to enter. Tanis is not his slave, though; she allows Babbitt to "beautifully come home" (296) in her "[s]elf-contained" living room, "warm, secure, insulated from the ha-rassing world" (269), to revel in his discontent, until "he discover[s] that she too had Troubles" (296). He loses interest in Tanis when she ceases merely to give him "sympathy" and begins to "make demands" upon *his* sympathy, "the way" "these women" (295) do. Tanis loses Babbitt by becoming just like Myra: a woman's discontent is inimical to the man's enjoyment of his.

Babbitt's resistance does not neatly resolve itself into an antinomy be-tween a masculine pursuit of freedom, on the one hand, and a feminine will to stability and civilization, on the other. Women are themselves rest-less, and the novel's plot of male discontent and relocation is driven by the desire for a home; Babbitt only flies from the suburban house and way of life in search of what they promise but do not deliver. Even the most conventionally masculine fantasy of escape, straight from Leslie Fiedler's script, is envisioned as domestic recuperation.[38] From a vacation in Maine, Babbitt "remembered Joe Paradise, half Yankee, half Indian. If he could but take up a backwoods claim with a man like Joe, work hard with his hands, be free and noisy in a flannel shirt, and never come back to this dull decency!" (242). A ritual of male interracial bonding and man-ual labor is proposed as a solution to one aspect of the problem of being Babbitt: it's boring. And yet a sentimental yearning for placement is fore-most when the white middle-class man runs off "to the guides' shack as to his real home" (243). But the guides at "the old home" (243) don't recognize him or themselves as frontiersmen. When questioned by Babbitt about his goals, Joe Paradise "brightened" and "bubbled" (246): he would rather move to town and open a shoe store than heal the spiritually sick businessman on holiday. Indeed, Joe Paradise wants to be that busi-nessman. He shares Babbitt's bourgeois ambitions but is unambivalent about them. A comfortable and dull middle-class life can look awfully good to the man in the shack.

During what turns into a mundane camping trip, Babbitt discovers the metaphysical oneness of all places: "he could never run away from Zenith and family and office, because in his own brain he bore the office and the family and every street and disquiet and illusion of Zenith" (247). An-other way to frame the power of Babbitt's mental map is to say that throughout the novel he possesses the freedom to explore the limits of his homelessness from the safety of a worldview that assures him that he can potentially be at home anywhere. The logic of standardization is such that it simultaneously fosters his displacement and ensures an irresistible location. Daniel Boorstin has described the emergence within modern consumer culture of abstract and impersonal "everywhere communities," through which standardization transformed basic notions of human affiliation. Statistical links between strangers supplemented and at times supplanted the particularized and immediate "world of the neighborhood," where face-to-face contacts among intimates prevailed.[39] The substitution of social impersonality for social intimacy also described a major geographical shift of modern life, according to prominent sociologists affiliated with the University of Chicago. In theoretical essays and case studies, they argued that the forces of urbanization, its scale and social complexity, dissolved the old kinship ties of the village; impersonal encounters became the rule of most interaction in the city.[40] Within the context of the suburb, however, *Babbitt* articulates an interesting convergence of the anonymous and the immediate, the "everywhere" and the right here.

Hana Wirth-Nesher has identified the modern urban novel with the erosion of the boundaries between public and private, the "parlor" and the "street," which occurs in such places as hotels and restaurants. These are the quintessentially urban adaptations of domestic habitats, where familiar activities are disclosed to the penetrating "gaze of the stranger."[41] In *Babbitt*, however, private space is made public not primarily through the conspicuous commodification of cooking and lodging outside the home, but with special reference instead to the standardization of the familiar interior. When the novel compares the Babbitts' bedroom to a hotel where people "stay but one night," it announces the Babbitts' estrangement by suggesting that they share the house, because they share their tastes, with strangers who never set foot in there. And indeed, the bedroom's decor, from the white woodwork and gray walls, to the "serene" blue rug and look of mahogany, are right out of home decorating articles in national women's magazines of the early twenties, linking their house to anonymous others.[42] But the novel's comment that "[e]very second house in Floral Heights had a bedroom precisely like this" indicates that they in fact share it with their actual neighbors as well, the people they not only live near but regularly visit and entertain. The parenthetical comments that punctuate the description of the Babbitts' living room also situate the Babbitts within a local community of consumption. "(Two out of every three houses in Floral Heights had before the fireplace a davenport, a mahogany table real or imitation, and a piano-lamp or a reading-lamp with a shade of yellow or rose silk.) . . . (Eight out of every nine Floral Heights houses had a cabinet phonograph.) . . . (Nineteen out of every twenty houses in Floral Heights had either a hunting print, a *Madame Fait la Toilette* print, a colored print of a New England house, a photograph of a Rocky Mountain, or all four)" (78–79). The fractions move closer to a whole and identify the Babbitts as inhabitants of their subdivision; the community created *is* the neighborhood.

These descriptions indicate that for Lewis one effect of standardization in the suburb is the substitution of middle-class community for isolated single-family houses. The problem with the house is not simply its disrespect for the Babbitts' individuality, but also its violation of their privacy. Historians of American architecture and of the suburb have noted that structural changes in the design of single-family house interiors by the 1920s—the virtual elimination of entrance halls, the ubiquity of open floor plans in the living and dining areas—made these areas less private and enclosed than before, more readily accessible to all family members and even to visitors. Meanwhile, the second floor of two-story houses like the Babbitts' became more privatized; bedrooms had ceased to be receiving areas for children or guests as they had often been in middle-class Victorian households.[43] By focusing on decor rather than on the architectural arrangement of the interior, about which the novel has very little to say, *Babbitt* imagines the irrelevance of the house's structure to either maintain or compromise privacy. Nor does it matter that the Babbitts are the first occupants of their house, which they had built for themselves. Although a disdain for "used" housing has been discussed as a post–World War II phenomenon by Kenneth Jackson and Gwendolyn Wright, writers in *Ladies' Home Journal, House Beautiful*, and *House and Garden* expressed or acknowledged a bias in favor of original ownership and habitation in the twenties, as though privacy were based on primacy: "An old house must be shared with those who lived in it before." Like other house owners in the 1920s, the Babbitts have chosen the "spotless unworn immaculacy of modernity," but the originality of their house does not preempt either its uniformity or its communality.[44]

As a receptacle for mass-produced commodities, in other words, the suburban house needs to be protected from other people, but most urgently from those who are just like the Babbitts, those whose desires are shaped by the same national magazines and advertisements, and who have the resources to indulge them. The white middle-class home in *Babbitt* is jeopardized by neighbors rather than aliens and outsiders. The relationship between the homogeneous community of consumption and homelessness is causal: because Babbitt is a member, he is also a guest. But as Lewis is aware, membership has its privileges. The consumer community that compromises one kind of home, the private, individualized, single-family suburban house, also fosters new ideas about the nature of the home and its boundaries. In the Real Estate Board address, Babbitt recites a poem by his friend and Floral Heights neighbor, Chum Frink, a nationally syndicated newspaper bard, that *celebrates* the hotel as the model of a new kind of national home and community:

[W]hen I get that lonely spell, I simply seek the best hotel, no matter in what town I be—St. Paul, Toledo, or K.C., in Washington, Schenectady, in Louisville, or Albany. And at that inn it hits my dome that I again am right at home. If I should stand a lengthy spell in front of that first-class hotel . . . if I should look around and buzz, and wonder in what town I was, I swear that I could never tell! . . . Then when I entered that hotel, I'd look around and say, "Well, well!" For there would be the same news-stand, same magazines and candies grand, same smokes of famous standard brand, I'd find at home, I'll tell! And when I saw the jolly bunch come waltzing in for eats at lunch, and squaring up in natty duds to platters large of French Fried spuds, why then I'd stand right up and bawl, "I've never left my home at all!" And all replete I'd sit me down beside some guy in derby brown upon a lobby chair of plush, and murmur to him in a rush, "Hello, Bill, tell me, good old scout, how is your stock a-holdin' out?" Then we'd be off, two solid pals, a-chatterin' like giddy gals of flivvers, weather, home, and wives, lodge-brothers then for all our lives! So when Sam Satan makes you blue, good friend, that's what I'd up and do, for in these States where'er you roam, you never leave your home sweet home. (156)

Lewis's characteristic irony pervades the euphoric poem, but just as characteristic is the difficulty of reading the poem as purely ironic. Babbitt's and Chum's allegiance to standardization is motivated by their commitment, like Lewis's, to home as a sentimental ideal; they love the home so much they never want to leave it. The standardization that makes Babbitt's house a hotel, by making it indistinguishable from its neighbors, enables him to feel "at home" in real hotels. The out-of-town business trip is supplanted by the circular journey of the domesticated consumer. He experiences consumption not as social competition, in the Veblenian account, but as social cohesion, or what Michael Schudson has called "social *membership*."[45] "First-class" hotels foster affective connections through a brotherhood of consumption, which liberates affluent members such as Babbitt and his Chum from the constraints of the suburban house and responsibilities to wives and families while allowing them to feel pleasurably connected to what they have left behind. The passage indicates that there is nothing uncanny about some compulsions to repeat; standardization can be utterly and desirably *heimlich*—literally like home—insofar as it destabilizes all sorts of boundaries, at least for this population: between the alien and the familiar, the national and the local, the stranger and the neighbor.

Lewis's interest in a world of standardized commodities and places, in middle-class homelessness, shaped his preoccupation with what we tend to think of as a postmodern sense of the possibilities and challenges implied by the erosion of conventional geographical, cultural, and conceptual boundaries. With *Babbitt* Lewis turned from the Midwest as an occasion for literary regionalism, in contrast with both *Main Street* and the fiction of his contemporary and rival, Sherwood Anderson, to heralding and enacting the demise of the regional: "no matter in what town I be." Put another way, Floral Heights residents are neighbors, but their neighborliness is defined more by similarity, the shared davenports and cabinet phonographs, than by proximity. By *Dodsworth* even the border between the domestic and the foreign, or the national and the global, is tentatively deconstructed through an empire of consumption, albeit only with reference to European capitals. Paris, where one can purchase American toothpaste, corn-plasters, Bromo-Seltzer, and Lucky Strikes is called the "largest . . . of modern American cities."[46]

As the examples of Babbitt's first-class hotel and the Americanization of Paris indicate, for Lewis the possibilities of unbounded location virtually always resolve themselves into the tentative freedom to approximate the feeling of home someplace else, for others as well as for oneself, for others more or less like oneself. At the end of *The Job* Una Golden gives up her career in real estate, providing "suburban homes for men and women and children" (281), because she conceives a higher mission, to "make homes for people travelling" (322). She invents the job of general manager of decoration, catering, and service for a new "syndicate of inns" (315), the first national hotel chain, where businessmen and vacationers can feel "at home" (322) through the standardization of good mattresses, coffee, and decor. Martha Banta observes of the final plot development, when Una marries a rootless sweetheart who strays back into her life but keeps her job, that as a woman she is doubly burdened by her private role and "public career as nurturer of wandering males."[47] But Lewis by no means envisioned a paid career of homemaking as a uniquely female enterprise. He shortly proposed the same ideas for hotel service in a series on automobile travel for the *Saturday Evening Post*, which noted the deplorable condition of American hotels outside big cities and called on a "young man . . . to start a chain of small, clean, pleasant hotels, standardized and nationally advertised, along every important motor route in the country," with "good coffee, endurable mattresses, and good lighting."[48] He anticipated the distinguishing features of the post–World War II motor-hotel (motel) chain, your home away from home: prominence along national highways, the emphasis on comfort over extraneous decoration ("he is not going to waste money on gilt and onyx"), and the importance of standardization.

In the twenties automobile tourism gained in mainstream popularity as national highways were constructed following the Federal Road Act of 1921 and a week's paid vacation became the norm for white-collar employees.[49] Kenneth Jackson has discussed the correlation between automobiles and suburbanization, but the car was an important factor in domestic life for other reasons.[50] In *Middletown* the Lynds observed that with the advent of automobility, the home no longer figured so importantly as the center of even routine social life and leisure, especially for the young. The car, in which no one lived, generated "emotional conflicts" and outcries that "the home is endangered" (255). As a novelist, Lewis functioned something like Una and the enterprising "young man": he was committed to bringing mobile middle-class Americans home, and continued to structure his fiction around that project. Indeed, *Dodsworth* concerns little else. In the way Lewis novels endlessly cite themselves, as a tribute to his powers as a sociologist, Sam Dodsworth is "not a Babbitt" (11). He is a "craftsman" (14), a "pioneer" (16) in the development of streamlined automotive design, and a successful national manufacturer. When the business is sold to a larger corporation, his wife, Fran Dodsworth, moves them to Europe and real hotels, which Sam mournfully considers "the home of the homeless" (125). Sam deals with his own homelessness through a plan to house others. He contemplates designing "one of those astonishing suburbs which have appeared in America since 1910" (194), garden suburbs like Roland Park and Shaker Heights, which I discussed in chapter 1. But Sam wants to return to "pioneering" (193), which means the "tradition of . . . pushing to the westward . . . never resting, and opening a new home for a hundred million people" (352). Pioneers express a dynamic national restlessness that also enables the affinity for home, and he decides to combine his personal, yet distinctively American, quest for comforting suburban placement with his professional experience in American mobility.

Seeking to create "an authentic and unique American domestic architecture" (363), the residential equivalent of the "skyscraper" (363), he finally revives an idea to design and manufacture "motor caravans" (19) that feature "a tiny kitchen with electric stove, electric refrigerator; a tiny toilet with showerbath; a living room which should become a bedroom by night—a living-room with a radio, a real writing desk. . . . He could see his caravanners dining on the verandah in a forest fifty miles from any house" (21). *Dodsworth* appeared in 1929, the same year as the first mass-produced trailer, named the Covered Wagon in honor of the nation's first mobile homes.[51] Whereas Sam once noticed his cars parked "before every other bungalow" among "miles of green and white little houses" (153), the caravan's innovation is to liberate people from the static suburban house by putting it on wheels, unifying the American "dialectic" between "the thrill of the open road and the certainty of home," "migration and habitation."[52] Five years later Lewis coordinated these tendencies again at the end of the egregious *Work of Art* (1934), a novel about a man's failed quest to build and operate the perfect hotel. The protagonist finally decides to experiment with "the newest thing in the world," a tourist court that offers automobile travelers shelter in "neat, clean cabins," "each with shower bath," good food, and amenities, to "persuade [people] to stay over a couple days" rather than drive on to the next random destination.[53] The natural love of home that Hoover attributed to Americans coexists in these novels with the indisputable fact of their restlessness, a paradox that struck other commentators in the twenties.[54] Lewis imagined a provisional resolution of these tensions. He thought of travel in terms of homecoming. The trailer and the tourist court do not express alternatives to the suburb and suburban house so much as better, because more flexible, versions of them.

By *Dodsworth* Lewis promoted ingenious commodities such as cars, caravans, plumbing, and dishwashers, in part because he believed that his attacks on standardization in *Main Street* and *Babbitt* had made Europeans patronizing and Americans overly "apologetic" (59) and "insecure" (76).[55] The endings of *Dodsworth* and *Work of Art*, like *The Job*, aspire toward, but never realize, the reconciliation of restlessness and home through which the standardization of such commodities might be acknowledged as an asset to the Babbitts of this world. Lewis does not deliver on his promise of a home away from home, despite an increasingly optimistic view of standardization. The boundaries between outside and inside, public and private, are already under assault in his fiction, but they continue to shape what is meant by *home*. The values do not keep pace with the realities. By ending with plans and propositions rather than concrete artifacts, these novels remain true in the end to the logic of homelessness in *Babbitt*: the home's interior should not be open to things exterior to it; to feel at home anywhere is in fact to be at home nowhere. Babbitt is subject to an unappeasable restlessness because "home" for him is always only a simulacrum of a thing he hasn't got. He cannot escape from places that remind him of what he has left behind and thus of what he has not yet found; he is perpetually in a position to realize that he has still to come home.

In domestic limbo, bounded and discontented, restless and displaced, Babbitt is suddenly returned to the family and community by "the standard and traditional realities"—and one should add, literary devices— "of sickness and menacing death" (311). Faced with his wife's emergency appendectomy, "he swore faith to his wife . . . to Zenith . . . to business efficiency . . . to the Boosters' Club . . . to every faith of the Clan of Good Fellows" (315, ellipses in original). Babbitt's pledge of allegiance isn't the disappointing reversal one might think. His break with Zenith's ruling elite is boldest when a series of strikes prompts his peers to quash the workers' political activities. Babbitt refuses to join the Good Citizens' League, but not for political reasons; actually, he refuses for no reason at all: "Babbitt could not recall his reasons for not wishing to join the

League, if indeed he had ever definitely known them, but he was passionately certain that he did not wish to join" (302). The recruitment committee waits for Babbitt's reply: "He thought nothing at all, he merely waited, while in his echoing head buzzed, 'I don't want to join—I don't want to join—I don't want to' " (303). The mechanical repetitions and banal petulance of his resistance replay the thoughtlessness of his prior conformity. He finally joins the Good Citizens' League, "almost tearful with joy at being coaxed instead of bullied, at being permitted to stop fighting, at being able to desert without injuring his opinion of himself" (316). His reluctance to belong has been a stand for his personal, rather than for others' political, freedom.

Babbitt has always been at heart a "domestic revolutionist" (317); even when his resistance seems most political, it must be seen as an effect of the suburbanite's burgeoning self-consciousness and not as evidence of a budding liberal conscience. His return to the good graces of his neighbors is thus described as a kind of homecoming that is associated with the security of a place like the suburb, where he makes something of a Tarzan-like entrance: "All his friends ceased whispering about him, suspecting him. . . . Babbitt felt that he was swinging from bleak uplands down into the rich warm air of a valley pleasant with cottages" (316). Back in the house and the neighborhood, however, he is more like the same old Babbitt than a Tarzan reborn. Discontent continues to be an essential condition of his middle-classness. As Babbitt packs Myra's bags for the hospital, he admits that his rebellion was the "last despairing fling before the paralyzing contentment of middle age" (314). He may be paralyzed, torn between desires and duties, but he isn't exactly contented: "He felt that he had been trapped into the very net from which he had with such fury escaped, and, supremest jest of all, been made to rejoice in the trapping" (323). Babbitt has learned to feel good about his advantages again, but he is still discontented—he feels caught. Rebellion also entails learning to feel good about his disadvantages. Discontent yields its own contentments. Shortly before the operation, he bullies Myra into accepting blame for his affair with Tanis: "He went to bed well pleased, not only the master but the martyr of the household" (301). Babbitt's rule is legitimated by a kind of moral authority that his suffering confers on him; his discontent makes possible a pleasurable sense of disempowered power.

Critics have long observed the "equivocation of values" and "split in sensibility" that make the boundary between satiric critique and sentimental sanction so uneven in Lewis's novels.[56] What it means for Babbitt to be the object of the author's sympathy as well as satire is that the white middle-class male is both a tyrant and the victim of his own tyranny, or in the terms Lewis used in the unpublished introduction to *Babbitt*, "the ruler of America" and "a god self-slain on his modern improved altar, the

most grievous victim of his own militant dullness."[57] Babbitt's shared
sense of victimization results in an "interesting martyrdom" (270) that
provides an antidote to dullness. Moreover, feeling bad about his affluence does not carry the penalties of actually having to give anything material up (he never does quit smoking). From beginning to end Babbitt has
done exactly as he pleased—betrayed his wife, antagonized fellow businessmen and friends, repudiated his lifestyle—and suffered no lasting consequences. At one point Babbitt wonders, "What was he getting out of
rebellion? Misery and shame" (241). Exactly. The challenge of being middle class, for Lewis, is to enjoy the trap, not to escape it, to feel sorry for
oneself as one struggles in and benefits from it. Babbitt's inability to find
his "real home" is the function of a productive rather than debilitating
disequilibrium that demands the feeling, if not the fact, of dispossession.
The suburb highlights the contradictions of white middle-classness in
Babbitt; as the place where his material advantages are most palpable, it
is almost automatically converted into the site of his oppression. And even
if he really wanted to abandon it, there is no other place for the tired,
homeless businessman to go.

BABBITT, *C'EST MOI?*

When will Sinclair Lewis write a satire of suburban life? Christine Frederick posed this question in a 1928 article denouncing the suburb, but she
did not attack it for isolating women or giving them too much or too little
to do. Indeed, the author of *Selling Mrs. Consumer* (1929), an advice
manual for advertising and marketing executives, professionally promoted consumption and suburbanization as means to the housewife's autonomy and fulfillment. She complained instead about its dullness for
cultivated people like her. The suburb "is a good temperamental fit" for
"the general run of people," but "the more sophisticated and individual
types" find it "sometimes utterly intolerable, and nearly always a disap-
pointment. It is the very apotheosis of standardization at its very worst."[58]
The article prompted a rejoinder by Ethel Longworth Swift, who con-
ceded her antagonist's point about the suburb while defending the suburbanite against it. She sarcastically wondered whether "our minds [are] so
dulled by the sugar-coated *bourgeois* existence of life in our little town
that we have lost, not only the ability to plumb the depths of cosmopolitan
life, but even the insight to recognize our own narrowness?"[59] The middle-
class suburbanite's mind *is* dulled, but not so dull that it cannot perceive
its limitations. Swift converts an awareness of the suburb's inferiority into
redemptive self-consciousness. She does not credit Lewis or Babbitt for

her insight, but merely ends the article with thanks to "that enterprising realtor, Babbitt, for the suburb" (558).

But Frederick's and Swift's debt is greater than they acknowledged, because both needed someone like Babbitt to define themselves against. Frederick did not count *Babbitt* as a satire of the suburb, because it insists that sophisticates and individuals, those like the Fredericks who can afford an urban apartment and a house in the country, are not the only ones who are alienated from the suburb. Lewis proposed that a sense of its failings was an intrinsic feature of white middle-class consciousness. Frederick cannot distinguish herself from the "general run of people" in her disdain for the suburb if the general run disdains it too. Similarly, it would drain some of Swift's satisfaction in the cool recognition of her narrowness were she to compare it with the analogous self-awareness of a character who had already come to stand for middle-class obtuseness. It was more pleasant to think of Babbitt as the person who sells suburban houses than as a next-door neighbor.

The tremendous success of *Main Street* and *Babbitt* had suggested to reviewers that "as a nation we were beginning to become self-conscious"; according to Edmund Wilson, Lewis's popularity—"not only among the intelligentzia [*sic*], but among the reading public at large—proves that there is a widespread feeling of disgust in America with the conditions of American life."[60] Lewis popularized his version of the intellectuals' critique, bringing it through best-selling fiction to the people who were its primary targets. But it may be more accurate to say that if anything, Lewis enabled the evasion of self-consciousness. He remarked on the irony of *Main Street*'s enormous success, in terms that apply equally to *Babbitt*: "here is a divine comedy! An earnest young man . . . writes a long book to slap the bourgeois—the bourgeois love it, eat it!"[61] Lewis thinks his audience experiences masochistic pleasure from the book; they love what slaps them. But the pleasure is perhaps not found in pain. For the spiritually "starved" middle class, to return to the metaphor of both Frank and Stearns, "eat[ing]" Lewis's indictment could provide it with a kind of nourishment. Carl Van Doren considered that "hundred of thousands" had read *Main Street*, "proof enough that complacency was not absolutely victorious" (410), proof, that is, of the readers' superiority to the inhabitants of Gopher Prairie. One might draw the same inference from the popularity of *Babbitt*. May Sinclair hinted in a *New York Times* review that readers identified Babbitt with other people they knew and never with themselves.[62] The question they asked of *Babbitt* was not *Am I Babbitt?* but *Are we Babbitts?* and the answer, she thought, was *Yes, they are.* If the success of *Main Street* and *Babbitt* implied a new national self-consciousness, it may have been directed against all those other

Americans. Readers might have loved these novels because they slapped someone else.

Babbitt was the object and emblem of the reader's "disgust . . . with the conditions of American life," but as I have argued, Babbitt not only exhibits disgust along with the reader, he is also disgusted with himself as the embodiment of those conditions. The response described by Van Doren, May Sinclair, and Lewis himself indicated the failure of his sentimental satire to produce *self*-consciousness on the order of Babbitt's, whereas Swift implicitly dissociated her own self-consciousness as a skeptical suburbanite from the novel. Like Mumford, Stearns, Frederick, and Swift, however, Babbitt knew that there was more to life than bathtubs. He prefigured by a few years Mumford's sense, in *Sticks and Stones*, of a growing revolt from the suburb: "Blindly, rebellious, men take revenge upon themselves for their own mistakes: hence the modern mechanized house, with its luminous bathroom, its elegant furnace, its dainty garbage-disposal system, has become more and more a thing to get away from."[63] Rebellion against the privileges of affluence again comes down to running away from home. Babbitt is self-conscious, rather than simply obtuse, and the novel suggests the limits of middle-class self-consciousness to generate transformative self- and social criticism, with the productive political and cultural effects anticipated by intellectuals of the period, what Warren Susman termed "[c]ritique as creation."[64] Given that self-consciousness in the novel signifies an uncritical acceptance of the proposition that a materially bountiful life is emotionally uninhabitable, the reader's insensibility to what Lewis conceived as *homelessness* seems hardly less liberatory than his or her abject recognition of it.

Escape from the Suburb

Laments about spiritual sterility in *Babbitt* are underwritten by the security of material abundance; concerns about dullness are measures of and never threats to prosperity. Lewis's understanding of white male middle-class consciousness remained fairly stable despite the tremendous social changes of the thirties and forties. Less than a decade after *Babbitt*, the Depression made spiritual homelessness and discontent more difficult to invoke and even more ludicrous to embrace as cornerstones of white middle-class identity. By 1933 there were one thousand house foreclosures per week in the United States, and nearly half of all home mortgages were technically in default.[65] The stakes of discontent were political and economic rather than loosely spiritual. The crisis of employment and property ownership had jeopardized or eliminated "the good life" for many middle-class people, and a pair of sociological studies published in

THE REVOLT FROM THE SUBURB 71

1935 claimed that the new "discontent" of the middle class had created a population that was ripe for either socialism or fascism.[66] Lewis Corey argued that the battered middle class would soon realize that their future under capitalism was as propertiless employees and that their real interests were aligned with the workers and a new socialist order. Alfred Bingham predicted instead that the middle class would selfishly commit to fascism to restore the security it had lost with the failure of capitalism during the Depression. "In a time of distress and disintegration there is nothing that terrifies the average man more than the thought that he may lose his home, his furniture, his personal belongings, his little savings account, or insurance policy," and he craves the "discipline" necessary to protect them.[67] The average man in the 1930s is terrified of poverty, not alienated from affluence; homelessness in the spiritual sense is a luxury this Babbitt cannot afford.

Lewis addressed such fears about the middle class and fascism in *It Can't Happen Here*. It conceives of fascism as "revolution in terms of Rotary," which draws heavily from the ranks of unemployed white-collar workers and "suburbanites who could not meet the installment payments on the electric washing machine."[68] Surprisingly, though, like Babbitt's "rebellion," resistance to fascism is rather Rotarian too. Doremus Jessup, the self-described "liberal" and "bourgeois" (53) owner/editor of a small-town newspaper, finds the underground movement a "delightfully illegal" (233) backdrop for his extramarital affair with a more committed revolutionist: "[H]e was utterly content. . . . They were going to be so adventurous together!" (241). If the discontent that produces Babbitt's affair sometimes expresses itself in remotely political terms, the political imperatives of *It Can't Happen Here* express themselves in terms reminiscent of the old middle-class desire for something besides a stable family life, a good business, and house ownership. Discontent and boredom are so constitutive of white middle-class male identity for Lewis that they motivate even a protagonist who faces national crises of total political repression and economic turmoil. Doremus succumbs to the romance rather than to the politics of revolution.

He eventually becomes a more committed revolutionary, however, after brutal courtroom and prison experiences convince him of his vulnerability "to all the risks and pain of ordinary workers" (264). He "who had thought of himself as a capitalist because he could hire and fire, and because theoretically he 'owned his own business,' had been as helpless as the most itinerant janitor" (272). Doremus's true rebellion is prompted once he identifies his suffering, and his interests, with the worker's, as Corey would predict. But if white middle-class self-pity is sustainable only in a prosperous world, actual hostility to capitalism cannot survive the social, economic, and political crises under which alternatives would appear most attractive. The antithesis of fascism in *It Can't Happen Here* is untheoretical capitalism. The novel is nostalgic for the old-fashioned tyrannies of the 1920s, as Doremus carries the revolution to small midwestern towns. Lewis disliked communism and fascism—both entail the abridgment of free speech and of the right to a private bedroom—and his prescription for their dangerously classless visions is to reclaim the old-fashioned bourgeois values of Main Street.[69]

Twelve years later, with the prosperity that followed World War II on the horizon, Lewis reexamined spiritual alienation for a now explicitly racialized suburbanite. *Kingsblood Royal* is a passing novel in which "a one-hundred per cent. normal, white, Protestant, male, middle-class, efficient, golf-loving, bound-to-succeed, wife-pampering, Scotch-English Middlewestern American" discovers that his great-great-grandfather was black and thus, according to the one-drop rule, so too is he.[70] Neil Kingsblood is at first a younger, less tortured Babbitt, who takes a certain comfort in his constraints: "he was caught and not at all unhappy about it" (30). What he learns about his ancestry alerts him to the trap of his former racial identity. With remarkable alacrity, he is freed from the myth of white superiority and his racism and is drawn instead to the wonderful exoticism of African American culture.

Neil doesn't merely accept the fact of his real racial identity, as he understands it; he embraces it. "[A]ren't you kind of overdoing your glee in becoming a colored boy? —Okay. I am" (74). On his first trip to the black part of town, he is amazed—and disappointed—to learn that the residents "were like any other group of middle-class church-going Americans" (92). Neil is dissatisfied with their proximity to his old white self: "He could have done with more tom-toms and jungle-dancing, more samples of what his darker ancestors might have been. . . . If I *am* going to be a Negro, I want my sermons hot. I might as well enjoy getting away from certifying checks and playing bridge, and roll the bones in the jook" (99). Like Babbitt with Joe Paradise, the plodding, conventional Neil seeks an exotic racial group to free him from what he has begun to see as the dullness of white privilege, but the middle-classness of the black churchgoers subverts their compensatory racial function. Neil's fascination with the racial other, or rather, his allegiance to an "authentic" racial self, converges with the inconvenient discovery that he is not relieved of the old class affiliations, which seem at first to supersede racial difference.

His protests against black middle-class respectability echo the objections of Langston Hughes some two decades previously, in "The Negro Artist and the Racial Mountain." Hughes, whom Lewis consulted during the composition of *Kingsblood Royal*, wrote that in its eagerness to "pour racial individuality into the mold of American standardization," "the smug, contented, respectable" black middle class cuts itself off "spiritually" from the folk and thus from the race; for example, the "drab melodies" and restrained behavior in church services, the very things Neil complains about, mimic their white counterparts: "'Let's be dull like the Nordics,' they say, in effect."[71] Sociologist E. Franklin Frazier supplied the missing analytical term when he observed that "New Negro" intellectuals sometimes denounced the "Negro business man" as "a Babbitt."[72] Hughes didn't want bone-rolling, but like Neil, he didn't want Babbitts. They both imagine an essential racial identity that is "colorful" and "distinctive" (Hughes 693) but rendered dull and standardized by a whitening effect associated with the middle class.

As someone who cannot escape the mainstream even with the discovery of a genuine African American ancestry, Neil is also not the marginal, rootless, rebellious "white Negro" described by Norman Mailer in the 1950s.[73] But he does at last find difference amid the comfortable familiarity. Once inside the house of a black middle-class family, which is "exactly like the house of any other middle-class Americans with ordinary taste and neatness" (107), Neil discovers that "these people—it was another shock—talked like the people he knew, like all the people he had ever known. . . . Only, more gaily!" (148). Even without the "voodoo altar" and "leopard skin" (107) he seeks, the black middle class withstands standardization because it is gratifyingly cool. "He felt that he had come on a new world that was stranger than the moon, darker than the night, brighter than morning hills, a world exciting and dangerous. 'I love these people!' he thought" (152). Neil ultimately differs from Hughes in the belief that the black middle class can't help but be more "colorful" than the same old unhip white middle class he has always known. Blackness is not just an identity for Neil, but an allegiance that has simultaneously introduced him to middle-class self-pity, which is by definition white in *Kingsblood Royal*, and offered him a way out of it.

In linking *Kingsblood Royal* to the narrative of discontent and self-pity that the chapter has traced, I do not want to overlook Lewis's ambitions for it. For a novelist of his stature to tackle the subject of racial discrimination meant that many white readers and reviewers would confront his critique before wartime patriotism had faded and at a time when agitation on behalf of African Americans would soon invite accusations of communism.[74] The novel is nonetheless on a continuum with *Babbitt*, insofar as it traces a dull middle-class white man's quest for spiritual salvation; it also, however, marks an evolution in Lewis's thinking about the suburb, which ceases to revolve around the problem of homelessness. Before his discovery, Neil's "normal, white, Protestant, male, middle-class" blandness is linked to his conventional Colonial house in a "new gray-shingle and stucco and asphalt-roof and picture-window real-estate development called Sylvan Park" (6). More homogeneous than Babbitt's, the suburban house plays a quite different role in *Kingsblood Royal* once the drama of Neil's racial identity unfolds. Unable to keep his race a secret—he is so excited that he can't resist telling all his racist white peers—he loses his white friends, family, and job at the bank. Neil's transgression of the values and conventions of his peers, which is established less by the racial revelation than his enthusiasm about it, has significant consequences for himself and his family. The only thing that remains to Neil and his wife, Vestal, who stands by him, is "their home, sacred and secure—and paid for!" (290). But as someone whom everyone in the novel now thinks of as black, Neil becomes the theoretical house owner. The one-drop rule operates on a spatial as well as biological plane. The "Sylvan Park suburbanites want to keep their tedious neighborhood lily white . . . " (336), and they remind Neil that the subdivision is covered by racial covenants that prohibit ownership by blacks. He must sell or be literally dispossessed.

At this point, spiritual alienation from the suburban house, from, for example, "the Model Kitchen that had replaced the buffalo and the log cabin as the symbol of America" (12), and the spiritual thrill of racial realignment are rendered absurd by the urgency of racial equality. Residential suburbs are attacked as bastions of racial exclusion, not as places where white rulers are discontented or bored. Published the year before the U.S. Supreme Court ruled in *Shelley v. Kramer* that racial covenants were legally unenforceable, *Kingsblood Royal* sees even the most ordinary house in the most monotonous subdivision as the "extreme symbol of dignity and independence" (308), an attitude that is inconceivable in *Babbitt*. There is a confrontation between the Kingsblood family and a few friends, black and white, and a hostile mob of white neighbors. The novel ends as police unjustly cart Neil and Vestal off to jail for protecting their house from vigilantes. Given the implausibility of Neil's joyous racial rebirth in his early thirties, not to mention the shoddy biological premise on which it is based, the scenario seems still to represent living how and where one pleases as the ambition of beleaguered white people. But the violent conflict between the rightful white-ish inhabitant and his racist white neighbors is nonetheless fought to extend to black people the right to live how and where they please as well.[75]

When it comes to race, the suburb is all about freedom and not the deadening forces of conformity or the divided mind of the suburbanite. This is true whether it is the now racially conscious resident fighting to preserve his home or Neil's equally race-conscious white neighbors evicting a long-term resident. While it may be tempting to applaud Babbitt's desperate, if temporary, retreat from a dull environment and the dull people who are exactly like him, especially in contrast with Tarzan's resolution to seek out people of his race and class, flight from and to the suburb are not unrelated moves. The achievement of racial and class homogeneity affords Babbitt the luxury of experimenting with resistance to his privileges. When the white male suburbanite is secure, with nothing much left to work for or fight against, he turns his critical energies inward and comes up with discontent. Twenty-five years after *Babbitt*, Lewis admitted that escape from the suburb is desirable only when no one questions one's right to be there.

CHAPTER THREE

Mildred Pierce's Interiors

BABBITT REDUX

S INCLAIR LEWIS'S placeless subdivisions in fictional midwestern cities present a homogeneous middle-class landscape, defined by the erosion of the boundaries between the local and the national, the familiar and the foreign, the boundaries upon which the condition of being at home in *Babbitt* may be said to depend. The opening of *Mildred Pierce*, James M. Cain's foray into the hard-boiled world of a suburban housewife who builds and loses a successful restaurant chain, draws instead upon the actual physical contours of southern California, the national center of decentralization, to dramatize the collapse of the regionally specific and the generically suburban:

> In the spring of 1931, on a lawn in Glendale, California, a man was bracing trees. . . . His name was Herbert Pierce. . . . It was a lawn like thousands of others in southern California: a patch of grass in which grew avocado, lemon, and mimosa trees, with circles of spaded earth around them. The house, too, was like others of its kind: a Spanish bungalow, with white walls and red-tile roof. . . . The living room he stepped into corresponded to the lawn he left. It was indeed the standard living room sent out by department stores as suitable for a Spanish bungalow, and consisted of a crimson velvet coat of arms, displayed against the wall; crimson velvet drapes, hung on iron spears; a crimson rug, with figured border; a settee in front of the fireplace, flanked by two chairs, all of these having straight backs and beaded seats; a long oak table holding a lamp with stained-glass shade; two floor lamps of iron, to match the overhead spears, and having crimson silk shades. . . . On the long table was one book, called Cyclopedia of Useful Knowledge, stamped in gilt and placed on an interesting diagonal.[1]

Despite exotic flourishes, the lawn, "like thousands of others," house, "like others of its kind," and interior decoration, "sent out by department stores," betray the commonplace uniformity of "an endless suburb" (9). Waldo Frank's grim observation about the deracinating "march of the bungalow" and the disappearance of the Mexican adobes, along with the unique regional traditions they represent, is advanced in Cain's depiction of the sterile reproductions of a more palatable European heritage, as whitewashed as the residents of Glendale.[2] The transition from pueblo to modern metropolis was accomplished largely by native-born white Americans, who poured into the Los Angeles area between 1890 and 1930, creating "a middle-class heaven" of "single-family houses, located on large lots, surrounded by landscaped lawns, and isolated from business activities": a vision of the residential suburb writ so large that it seemed almost to dispense with the notion of the urban, as the region came to be known as "nineteen suburbs in search of a city."[3]

Although the details of Cain's southern California landscape are new, we are, nonetheless, on familiar ground. Lewis's turgid prose in *Babbitt* has given way to Cain's leaner literary style, but their critiques have much in common; the Spanish style is a vernacular expression of a problem that exceeds the particularity of the historical referent and immediate location. The placement of the Glendale resident in his Spanish residence is defeated by the predictable deficiencies of a "standard living room" and its lamentable middle-class aesthetic of impersonality. Indeed, the unexpected reference to the *Cyclopedia of Useful Knowledge* evokes Babbitt's "standard bedside book" and coffee-table "gift-books" (78) "laid in rigid parallels" (79), and situates the Pierce house within broader literary and national contexts.[4] Bert is "vaguely proud of" the living room, but the narrator knows better. It "achieved the remarkable feat of being cold and at the same time stuffy, and . . . would be quite oppressive to live in." The effect is so alienating that Bert's uninterrupted passage through the living room, with "neither a glance nor a thought," is sanctioned by a pronouncement on its functional failure—"As for living in it, it had never once occurred to him" (4)—Cain's not much less plaintive version of Lewis's commentary on the Babbitt house: "It was not a home."

In *Mildred Pierce* the democracy of consumption enables a Tarzanian fantasy of aristocratic suburban house ownership, manifested in the coat of arms, but once again it reduces the male inhabitant to something less than the lord of the realm. Bert's dislocation is especially striking because his connection to the house is otherwise so intimate. He inherited a ranch "in the exact spot where people wanted to build" (9); the Spanish bungalow is in fact a Pierce Home, built on Pierce Drive, in a three-hundred-acre subdivision owned and marketed by Pierce Homes, Inc., all products of the regional real-estate boom of the 1920s, "such a boom as has rarely been seen on this earth" (9). His success was an accident of location, but in constructing the suburb he constructed himself, or at least his sense of himself, as an astute professional: "a subdivider, a community builder, a man of vision, a big shot" (9). By the novel's opening in 1931, economic prosperity has given way to Depression, and steady suburbanization to stagnation. His house is "a mockery" (9) of his status and his tenancy;

the company is bankrupt, Bert unemployed, and the "place . . . mortgaged and remortgaged" (9–10). The Pierce Home is about to become "the bank's house" (18). The pending crisis of houselessness short-circuits the homelessness narrative, but Bert's relation to ownership is not so tenuous as to avert Cain's criticism of the middle-class standard that Bert mistakes for the sign of a home, nor to neutralize altogether the novel's investment in personal living spaces that generate meaningful affective connections.

Mildred Pierce, which Cain worked on from the early thirties, is driven by the desire to make the generic Pierce Home the Pierces' home, to imagine living rooms that express the owner rather than the department store and that are places people can live in. From instructions in the fine points of interior decoration to the manufacture of domestic comforts in Mildred's restaurants, the novel is obsessed with the limitations and possibilities of house and home as commodities in an age of mass production. The exigencies of the Depression are treated as an opportunity for rethinking the basic structure and services of the home; the projects of economic and emotional recovery are linked to the housewife's work of commodifying her not-quite-so-separate sphere. If homes in *Mildred Pierce* must always be made, they are then subject to remaking, to reproduction, and in places other than their conventional locations. This chapter analyzes Cain's elaborate model of homemaking as an aesthetic and affective practice in and out of the house. Far from opposing the replication and marketing of the home and its traditional associations, Cain finally points to the aesthetic and emotional, as well as the economic possibilities of mass production. In ways not envisioned by even the most ardent supporters of mass-produced housing in the thirties, the more manufactured the home in *Mildred Pierce*, the more sentimental one can be about it.

The psychical and physical displacement of men like Bert becomes Mildred's entrepreneurial opportunity. Both of the men in Mildred's life are disabled by the Depression: Bert cannot cope with "things that lay beyond his control" (7), and he "lives in a world of dreams" (10), while Mildred's second husband, Monty Beragon, who is from an elite Pasadena family that has lost its fortune and is also on the brink of losing its house, is "like Bert," unable to "adjust" to "catastrophic change" (167). By contrast, Mildred "can't take things lying down" (13). The Depression mobilizes her because it paralyzes men, and the consolation of dislocated men like Bert and Monty, whom she first meets while waitressing, becomes the focus of Mildred's paid domestic labor. As Mildred Pierce, the protagonist caters to the needs of her husbands; as Mildred Pierce, Inc., she perceives the economic value of the comforts of home and stops giving them away for free. The novel eschews the critiques of a moribund and monolithic capitalist economy that were the mainstay of proletarian literature in the thirties; it defies as well the particular association of hard-boiled literature by writers such as Cain and Raymond Chandler with emotional evacuation, the "tough guys" turned out by an "unusually tough era."[5] What *Mildred Pierce* envisions is a cozy sort of middle-class capitalism, with a mother's face, that is neither disconcertingly abstract nor in decline, but thrives precisely because of its capacity for generating sentimental investments during hard times. In bringing the hard-boiled style to bear on suburban lives in the Depression, *Mildred Pierce* not only examines the interplay between the sentimentality and toughness of the working mother, one who seeks to save her home by taking it to market; it further reveals the emotional stakes of the toughest of literary genres.

MASS PRODUCTION AND THE MODERN HOME

Mildred Pierce's aversion to homogeneous Spanish houses and their impersonal living rooms, and its commitment to modern technologies of homemaking, attend to a larger cultural preoccupation with the relation between house and home during what Siegfried Giedion called "the time of full mechanization" between the wars.[6] Mass production played a significant role in discussions of housing in the 1930s, which were rich with implications for the suburb, as the collapse of the construction industry and real estate market contributed to an acute shortage of dwellings across the United States and prompted demands for changes in the production, design, and economics of housing.[7] Mass production had already widely influenced American single-family house construction by the 1870s, when factory-made building materials, columns, cornices, and other decorative facade work came to form and adorn many Victorian residences. From 1904 through the midthirties, small building firms as well as national mail-order giants Sears, Roebuck and Montgomery Ward brought mass production to bear on "ready-built" houses, which they sold by catalog, primarily as suburban residences at the height of their popularity in the twenties. They advertised the efficiency and economy of houses that were precut by machine in the factory, "more accurately than hand labor ever could," rather than built on site to individual specifications.[8] At the same time, however, they sought to distinguish between the mode of production and the resultant domestic artifact. As Martha Banta notes, with reference to Leo Marx's *The Machine in the Garden*, mail-order houses had to be "located, as it were, in 'the middle landscape,' away from the factory yard."[9] The relocation efforts are evident from the catalogs. For example, at first Sears identified its houses only by number, but in 1918 the firm decided to name them as well—"Homeville," "Avalon," "Arcadia," and so forth—presumably to make them seem more intimate and homey, less mass-produced and mass-purchased, than #17 and #152. Innovations in design also did not follow from innovations in production and marketing. Mail-order houses featured conservative variations on traditional architectural styles; they were not influenced by the aesthetic of the machine and mass production in the way that the streamlined look of many appliances and other consumer goods was in the late twenties and thirties.[10]

In the thirties a new generation of house builders began frankly, even proudly, to announce rather than obscure the factory origins of their products. Experimenting on a mass scale with nontraditional materials such as asbestos and aluminum, and with simpler, more minimalist designs— with just about everything except the baseline of the freestanding single-family residence—new prefabricated houses were quickly stereotyped by their "box-like appearance and flat roof," a design "indigenous to the machine age."[11] While the mail-order catalogs advertised the virtues of the machine as an efficient tool in building utterly conventional houses, in the rhetoric and design of modern prefabrication, the "engineer's ideal of shelter" became itself a machine: machines were building other machines, and people were going to be living in them.[12] It was the French architect Le Corbusier who first described the house as "a machine for living in," but writers in popular and trade periodicals of the thirties freely borrowed the phrase to describe the designs of American building entrepreneurs.[13] Their housing was also often loosely labeled "functionalist," in recognition of its (superficial) similarity to the work of Le Corbusier and the figures associated with the Bauhaus school in Germany, who as social theorists and architects sought to eliminate all preconceptions about what buildings should look like in the practical and economical alliance of function and form, utility and aesthetics, through the design and manufacturing possibilities inherent in the machine.[14]

Commentators as divergent as the editors of *Fortune* and architectural critics and reformers Catherine Bauer and Lewis Mumford anticipated that mass-produced housing would soon be a financial imperative for most American house owners. They argued that houses built singly or a few at a time were becoming a "luxury product," an "economic anachronism . . . that none but the wealthiest can afford."[15] They also justified machine-made houses on the grounds that they might solve a problem of middle-class aesthetics as well as a housing shortage. "No cluster of prefabricated houses can ever attain a drabber, more monotonous pattern of standardization than in the 'developed' neighborhood which every man can point to in his own town"; such houses might "take the place of the more competitive chaos that provides our more traditional forms of monotony and squalor, or, as in the well-to-do suburb, of standardized 'variety' and fake elegance."[16] In the early twenties Sinclair Lewis did not yet see the architectural exterior of houses as especially worthy of his satire, but by the end of a decade of abundant single-family house con-

struction, the "depraved state of middle-class taste" had created a suburban vista of "pseudo-Spanish or pseudo-Colonial" houses, built from "a
few stereotyped plans," as uniform as anything that might come out of a
factory. Such "imitation" houses lacked both the "charm of good building," with a feeling for the site and materials, and "the austere clarity of
good machinery."[17] Sensible mass production in the factory, in conjunction with intelligent community planning, was aesthetically as well as economically and socially preferable to the spurious individuality of houses
that were randomly scattered across the landscape and effectively cast
from a single mold: "The words *Colonial, Cotswold, Tudor,* in suburban
architecture are mere attempts to cover by literary allusion the essential
standardization that has taken place."[18]

New forms of mass-produced houses may really have been no more
standardized than existing single-family houses, but only the former was
assumed to militate against the conventional affective associations of the
home. Mumford urged that "[i]f we wish to retain the single-family house,
we shall have to accept it as a completely manufactured article; and in
this event, we must throw overboard every sentimental demand."[19] A later
article elaborated on what he meant by *sentiment*—"the notion that the
house should express personality," which he opposed to thinking of it "in
terms of its essential functions."[20] In contrast with its ungainly, imitation
predecessors, the "modern house [is] not built for show but for living in"
(477). But would middle-class Americans want to live in mass-produced
houses that didn't feel personal? Would they jettison sentiment in favor
of function? As a writer noted in *Scientific American,* "home ownership"
was generally thought to be anything but scientific; it is "largely a matter
of heart rather than of head."[21] Factory prefabrication promised to re-
dress "the stone-age methods" of house construction, but not necessarily
to resolve the problem of housing: "unlike Europeans, Americans refuse
to be 'housed.' They want homes—not an efficient cubicle in a long row
of other efficient cubicles."[22] This writer for *American Home* implied that
the American home meant a house that expressed familiar domestic associations rather than the machine; the architectural expression of economy
and efficiency could not triumph at the expense of emotional investment.
In *Housing America,* the editors of *Fortune* warmly endorsed prefabrication but acknowledged the consumer's potential resistance: "What the
intending owner is theoretically buying is shelter. What he is actually trying to buy is a home" (51). The mechanical production of shelters in the
factory was not followed by mass consumption in part because they could
not overcome the problem of "satisfy[ing] the idiosyncratic, highly personalized tastes of the American home buyer."[23]

In Cain the "literary allusion" of familiar architectural styles, which
hides their real relation to standardization, becomes instead the literary

exposure of them and of the interiors with which they are exactly coextensive. Inside and out, Bert Pierce's Spanish bungalow, "like others of its
kind," is the imitation masquerading as the organic, a cliché that cites the
regional, while embodying the failure of conventional design to promote
an alternative to the mechanical uniformity portended by the factory. In
1941 the modernist architect Richard Neutra argued on behalf of the
"intrinsic esthetic possibilities" of new construction technologies and materials in southern California housing and against the reflexive "commem-
orating [of] historic styles."[24] His protest against "[t]he often deadly regu-
larity of the subdivision" (194) found a more literal counterpart in the
"House of Death" from Cain's crime novella *Double Indemnity* (1935).
"It didn't look like a House of Death when I saw it. It was just a Spanish
house, like all the rest of them in California, with white walls, red tile
roof. . . . [The press has] made a lot of that living room, especially those
'blood-red drapes.' All I saw was a living room like every other living
room in California, maybe a little more expensive than some, but nothing
that any department store wouldn't deliver on one truck. . . . The furniture was Spanish, the kind that looks pretty and sits stiff."[25] The department store did not forget the "coat-of-arms tapestry over the fireplace"
(4–5). The passage shares with the writings of Raymond Chandler a general association of private houses with perverse secrets, and it directly
links the tawdriness of the standardized Spanish style to the sinister murder plotted there, as though the house were an accomplice and bad taste
a crime.[26] Here in the deadening impersonality of the architecture and
furnishings is the hard-boiled commodity anaesthetic, the design equivalent of the criminal narrator's affectless prose.

Less sensationally, in *Mildred Pierce* the living room is used only once,
for viewing the body of the younger daughter, who dies of the flu. It
doesn't kill anyone, and yet the reiterated connection between living
rooms and death underscores Cain's sense of the discrepancy between the
conventional, impersonal aesthetics of standardization and places that are
for "living in" and feeling strongly about. But whereas mass production
seemed to suggest a necessary sacrifice of structure for sentiment, house
for home, Cain envisioned a model of homemaking in *Mildred Pierce*—
as a structural relation between the interior of the house and the inhabitants, as a mode of decoration, and as a form of household labor—whose
intimacy is brought off by its amenability to mass production.

For Cain, the most typically impersonal rooms of the house can be the
most intimate domestic spaces. He expresses contempt for the Pierce family taste but admiration for their pragmatism: "whereas it was, and still
is, a civilization somewhat naive as to lawns, living rooms, pictures, and
other things of an aesthetic nature, it is genius itself and has forgotten
more than all other civilizations ever knew, in the realm of practicality"

(5). It develops, however, that the practical genius has fostered the aesthetic at the same time. The living room is contrasted with the bathroom, a wonder of modern technology, in which function is perfectly realized; Bert does not live in the living room, but he bathes as soon as he reaches the bathroom. "[I]t was in green tile and white tile; it was as clean as an operating room; everything was in its proper place and everything worked" (5). The description harmonizes color, hygiene, organization, and performance into an integrated whole. It is, as Roland Marchand has argued about the bathroom in modern advertising, a "showplace of style and opulence," a tribute to the elevation of mundane commodities above their "mere utilitarian serviceability."[27] But the Pierce bathroom does not substitute art for use; it inextricably links them. Cain calls the bathroom a "utile jewel" (5), a term that discovers a provocative connection between the aesthetic and the pure expression of function, where "working" is as attributable to the right color scheme as the right equipment.

Mildred's kitchen is "a counterpart of the bathroom" (6), the "two rooms" that Cain elsewhere praised as "built with the best of skill, and polished with the utmost care," the saving grace of southern California houses.[28] As the mechanical nerve centers of the house, the bathroom and kitchen were the easiest and most obvious spaces to design in terms of function and were the first rooms in the house to be utterly transformed by mass-produced appliances.[29] Unlike the impersonal aesthetic of the machine, however, which marked the difference between the house and the home, not only for commentators on mass-produced housing in the thirties but also in *Babbitt*'s hostility toward such useful technological advances as radiators and bathtubs, the functional aesthetic of Cain's "utile jewel" mediates between the utilitarian view of the house ("consider[ing] it in terms of its essential functions") and the sentimental view ("the notion that a house should express personality"). The novel repeatedly insists that Mildred's most basic traits are her "literal-mindedness," "matter-of-factness" (20), and "common sense" (151). As the domestic "realm[s] of practicality," the bathroom and the kitchen, where she first develops the techniques of domestic efficiency that build her restaurant chain, give direct expression to Mildred's pragmatic personality.

The idea that homes express the people who live in them is advocated more conventionally in *Mildred Pierce*'s "lesson in interior decorating" (263). The "lesson" is administered to Mildred by her second husband, Monty Beragon, when they undertake extensive renovations on his Pasadena mansion, which she has purchased from him. He may have lost his old money, but he retains the innate good taste that Cain identified with upper-class sensibilities. All it takes for Mildred to move from Glendale to upscale Pasadena is money, but the move from middle-class mediocrity to refinement is more complicated. Mildred is judged a woman of inferior tastes, which Monty associates with the deficiencies of the Pierce living room:

> "Sit down a minute, and take a lesson in interior decorating."
>
> "I love lessons in decorating."
>
> "Do you know the best room I was ever in? . . . It's that den of yours, or Bert's rather, over in Glendale. Everything in that room meant something to that guy. Those banquets, those foolish-looking blueprints of houses that will never be built, are a part of him. They do things to you. That's why the room is good. And do you know the worst room I was ever in?"
>
> "Go on, I'm learning."
>
> "It's that living room of yours, right in the same house. Not one thing in it . . . ever meant a thing to you, or him, or anybody. It's just a room, I suppose the most horrible thing in the world. . . . A home is not a museum. It doesn't have to be furnished with Picasso paintings, or Sheraton suites, or Oriental rugs, or Chinese pottery. But it does have to be furnished with things that mean something to *you*." (263–64, Cain's ellipses)

The den to which Monty refers is furnished to be "comfortable" (31). In lieu of the stock paintings of cowboys and wagon trains that round out the decor of the living room, the walls of the den feature framed photographs taken at Pierce Homes banquets and blueprints of its houses. Photographs typify what Walter Benjamin called the "mechanical reproduction" of the work of art.[30] No "authentic" original of the endlessly reproducible photographic print exists, but it is the print, rather than the unique negative, that counts as "art." Analogously, blueprints can initiate one house or a thousand, although only the final, realized architectural products, where one could also never locate an authentic original, generally merit aesthetic consideration. Hanging a blueprint on the wall is like displaying a photographic negative, a sheer sign of reproducibility, rather than an intelligible and discrete aesthetic object in its own right.

According to Monty, the photographs and blueprints are also trophies of Bert's personal achievements that locate him within the subdivision and the house that bears his name. The blueprints and photographs reproduce and are "a part of" Bert; they refer unproblematically to an original, to the person they represent, furnishing material evidence of his identity that makes the den a home. Monty gently mocks Bert's pride in his symbols, even as he approves their effect as personal touches. It is because they look "foolish" that they also look "good." By comparing them to Picassos and Chinese pottery, Monty validates their aesthetic, while denying that the homely aesthetic of interior decoration aspires to great art. Museums are for contemplating works that express the artists who make them. As a place where *you* live, the home is for expressing oneself with objects that "mean something to you," with things that are good because they "do things to you," by way of generating proper emotional attachments.

Monty's "lesson" in decorating theorizes a correspondence between the interior of the home and the interior of the inhabitant that was central to the popular discourse of interior decoration and its overriding rhetoric of "personality." By 1930, according to Karen Halttunen, the concept of "personal decorating" had become commonplace in interior decoration literature, establishing the centrality of the home and the living room in particular to a new sense of the meaning of things, that collapse of selves and commodities, which "proved crucial to the emergence of mass consumer society in the twentieth century."[31] Etiquette expert Emily Post proclaimed in a seminal four-part series, addressed to the largely white middle-class female and suburban readership of *Ladies' Home Journal*, that the personality of the home and the housewife were identical: "Its personality should express your personality."[32] For another adviser, the main criterion for judging a decorating scheme was its accuracy in mirroring the housewife: " 'Is your home furnished as it should be?' 'Yes,' answers Dorothy Dix, 'If its furnishings express YOU.' "[33]

Interior decorating literature suggests that personality might also accomplish for houses what it was supposed to do for people, according to Warren Susman's argument about the imperative of distinguishing oneself from "the crowd" in a faceless mass society.[34] In a residential landscape characterized by "standardized 'variety' " and confronted with the possibility of prefabricated uniformity, individuality was to be fostered within the house, "to distinguish it from all other houses."[35] The question was how best to bring the housewife's interior to the surface. Readers were encouraged not to excavate alone and if possible to hire a decorator, an expert in the interiors of both houses and people. The interior decorator serviced clients by facilitating self-expression; more specifically, the decorator infused "the needs and individual preferences of his client into walls, floor coverings, furniture, draperies and accessories," carefully forging the link between selves and things.[36] And yet the very importance of the expert, often but not always assumed to be a man, implies that the tastes and, by implication, the personality of the untutored client, often gendered female, were somehow suspect. Put another way, how could someone else possibly express a client better than she could express herself? Wouldn't the client's individual preferences automatically find a voice if she furnished her house with things that she preferred? Decorators did not simply "express" their clients, however; they "always interpret . . . the personality and character of the individual house-owner."[37] The author of "Personality in the Small Home" was more direct about what the labor of interpretation might entail. She advised her California readers that the decorator "must know . . . what [the client's] general tastes in decoration are, if he is to help her to express her own personality in her home; if she is wrong about some of her ideas, he will make suggestions."[38] The notion that her "ideas," her tastes and personality, could be "wrong" but might be improved indicates that the decorator developed the interior of the client as well as correlated it with her home. "Men often believe that women instinctively know how to decorate a home," but that putatively natural connection in fact required nurturing.[39] The task of the decorator and the literature was to train the client/reader to express herself tastefully and to express a tasteful self.

This brief treatment of interior decorating suggests that the project of creating the home was related to the project of cultivating the housewife. *Translation* and *reconstruction* are the terms used to describe these processes in *Mildred Pierce*. For the expert interior decorator the novel substitutes the "expertness" (262) of Monty. Mildred is delighted with his ability "to translate her ideas into paint, wood, and plaster" (262). Mildred's "ideas" are her own, but she requires a translator to communicate them. Monty gives them form, expressing Mildred better than she can express herself. "About all she was able to tell him was that she 'liked maple,' but with this single bone as a clue, he reconstructed her whole taste with surprising expertness. He did away with paper, and had the walls done in delicate kalsomine. The rugs he bought in solid colors, rather light, so the house took on a warm, informal look. For the upholstered furniture he chose bright, inexpensive coverings" (262). The talented decorator manages to convey a preference for maple through a design scheme that does not seem to include maple. Monty is credited with having "reconstructed" Mildred's "whole taste," which suggests that he does not simply copy her taste in the furnishings of the home, but that as he decorates, he alters and improves her taste. In the process of expressing Mildred, Monty transforms her, with the understanding that both Mildred and the mansion needed to be redone. Monty is the ideal decorator who develops his female client's taste. Mildred is the ideal client, whose personal taste, what she thinks she wants, is reinvented by the decorator and the home's new interior, "what [she] really want[s]."[40] His successful efforts and Mildred's response to them attest to something implicit in assumptions about the putative benefits of interior decorators: middle-class women need and want to transcend (rather than express) their middle-classness. Monty's lesson in interior decoration specifically impugns *her* taste; Bert gets credit for the den, while she is blamed for "that living room of *yours*." Her middle-class preferences are converted through Monty's standard of good taste, as he strives to fashion a classy Pasadena wife out of a former Glendale waitress.[41]

Mildred's progress is evident in her response to the elimination of the exterior Spanish "incongruities" that Monty's grandfather added to make the "large but pleasant" Colonial house "a small but hideous mansion." Once the "porticoes were torn off, the iron dogs removed, the palm trees grubbed up," she "suddenly began to feel some sense of identity with the house" (262). Monty claims that the name *Beragon* is really a corruption of the Italian "Bergoni" (107). Monty is a faux Spaniard, as inorganic as the architecture, who makes the house pure Pasadena again by exorcising the Spanish traces that for Monty, as for Cain, have come to signify a meaningless, middle-class landscape, rather than the aristocratic privilege of old California. With the Glendale going from Mildred as well, she identifies with the house's original Anglo-Saxon restraint over its mangled Spanish excess. But houses are for living in, not looking at, and her connection to it is most deeply expressed and felt inside: "In what was no longer a drawing room, but a big living room, he found place for a collection of Mildred Pierce, Inc.: Mildred's first menu, her first announcements, a photograph of the Glendale restaurant, a snapshot of Mildred in the white uniform, other things that she didn't even know he had saved—all enlarged several times, all effectively framed, all hung together, so as to form a little exhibit" (263). A home can be a museum after all, as though photographs, blueprints, or even menus are domestic versions of Picassos and Chinese pottery. As curator, Monty employs technologies of reproduction in a tribute to Mildred's corporate identity. He substitutes enlargements for originals, and of course the exhibit itself is a reproduction of Bert's den, which becomes a decorating standard in its own right, but one that places Mildred in her home. If department stores were to begin selling Mildred Pierce exhibits, such a decoration in someone else's house, in a Glendale house, would function as the Western paintings in the Pierce living room, a mechanism of dislocation. And yet even a mass-produced exhibit of her career would still "mean something to [her]"; it would always generate emotional connection.

The novel's principal lesson of decorating, preached and practiced, is that interiors can be designed, engineered, and, emphatically, reproduced with remarkable effectiveness, that is, with respect for the affective requirements of the home. The exhibit of Mildred's career is explicitly affiliated with home life because it accompanies the transition from drawing room, a formal space for entertaining visitors, to living room, the place where the family also entertains itself, the room that exists only nominally in the Glendale house. But the exhibit indicates more than the ambition to modernize the house's interior in line with a more personal, less formal twentieth-century model. Its emphasis on Mildred's professional achievement as Mildred Pierce, Inc., reveals the depth of Cain's commitment to the reciprocity of homes and commercial enterprises, whether in the domesticated professional exhibits of Bert and Mildred, or the professional, domestic nature of the real estate and restaurant businesses, the provision of the structure and the services of home. Men—Monty, Bert, and Cain as well—reveal their investment in the home through insights into the aesthetic and sentimental construction of the house. Mildred, ever the pragmatist, takes her lesson a step further. Impressed by the model of the home that Monty has taught her to appreciate, she "went around meditating about it, and thinking how she could apply it to her restaurants" (263). She assimilates Monty's theory of home decoration to her already successful platform of professional homemaking: she perceives that the aesthetic of the home, like its comforts, can be reproduced in places other than the traditional house. It is Mildred's practical understanding of the mechanics of the home that facilitates her venture in duplicating its emotional effects elsewhere. Or rather, given that she locates two of her three restaurants in houses, her success as a businesswoman is linked to her ability to make them seem more like home than the places people are actually living in. Where William Marling has argued that the "dark" or hard-boiled style developed in the twenties and thirties as "the perfect vehicle for a master narrative about consumerism" within the "emerging techno-economic" order, *Mildred Pierce* reminds us that in a hard-boiled world, few things have greater commercial possibilities than the affect of home.[42]

Homes Just Like Mom Used to Make

As I explained in the introduction, the study of the home in American literature has focused almost exclusively on its manifestations in nineteenth-century domestic fiction, which pits it, the most sentimental of institutions, against the impersonal and exploitative market (even or especially, as Gillian Brown has demonstrated, as it sanctions and enables the logic of the marketplace). One might say instead of *Mildred Pierce*'s hard-boiled domestic narrative that homes thrive because there is always a market for them. The reader first glimpses Mildred in her kitchen, a typical suburban housewife baking a cake. Women's unpaid labor of cooking in the home is a classic illustration of the split in capitalism between productive economic activity and caring for the family, but Mildred's anomalousness is soon made manifest.[43] The cake is for profit, not for her family; she sells it to a neighbor for three dollars. The suburban house is a site of production as well as consumption; however, the kind of labor-intensive, handcrafted goods Mildred makes there cannot resolve her troubles in a modern economy. She starts to panic about money, and her neighbor, Lucy Gessler, has a plan. When the newly separated Mildred is invited to dinner by Bert's former business associate, Wally Burgan, Lucy advises her to refuse his invitation to eat out and instead "sit him right down for one of those Mildred Pierce specials," as "an investment" (29). Before such a thing as a Mildred Pierce special exists, which is to say, in anticipation of marketing Mildred Pierce specials at her restaurants, Mildred markets her talent in an analogous but far more traditional way. In financial desperation, she tries to sell herself as a wife by selling the potential provider on her wonderful talent for cooking.

She feeds Wally chicken and pie, the very things she features at her first restaurant. The possible husband is presumed to want exactly what the future paying customer wants, and he does. Wally Burgan is "enthusiastic about everything, but when she came in with the pie, he grew positively lyrical. He told how his mother made such pies" (34). Mildred's plan to snag a husband fails after a wild night with no proposal, perhaps because men want to eat food prepared by their mothers, and even to sleep with their mothers, but aren't really interested in marrying them. Or put another way, Wally likes the comforts of home but refuses to shoulder its responsibilities. He wants to be taken care of by Mildred but doesn't respond with the desire to take care of her.

Failing to get a husband, "Mildred knew she had to get a job" (39). With no work experience outside the home, she starts taking care of men for money as a waitress. The principle of direct economic exchange for domestic service at first entails a class violation that disturbs Mildred.[44] "The idea of putting on a uniform, carrying a tray, and making her living from tips made Mildred positively ill" (43). The work of waitressing, in which tips, not wages, are paramount, simply shifts the burden of economic dependence from a husband to her customers; as a badge of subordination, the uniform further signifies a presumed sexual availability to men:

> She cultivated men, as all the girls did, as they were better tippers than women. She thought up little schemes to find out their names, remembered their likes, dislikes, and crotchets, and saw that Archie gave them exactly what they wanted. She had a talent for quiet flirtation, but found that this didn't pay. Serving a man food, apparently, was in itself an ancient intimacy; going beyond it made him uncomfortable, and sounded a trivial note in what was essentially a solemn relationship. Simple friendliness, coupled with exact attention to his wants, seemed to please him most, and on that basis she had frequent invitations to take a ride, have dinner, or see a show. At first she didn't quite know what to do about them, but soon invented a refusal that wasn't a rebuff. She would say she wanted him to "keep on liking her," that he "might feel differently if he saw her when she wasn't in uniform." This had the effect of rousing a good lively fear that perhaps she wasn't so hot in her street clothes, and at the same time of leaving enough pity for the poor working girl to keep him coming back, so she could serve his lunch. (74–75)

A waitress sells related but separately remunerated commodities—food and herself, or her service—and it was the idea of an unregulated payment by men that led waitresses to be associated with sexual and moral looseness.[45] Mildred's customers want exactly what Wally did, a good meal followed by a good time, but Mildred refuses to go out with any of them. She achieves "intimacy" with men simply by serving them food, not by flirting, because men ultimately find sedulous attention to their domestic comforts more desirable than outright sexual advances. In the restaurant, they are willing to pay well for what she used to provide for nothing in her home; the intimacy of serving men food is uncompromised by its concrete economic value. Meanwhile, the uniform protects Mildred even as it attracts men. It displays her body, which Cain goes on about at some length, but provides the excuse by which Mildred converts their sexual interest in her and her caretaking into their emotional involvement on her behalf.

The emotional and economic issues that surround Mildred's labor are inflected by some of the concerns generated by working women during the 1930s. With Bert's desertion, Mildred becomes a troubling archetype of Depression womanhood: "the great American institution that never gets mentioned on Fourth of July—a grass widow with two small children to support" (13). Her situation as a mother who must work is imagined as both essentially American and vaguely unpatriotic, if not subversive, as the need for money and the duties of maternity pull uncomfortably at one another. The 1930s witnessed a backlash against working women, who were actively discouraged from entering or remaining in the workforce at a time when so many men were jobless. In some accounts of women's labor, men could begin to look less like victims of the Depression per se and more like victims of women, who were blamed both for perpetuating desperate economic conditions and for depriving men of the emotional support needed to face and triumph over them.[46]

Arguments against women's employment included the obvious tirades about marriage as the ideal career for women, the kind of thinking Mildred rather cynically tries but fails to put into practice with Wally, and the complaint that work for mothers outside the home was "ruining the children of these women."[47] On a different note, some critics charged that in the process of entering "the business world," women were becoming too tough, too much like the men whose "places" they were "usurping." In *Middletown in Transition*, the Lynds observed the problems of adjustment in the families of working women. These women needed "male traits of drive, single-mindedness, the qualities associated with power," which diverged sharply from "the feminine traits of gentleness, willingness to be led, and affection" that women brought to their role "in the home."[48] A defender of women in the workplace argued that men had "made a hard, ugly world," and if to "endure" woman "had to change" "her nature," to become, "like the American man, a self-charging dynamo in a world of dynamos," it was hardly her fault.[49] Another woman who worked outside the home acknowledged that making a place for themselves in the job market was "apt to produce a certain hardness."[50] Hard times made for hard women, just when there existed a "desperate need of her counterbalancing influence" to soften the traumas of the Depression; women were called upon to provide their usual "emotional balance."[51]

Mildred's practical calculations about the work of intimacy with men hints at the hardness about which these writers complained, and yet she is hard in the service of making things soft for others, for men in particular. What she exploits economically is precisely the sentimental value of her labor in a hard world. In contrast with the unemployed male workers whose hunger symbolized, for intellectuals on the left, "the body's deprivation of . . . labor" as well as food, Mildred's hungry male customers want to be filled with food and the right kind of feelings. [52] As a shrewd reviewer noted, Mildred's "talents" are as both "a good cook and a caterer to the inner man."[53] Men are better tippers than women because restaurants and waitresses respond so well to their "ancient" emotional needs. The crafty waitress also stimulates their sympathies without emasculating them. She is not a powerful working woman, but a "poor working girl" who makes dining out and tipping a kind of noble gesture. She bolsters male egos by fostering their pity, a more lucrative feeling than self-pity.

The problem with Mildred, it will turn out, is that she is never hard enough. She is not a machine, a "dynamo," but her sense of the machinery of home-making allows her to found a restaurant chain based on the insight that the traditional home is not a privileged place for sentiment, that sentiment is compatible with and even enabled by economic activity and mass production. She converts financial dependence on her customers and their emotional dependence on her into an entrepreneurial chance. She "really was a marvelous cook" (33) and puts her "fine domestic efficiency" (49) to work by soliciting restaurant contracts for pies. She succeeds as a professional housewife by Taylorizing her operation, first baking pies in the house according to the "principles" she learned at the restaurant where she waitressed—"Now she put them in by the clock and took them out by the clock, and saved herself much fretting, and made better pies" (114)—and later in her first restaurant. The rhetoric of the domestic science movement infuses Mildred's career and provides an instructive counterpoint to the problem that the house as machine was imagined to raise for sentimental occupation of it, and to the idea that laboring outside the home might turn women into machines. When it came to domestic labor within the house, mechanization was seen not as hostile but as conducive to the home. A woman's touch was abetted rather than diminished by streamlining it, because the scientific housewife ran the home like a factory out of a primary commitment to her family, whom she would better service by rationalizing her work, and with whom she would spend additional leisure time (if any). Domestic scientists argued that efficiency in the home enabled her to thrive in wifely and maternal roles and to feel good about her work.[54] In contrast with *Babbitt*, where domestic efficiency is imagined to turn the housewife into a bored and disgruntled consumer, *Mildred Pierce* uses it to foreground the role of production in domestic labor. As a "grass widow," Mildred cannot afford to learn how meaningful unpaid work can be. She is so ideally suited to the pragmatic and sentimental lessons of household efficiency that she responds by extending the principles of domestic science to unite home, factory, and restaurant, turning the drudgery of housework into lucrative, and even glamorous, labor.

The intricacies of Mildred's project are established in the first restaurant, located in the former "model home" of the Pierce Homes' subdivision. Model homes began appearing in subdivisions in the early 1920s to show customers the kind of structure, and sentiment, they might have for themselves if they bought a lot to build on. Its purpose was in part to establish an appropriate standard for the neighborhood, to "set the style of the houses suitable for the property."[55] What is so "model" about this home is that it is a kind of factory, and its products reproduce those of the home and offer the same emotional gratification:

> She had a moment of complacency as she reached for the chicken: now she would reap her reward for all her observing, thinking, and planning. She had had the free parking located in the rear, so she could see exactly how many customers she had, even before they came in; she had simplified her menu, so she could start the chicken without waiting for the waitress to report; she had placed her icebox, range, materials, and utensils so she could work with the minimum of effort. (141)

The restaurant, with its "streamlined" (92) kitchen, is a "well-tuned machine" (141) that characters continue to refer to as the "model home" long after Mildred has gone into business there. By standardizing her tasks and menu, she takes an architectural shell, a "dump" that "[n]obody can live in" (92), and generates a "warm, clean, and inviting" (136) atmosphere. "[T]hey never got such waffles since they was little" (148), a waitress boasts, because Mildred decides to cook them on "a gas waffle [iron]," "the old-fashioned kind . . . that people really like" (140). Like the "ancient intimacy" of serving men food, home cooking enables Mildred to market homeyness as an effect and affect that can be detached from the home and reproduced, with even greater success, in places like restaurants. The restaurant collapses homey and commercial environments—witness "the snug little gold mine" (206) she subsequently opens in Beverly Hills—but her business does so well because she successfully commodifies sentiment. She limits her menu because it is convenient, but she also sells waffles, chicken, and pies in particular because they are comfort foods, the kind of food people haven't had so good since they were little. What is so special about Mildred Pierce's is that it sells the consolation of an "old-fashioned" home that no longer exists.

The fluidity of the home is so attractive and its affect so marketable in part because of the economic crisis, which produces a disorienting world where, for example, mothers have to work in restaurants to put food on the kitchen table. As a restaurateur, Mildred ministers to those who have been economically and emotionally dislocated by the Depression. "People *eat* . . . even now" (60), and they don't need to own a Pierce house to enjoy Mildred's "model home." Given her plight when she opens the restaurant, it is not difficult to see why it could seem more like home than the place where one actually lived. Bert divorces her before she goes into business and makes her a present of the remortgaged Glendale house. "Mildred, caught wholly by surprise, wanted to laugh and wanted to cry. The house had long ceased to be a possession, so far as she was concerned. It was a place that she lived in, and that crushed her beneath interest, taxes, and upkeep" (100). Her unstable economic relation to the house prevents her from conceiving of it as either a possession or a home; as the place where "you live," the home must also be the place where you do not fear imminent eviction. Crushed beneath the financial obligations of the so-called owner, Mildred experiences a paralysis of emotional response: *outright* ownership and sentimental possession seem to be linked. Restaurants are different. She finds that with almost no capital she can get the property and equipment on credit from restaurant suppliers and the bankrupt real estate company. "If you don't look out, I'll cry" (92), she blurts out with this discovery. The Depression that severs owners from their houses also dissociates ownership from emotional connection and the making of homes.

People want to eat in places that remind them of home and to indulge in the experience of home, but the restaurant is sweeter for making that experience available some place besides where they live. Mildred doesn't even have customers, but rather "guests" (141), many of whom are Bert's former customers: "every person who had bought a [Pierce] home, or had even thought of buying a home" (137) is invited to the restaurant opening. She is thus more than a surrogate wife and mother; she is a good neighbor, whose restaurant models the suburb as well as the private home. Providing a point of social contact, the restaurant makes a place for community and domestic comfort in the "fragmented metropolis" of isolated freestanding houses. Just as customers are guests, coworkers in the novel are friends. The first night at the restaurant the "well-oiled machine" becomes "stalled" (143) when Mildred is temporarily overwhelmed by all the people who want a Mildred Pierce special. Lucy, the next-door neighbor, starts selling pies, while Ida Putiak, the hostess at the restaurant where Mildred waitressed, lends a hand in the kitchen. Lucy and Ida eventually become the managers at the Beverly Hills and Laguna Beach branches and codirectors of Mildred Pierce, Inc. Professional homemakers are distinguished from amateurs not only because women are compensated for their labor, but they perform it collectively rather than in isolation, in a market that values their labor because it so highly values the institution represented and re-created by that labor. As the place where the paid cook produces home cooking just like mom *used* to make, but seems "never" to have made quite as well as Mildred, the restaurant and the women who work there deliver the emotional comforts of home more effectively than the home itself does.

Mildred's primary commitment as a career woman, however, is neither to a surrogate family, friends and neighbors, nor to the career itself. The point of manufacturing the home for others is always understood first and foremost as a commitment to her daughter, Veda. The businesswoman's problem is not, as one might suspect, that she is insufficiently motherly—too hard. Rather, she cares for her child excessively, to the extent that mother love interferes with the fiscal responsibilities. In the end, Mildred loses the business through emotional and financial overinvestment in the family. She drains capital from the restaurants to subsidize the lifestyle of Veda and Monty: "All four units of the corporation . . . would be showing a profit if it were not for the merciless milking that Mildred was giving them in order to keep up the establishment in Pasadena" (282). When asked about "home finances" (282), she responds that it's "nobody's business but mine" (283), but it is precisely her failure to run the home in a businesslike way that makes it the business of her creditors. Veda and Monty bring "endless guests" to the newly redecorated house and run "up the bill for household entertainment to an appalling figure" (279). As a personal and aesthetic artifact, Mildred Pierce, Inc., helps to make the Pasadena house a home, but photographic reproductions of Mildred and her business practices are no substitute for the corporation's economic efficiency. Something happens in the transition from Glendale entrepreneur to Pasadena hostess. In the process of improving her tastes, she loses some of her commercial shrewdness. The corporation is going bankrupt because she is running what amounts to an additional establishment for people who really are her "guests," taking for free in her home what they are supposed to be paying for in her restaurants. Mildred, in turn, is imagined as an overly generous creditor of Veda, who as a renowned singer now makes plenty of money in her own right. Veda has "run a lengthy bill" and ought to "pay in," but Mildred refuses to collect:

"I don't keep books on her" (283). She eventually loses Mildred Pierce, Inc. She cannot "pay" "her creditors" (285) because she will not charge Veda.

Mildred manufactures sentiment for restaurant customers but cannot regulate her own. Pragmatism fails when it comes to her selfish daughter. Mildred's misplaced allegiance led her to a bad bargain with Monty; she married him for Veda, who coveted his social connections and society address, commodities whose value is low as a result of the economy. Like the relationship between waitresses, cooks, and patrons, families are constituted through economic and emotional exchanges, but they are not particularly good investments. The lesson of *Mildred Pierce* is not that working mothers destroy their families, as some commentators in the 1930s feared, nor merely that the housewife who wishes to enter the commercial world needs to manage her family as scrupulously as her business.[56] More to the point, Mildred's marketing of the home and its affect successfully imitates the work of the family, while the dissolution of the family points to its deficient imitation of the restaurant, the factory, and the corporation.

Mildred argues for the perfect efficiency of her planned venture: "What costs in a restaurant is waste," but if "[e]verybody gets a chicken-and-waffle dinner," "there wouldn't *be* any waste. All the leftovers would go into gravy and soup" (91). In contrast with the disabled economy of the Depression, in her restaurant there is no such thing as underconsumption.[57] Mildred imagines reproducing something close to this efficiency in the home, when the Pierce family unit temporarily re-forms and returns to Glendale in the last chapter. She has lost her restaurants and left Monty but is thinking about going back into business: "Bert said if she felt like making pies again, just leave the rest to him. He'd sell them. Veda laughed, pointed at her mouth, whispered that she'd eat them. Mildred wanted to jump up and kiss her, but didn't" (296). The family is envisioned as a tidy, self-sufficient cycle of production, distribution, and consumption, and Mildred immediately gets emotional about it. But families for Cain just aren't this efficient, and they don't sustain or reward emotional investment as restaurants, or a well-decorated room, do. In *Mildred Pierce* no good can come from a woman who only ever consumes food and produces none herself. In the next paragraph, a taxi arrives for Veda, and she flies to New York with Monty, recycling Mildred's lover, but otherwise refusing to participate in a thrifty domestic economy. In the end, the writer best known for murder fiction finds that he can't do without a criminal after all: "Mildred's only crime, if she had committed one, was that she had loved this girl too well" (297). Obsessive familial love is a crime that does not pay in any sense; it defeats affective and economic recovery.

As the owner of Mildred Pierce, Inc., Mildred discovers that what remains of her personal assets are protected from her creditors, but she is distraught to learn that because she has incorporated, she is unable to protect her name. She is still Mildred Pierce, and she can still make pies, but she can no longer make and market Mildred Pierce pies, because the corporation owns the right to do so: "The loss of Mildred Pierce, Inc., had been hard. . . . And it had been hard, the wilting discovery that she could no longer do business under her own name" (293). Only with the loss of the business does Mildred experience herself as radically alienated from the capitalist public sphere, which severs the link between a woman and her corporation in order to maintain those between the woman and her private money.[58] Like Bert and Pierce Homes, however, Mildred feels a powerful sense of identity with the business that bears her name, even after its products have long since ceased to be hers in the sense that she no longer makes them herself. A few months after opening the restaurant in the model home, she hires a baker, and by the time she is running a third place, "Mildred never cooked anything herself now, or put on a uniform" (208). When Mildred Pierce pies continue to roll off the corporate assembly line, after she no longer bakes them and even after she ceases to be affiliated with the bakery and the restaurants, the factory has indeed successfully imitated the housewife. In a sense, Mildred succeeds too well; the pies just like the ones mother used to make are now the pies just like Mildred used to make.

And yet the novel suggests that without Mildred, Mildred Pierce, Inc., really cannot make Mildred Pierce pies. Shortly after the corporation passes to receivers, a former customer expresses dissatisfaction with the pies he is getting, and to his delight she asks him "how he'd like to have some of *my* pies" (296). Pies manufactured by the corporation just don't taste as good when Mildred is no longer at the helm, regardless of who bakes them. In *Mildred Pierce*, corporations not only protect personal wealth and provide consumers with products that are designed to strike an emotional chord, but they are themselves personal artifacts, preserving rather than abolishing the intimate identification between founder and product. It is her immediate relation to the corporation that counts; it gives Mildred an immediate relation to the pies. Mildred Pierce, Inc., is no less a personal expression of its owner than the exhibit to which it gives rise. The sentimental possibilities of Mildred Pierce, Inc., are suggested by the domestic places associated with it: Mildred's kitchen, the Pasadena living room, the model home. Corporations may be economic abstractions, but *her* corporation also locates Mildred, as the restaurants that constitute its primary assets do her customers. In *Mildred Pierce*, the restaurant, the factory, and the corporation are better at delivering the sense of emotional gratification, for the producer as well as the customer, that the home was always imagined to provide.

SOFT-BOILED FICTION

In *Mildred Pierce* mass production and sentiment come together finally at the level of its form. The hard-boiled style of the twenties and thirties has roots in one version of late-nineteenth-century literary realism, with which it shares a commitment to verisimilitude of speech and character and to representations of the commonplace, but Cain's prose can also be described as a kind of functionalist writing. Cain provided this account of his style: "I merely try to write as the characters would write, and I never forget that the average man, from the fields, the streets, the bars, the offices, and even the gutters of this country had acquired a vividness of speech that goes beyond anything I could invent, and that if I stick to this heritage, this *logos* of the American countryside, I shall maintain a maximum of effectiveness with very little effort."[59] This passage has been read as an extension of realism's naive and repressive fallacies, the idea that "hard-boiled language [is] a transparent transmitter of documentary evidence."[60] But the alleged transparency of the language is only one of its attractions for Cain. Just as Mildred organizes the restaurant kitchen so that she may cook "with the minimum of effort," Cain is also drawn to the efficiency of speech that is easily produced. The bias in favor of the practical and reproducible, or the "formularized," as Edmund Wilson described it, is combined with the aesthetic contribution of its "vividness."[61] Cain's hard-boiled prose is the linguistic equivalent of the utile jewel.

A review of Cain's first novel, the best-selling *Postman Always Rings Twice* (1934), praised Cain for having "developed the hard-boiled manner as a perfect instrument of narration" that matched elemental style and concerns. Getting "down to the primary impulses . . . in fewer words than any writer we know of," Cain achieved an effect of lean literary minimalism with a "toughness" that "makes . . . [Erskine] Caldwell [look] like a sob sister at her first eviction."[62] The hardness of hard-boiled prose—"a carefully controlled blend of colloquialisms, terse understatement, objective description, all narrated in a detached tone"—and of its male protagonists is a critical given.[63] But just as Mildred coolly calculates and streamlines to facilitate the production of the sentimental associations of home, one might say as well that in *Mildred Pierce* Cain's efficient prose is hard-boiled only so that it may be soft. His metaphors have nothing on Chandler's for sheer corniness, but they express a "sob sister" side via the literary sob sister. When Monty first asks Mildred out, she realizes that after weeks of ceaseless activity preparing for the restaurant opening, she has nothing to do that day: "It was as though for a little while she was unlisted in God's big index" (105). After the successful opening, Mildred "went to bed . . . tired, happy, and weepy, and Bert, Wally, Mrs. Gessler,

Ida, Monty, the sign, the restaurant, and the $46 were all swimming about in a moonlit pool of tears. But the face that shimmered above it, more beautiful than all the rest, was Veda's" (150). The last example in particular suggests that underlying her matter-of-factness is some serious sentimentality—about family, friendship, lovers, community, and, of course, commerce—but one might make precisely the same point about Cain. In his previous novels, which are narrated in the first person, Cain could indulge in such mawkish moments and palm the responsibility off on the character; the softness was the speaker's, not his.[64] But the third-person narration of *Mildred Pierce* blends the voices of Mildred, narrator, and author, implicating Cain in the emotional excess that underlies the rhetorical excess.

Sentiment intrudes upon stereotypical hard-boiled moments as well. After Mildred and Bert discuss their pending divorce in characteristically practical terms, Bert "doubled his fist, brushed her chin with it," and at that point they "burst uncontrollably into sobs" (128). Tough-guy gestures are only gestures; they enable the expression of emotion rather than shutting it down. On its rough surface, the hard-boiled novel would seem uniquely, hopelessly unsuited to the demands of domestic fiction. Knopf's advertising campaign for the book played up Cain's popularity as a tough-guy writer and obscured its melodramatic elements: "It's a hard-boiled book, but the world today isn't exactly a cream puff."[65] Mildred's lovers and her male patrons *are* cream puffs, wanting to be flattered, shielded, taken care of, consoled. But as the complementarity of the culinary metaphors in the advertisement suggests, Mildred's world of chicken, waffles, and pies is a bit of both. Hard-boiled prose that mediates between aesthetics and efficiency, bringing together sentiment and a stylistic counterpart to mass production, like the house, like the restaurant, like the corporation, proves a logical medium for Cain's alternately tough and tender exploration of suburban domestic culture during the Depression.

CHAPTER FOUR

Native Son's Trespasses

BIGGER'S JUNGLE

IT WASN'T UNTIL 1932 that Johnny Weissmuller, the seventh Hollywood Tarzan and the first to speak, transformed Burroughs's blue-blooded hero into the ungrammatical, uncivilized ape-man of American popular culture. Although no cinematic Tarzan ever uttered the celebrated line "Me Tarzan—you Jane," director W. S. Van Dyke's lavish MGM production replaced the nobleman-savage version of Tarzan with a simpleton. The extent of Tarzan's devolution is captured in the following exchange. "Oh my dear, he's not like us," Jane's father assures her when she mentions Tarzan's sorrow at the death of an ape. Jane responds, simply, "He's white." "Well, whether they are white or not, those people, living a life like that, they have no emotions, they are hardly human." The jungle environment has tainted Tarzan, whose white skin no longer guarantees "white" sensibilities. According to Jane's father, Tarzan is more black than white, more alien than neighbor. It is almost as though the Weissmuller films, which Burroughs openly criticized, realized his worst fears about the consequences of black and white cohabitation. Tarzan, his basic humanity in question and even the rudiments of English perpetually beyond his grasp, has changed from a superhuman white aristocrat into a subhuman black primitive.

The year before the release of *Tarzan the Ape Man*, Van Dyke had already revitalized the "jungle pic" for MGM; he was chosen to direct *Tarzan* based on the commercial and critical success of his first African adventure film, *Trader Horn* (1931), which purported to set new standards for cinematic realism in its depiction of African people and animals in their native settings. For one reviewer, the pleasure of *Trader Horn* lay in its "undiluted realism" and the provocative collapse of African and urban American jungles: "We watch their rude sport in the heart of darkest Africa as immediately as if they were alley cats in our own back yard."[1] It is *Trader Horn* that Bigger Thomas watches in the early pages of Richard Wright's own revised and cautionary jungle epic, *Native Son*. The immediacy of the African cannibals onscreen does not occur to Bigger, but not for the obvious reason that they perform a concept of Africa designed to shock and titillate white audiences. In fact, the Africans seem quite real to him, but only as they represent a reality in which he does not share: "He frowned in the darkened movie, hearing the roll of tom-toms and the screams of black men and women dancing free and wild, men and women who were adjusted to their soil and at home in their world, secure from fear and hysteria" (36). Here are the exotic primitives that Neil Kingsblood first hopes to discover among the people with whom he comes to identify. Here too are the hysterical cannibals envisioned by State's Attorney Buckley, when he later condemns Bigger as a "demented savage" (346) who burned Mary Dalton's body to hide "the marks of his teeth . . . on the innocent white flesh" (344). But Bigger is neither thrilled, frightened, nor outraged by the screaming tribe of *Trader Horn*; he perceives instead a powerful instance of black men and women, "adjusted" and "at home," celebrating an experience of confident placement that is inaccessible to him.

Trader Horn forces Bigger to confront his isolation, but it also stimulates the desire for connection. "It was when he read the newspapers or magazines, went to the movies, or walked along the streets with crowds, that he felt what he wanted: to merge himself with others and be a part of this world, to lose himself in it so he could find himself, to be allowed a chance to live like others, even though he was black" (226). For Wright, movies and newspapers point Bigger in the direction of needs they can identify but never fulfill; they teach Bigger about mass culture's inability to sustain the individual as substitutes for genuine connection and community. He wants to be "at home" in "this world," not in the movies or the movie jungle—"*their* world"—of *Trader Horn*. Bigger's attraction to mass culture, to the pleasurable possibility of losing himself in the mass, in a world without boundaries, expresses a longing for recognition and acceptance through which he might also "find himself" and emerge from it. When contemplated by Bigger, who is excluded by his race, the fantasy of joining the mass is not depersonalizing; rather, it represents the freedom to merge with others as an individual, to live like them and with them.[2]

If *Tarzan of the Apes* aspires to demonstrate the benefits of isolating white skin—with the witless, inarticulate Tarzan of the movies reinforcing the urgency of this proposition—*Native Son* is dedicated to revealing the devastating consequences of isolating black skin. Hollywood Africans feel adjusted and "at home" in the jungle, but Bigger does not. Abandoned to "the wild forests of our great cities . . . the rank and choking vegetation of the slums" (362), Bigger responds by killing two women, including the daughter of Henry Dalton, slumlord of the jungle. His attorney, Boris Max, represents these crimes not simply as an accommodation to jungle violence but as a strategy "to achieve that feeling of at-home-ness" (365) Bigger envies in *Trader Horn*, but that proves unavailable within his segregated sliver of Chicago, "a city within a city," seven miles long and one mile and a half wide, "an island in a big white sea."[3] Early in the novel he complains about the racial divisions that enforce his seclusion: "We live here and they live there. We black and they white. They got things and we ain't. They do things and we can't. It's just like living in jail" (23). Residential segregation is Bigger's basic condition of impossibility; anticipating and generating other disparities in freedom, it seems anterior even to racial difference itself.[4] The novel focuses on the inexhaustible effort of white people to link and police these physical, social, and psychological borders, to deprive Bigger of a home by turning the color line that isolates the rest of Chicago from what Wright called the "locked-in life of the Black Belt" into an impassable racial wall.[5] The prior experience of "living in jail" portends and is conflated with Bigger's eventual relocation to prison.

For many critics, the most troubling aspect of *Native Son* has been precisely the degree to which it insists upon the destructive effects of white racism on black personality, culture, and community, from James Baldwin's eloquent attacks on the novel's representation of black life as "debased and impoverished," to studies of Bigger's allegiance to mass culture, to critiques of Wright's misogyny, and to the recentering of the twentieth-century African American literary tradition around the work of Zora Neale Hurston.[6] For example, although Houston A. Baker Jr. initially identified Bigger with "the survival values" of a black folk tradition, in a fine essay on the "dynamics of place" in *Native Son*, he recasts Bigger as a lost cultural outsider. Wright ignored the rewarding folk culture that could "place" black men and women in the northern industrial city and without which "Bigger is doomed."[7] Such analyses highlight the insufficiency of Wright's structuralist critique of racism; although Bigger is not "essentially and organically bad," to blame "American oppression" for his "lack of inner organization," "spiritual sustenance," and "culture" is still to privilege racism as the defining fact of black life that eclipses everything else.[8] In this account, Bigger is imprisoned as much by Wright's narrow view of black urban culture as by the particular economic and social conditions that shape his life.

In a fine book on the relationship between Chicago novelists and sociologists, Carla Cappetti argues that Wright's dismissal of folk culture ought to be understood as an informed response to prevailing sociological theories of migration and cultural transformation. Cappetti argues that he wrote the autobiographies *Black Boy* (1945) and *American Hunger* (1977) out of the Chicago school sociological tradition, which perceived the individual to be in fundamental tension with the group and the community, and with the cultural consensus and authority they seek to impose. Wright's hostility is directed more toward the tyranny of community and culture as such than toward black culture in particular; in this light, his repudiation of the Communist Party in the North is structurally identical to his rejection of black family life and tradition in the South.[9]

Cappetti's work is an important addition to Wright scholarship that demonstrates why we must give his abiding interest in sociology at least the same weight that critics have always put on his more vexed encounter with communism. But the insignificance of *Native Son* to a book that addresses the novelistic and sociological activities of "writing Chicago" is surprising.[10] In *Native Son* the relationship between community and authority is not simply homologous; rather, the novel demands that we consider the ways in which communities are authorized. Bigger's failure to connect with other African Americans exceeds *Native Son*'s problematic diagnosis of personal pathology and diminished culture, marking Wright's refusal to accept the bounded community—and the very concept of boundaries—generated and enforced by white real estate interests (Dalton) and their political and legal henchmen (Buckley). Through the connections between Bigger's spatial and psychological isolation, Wright explodes the explanation that men like Dalton give about discriminatory real estate practices: "I think Negroes are happier when they're together" (303). In creating a character who refuses to "make believe that he was happy when he was not" (240), Wright explicitly rejected the kind of argument that justified techniques of residential exclusion by masquerading them as policies of inclusion. Bigger must belong everywhere, or he will be at home nowhere. By focusing on the harmful effects of bad housing in an artificial community, rather than on a compensatory shelter of black culture, Wright sacrificed what we would today call a cultural politics of identity to insist, as the *Crisis* would shortly put it in an article on residential segregation in Chicago, that "[t]here is no right more elemental, nor any liberty more fundamental in a democracy than freedom to move where and when you please."[11]

Like the sociologists upon whose insights he drew, Wright asserted that the color line dividing the Black Belt from hostile white neighborhoods was both an intractable fact and an unstable artifact, its borders permeable and elastic. This chapter argues that as housing was about to become Chicago's "most explosive racial issue," according to historian Arnold Hirsch, Wright produced not only, obviously, a novel of racial conflict but also of racial transition.[12] Once the oldest and among the most exclusive suburbs of Chicago, the Daltons' "quiet and spacious white neighborhood" (45) of Hyde Park–Kenwood had by the novel's publication reformed as a hostile and self-protective urban neighborhood, just one block from the Black Belt. Mary's death represents Bigger's attempt to achieve what the Daltons have by virtue of their race and wealth—more room—and incarnates the desperate dynamics of segregation: the forces of containment and compression by white Chicago, and the confinement and countervailing expansiveness of the Black Belt.

Native Son is one of the great novels of the urban experience, but a reading of its spatial and racial politics is crucial to a study of the suburb's significance in American literature. Fundamentally related but irreducible to the problem of housing, Bigger's preoccupation with the feeling of "at-home-ness" is linked to the project of self-determination, in particular as it is manifested in the desire to inhabit the city fully by living where and how he pleases. This ambition is associated with the achievement of privacy and community, free isolation as well as free association, but a premium is placed on racial and class inclusion. At the most obvious level, *Native Son* is relevant for a project on the suburbs because it supplies an important piece that is missing from the other novels examined in this study: the fate of someone who is walled off and left behind. *Native Son* allows us to examine the logic of homelessness when the privileges of home are really taken away. Its insistent rhetoric of confinement accounts in part for my emphasis on the Chicago experience in particular, even as the discussions of Lewis and Cain have called attention to the generic aspect of their suburban representations. While *Mildred Pierce* is predicated on mobility, not only through the fluidity of abstract boundaries such as homes, restaurants, and corporations, but also in Mildred's quite concrete and unrestricted migration from Glendale to Pasadena as the measure of her economic rise, *Native Son* is obsessed with the effects of immobilizing boundaries, Bigger's isolation in and within Chicago. *Native Son* is a useful text because it is committed to revealing what remains obscure in a novel like *Mildred Pierce*: the extent to which the freedom of white people to exercise the right to live where and as they like, in city or in suburb, is enabled and underwritten by the constraint of others. If Wright comes down too hard on the side of victimization, it is a situation that gives maximum credit to Bigger's claim that he is Mary's murderer rather than an accidental killer, an agent not a victim. *Native Son* reminds us more forcefully than any analysis of the other novels alone could how bankrupt are propositions that put forth the homelessness of the white suburbanite and the suburb's narrative of intrinsically soulless prosperity.

Rewriting the Renaissance

In an essay written after Wright's death, Nelson Algren explained his friend's motivations for moving to Chicago from the South: "Richard Wright came to Chicago because there was no other place for him to go."[13] Algren conveys the tension between mobility and constraint, and the sense of permanent displacement, that characterized Wright's experience of migration generally and of Chicago, the first of several destinations, in particular. Chicago, where Wright struggled for a few years of so-called national prosperity before the privations of the Depression, hardly fulfilled the promises of urban opportunity for which Harlem had been lauded just a few years before; in *Native Son* he would revise, indeed, reverse, the celebratory account of black residents in the northern metropolis.[14] Among literary critics, the connection between home and Harlem in the 1920s has become commonplace. Sidney Bremer distinguishes literary Harlem as an "urban home communit[y]" that disavowed the mechanistic and dehumanizing depictions of urban life so popular among white American modernists, while Ann Douglas has recently described Harlem as akin to an African American "homeland."[15] In a compelling reading of the essays in *The New Negro*, however, Charles Scruggs argues that in the 1920s such identifications depended upon a careful reconstruction of what counted as home. As *The New Negro* evolved from a special issue of the *Survey Graphic*, editor Alain Locke's seminal predictions for "a new dynamic phase" in "the life of the Negro community," locally and nationally, apparently required the elimination of articles such as "Harvest of Race Prejudice" and "Ambushed in the City," which focused on the ill effects of racism and poverty in Harlem, and the addition of articles on the middle class.[16] The multidimensional glimpses of Harlem as broken promise and promised land gave way to a partial portrait of a thriving cultural and economic community.

The spirit of *The New Negro* is evident in James Weldon Johnson's contribution, "Harlem: The Culture Capital," which had little to say about culture but much to report on rates of black property ownership. The essay extols Harlem as the northern capital of black capital, suggesting that its cultural vitality and independence rested solidly on economic autonomy. Prosperity was not inimical but advantageous to cultural expression and spiritual life, in striking contrast with frequent presumptions about their incompatibility for middle-class white people, which I explored in relation to Lewis. Moreover, capital brought Harlem together as a community. Harlem had established "group consciousness and community feeling" because it was "well-defined and stable, anchored to its fixed homes, churches, institutions, business and amusement places, having its own working, business and professional classes" (309). The local ownership of private and civic property stabilized the residents affectively as well as economically. Furthermore, class differentiation did not seem to entail economic disparities and thus did not compromise the sense of community. Even people named "Pig-Foot Mary" laid claim to Harlem by profitably investing in residential real estate worth tens of thousands of dollars. While Sinclair Lewis was busily associating middle-class white people with bland homogeneity, the assertion of the existence of black middle classes proved the race's heterogeneity. And the impossibility of continuing to "regard and treat the Negro *en masse*," as "a homogeneous mass" of the masses, paradoxically advanced a coherent group identity.[17]

Despite what has been called "persuasive" "evidence" to the contrary, Johnson marshaled anecdotes and descriptions to insist, it seems almost defensively, that Harlem "is not a slum," nor "a 'quarter' of dilapidated tenements" (301) "cut off" (309) from the rest of the city.[18] In the foreword Locke dismissed "the darkened Ghetto of a segregated race life" (xxvi) as a matter of aesthetic interest or social consternation. As late as 1941, Claude McKay, author of the novel *Home to Harlem* (1928), defended the "community" by arguing that "[n]ot by the greatest flight of the imagination could Negro Harlem be considered a segregated area."[19] For these writers to think of Harlem as home was to ignore the disordering facts of segregation and poverty. These writers asserted a community based on "self-dependence" (Locke 4) and "positive self-direction" (8)— the thrill of economic autonomy and residential choice.

By 1937 Wright, as chief Harlem correspondent for the *Daily Worker*, knew firsthand of dire living conditions, and he wrote articles on both poverty and racist housing practices among white landlords. That year he published a manifesto of his own, "A Blueprint for Negro Writing," which criticized the bourgeois preoccupations and political ineffectualness of the Harlem Renaissance. In Barbara Johnson's pithy formulation, "Blueprint" challenged contemporary black writers to abandon Harlem antecedents and become "at once red and black," class- and race-conscious, politically engaged and culturally situated.[20] Despite the obvious political differences, however, there seems to be a telling correspondence between Wright and the strain of Harlem Renaissance thought outlined above. Community in *Native Son* is defeated by just those elements—segregation and poverty—that threatened to compromise or destroy it for the *New Negro* writers. But while Locke and Johnson insisted that all the conditions for community were firmly in place, in *Native Son*, as in "Blueprint," Wright challenged evasions of economic and political reality.

In landmark sociological studies of Chicago's segregated South Side, *The Negro Family in Chicago* (1932) and *Black Metropolis* (1945), to which Wright contributed the introduction, E. Franklin Frazier, St. Clair Drake, and Horace Cayton came closer to realizing Wright's blueprint for treating African American experience in all its complexity. The sociologists examined nuances of class distinction within a variegated group, identifying patterns of black middle- and upper-class life, but also documenting at length the plight of the impoverished majority. For Drake and Cayton, whose study was more concerned with subjective experience than was Frazier's, the "Black Belt" of white determination coexisted with the "Bronzeville" of black freedom. Although oppression worked to keep residents in "their 'place' " (198) and poverty made "home life" (581) difficult for most residents, "[w]ithin Bronzeville Negroes are at home. They find rest from white folks as well as from labor, and they make the most of it" (387). Bronzeville was shaped by racism but nonetheless served as a physical and psychical refuge from it, an "object of pride" (114), something *all our own"* (115), regardless of the residents' relation to property ownership. *Native Son* registers its objection to Harlem Renaissance complacency by erring in the other direction; Wright reversed the excision performed by his predecessors, making the Chicago Black Belt all slum and evacuating the black middle class. In writing the middle class and the gratification of "Bronzeville" out of the "Black Belt," he reduced the very complexity he claimed to seek in the interest of indicting a city where the only place for the most disenfranchised was in jail.

RACE AND PLACE

From the blueprint of Wright's essay comes in *Native Son* the architecture of the kitchenette, a one-room apartment with minimal cooking facilities and no private bathroom. Mrs. Thomas has brought her three children to Chicago from the South and has "tr[ied] to make a home" (13) for them, but she is defeated by the closeness and squalor of the quarters and the poverty that forces her to transform their fraction of domestic space into a workroom for doing other people's laundry. In contrast with the work in *Mildred Pierce* of making the home pay by re-creating it for other people at a profit—and the farther from the kitchen Mildred gets, the more lucrative and glamorous her work becomes—the hard labor of laundering in the kitchenette divides the home against itself, forcing Mrs. Thomas to eject her children from the flat to earn the money that keeps them there. The family cannot unite in anything but a "conspiracy against shame" (8), which serves only to drive the Thomases apart in the urgency of dressing as privately as possible in a one-room apartment. Given the arguments, reproaches, and conflict generated by so many people sharing so small a space, the trauma of the enormous rat is in part attributable to its insulting presence as one more body to be crammed into it, an extra, unwanted tenant.

The famed opening scene highlights the problem of establishing family closeness when a family has to be that close. The thematic significance of the walls that Wright invokes throughout the novel to express Bigger's feelings of constraint and isolation from his family, his peers, the city, the world, develops first in the context of the kitchenette's absent interior walls:

> He knew that the moment he allowed himself to feel to its fullness how they lived, the shame and misery of their lives, he would be swept out of himself with fear and despair. So he held toward them an attitude of iron reserve; he lived with them, but behind a wall, a curtain. And toward himself he was even more exacting. He knew that the moment he allowed what his life meant to enter fully into his consciousness, he would either kill himself or someone else, so he denied himself and acted tough. (13–14)

As the most pressing evidence of the family's poverty, and the instigator of the shame that is presented as the most salient feature of their relations, the lack of physical walls within the kitchenette demands the construction of mental walls; the psychological and the spatial are indissolubly bound.[21] Bigger lives with his family, but keeping himself together means that he must keep them at arm's length. It also requires a mental partitioning that divides Bigger from himself. Whereas in *Mildred Pierce*, the suburban house's multiple walls enable the expression of the occupants' personality, here the absent walls repress it. Intimacy with oneself, like family closeness, is a luxury of physical privacy.

The metaphor of the wall delicately establishes the role of residential segregation in the passage's drama of dissociation. In *The Negro Family in the United States*, Frazier referred to "the walls of segregation" three times in two pages, as if the color "line" were conceptually insufficient to convey the white imperative to keep black people in their place.[22] Moreover, *iron ring* was a term used to protest the boundaries that white property owners and realtors tried to maintain through restrictive covenants that barred African Americans from owning or renting property in many areas and through physical violence. The "iron reserve" Bigger holds toward his family and himself is a fit expression of the "iron ring of housing" that keeps them apart from white Chicago.[23]

The kitchenette was notorious in sociological literature of the period as the worst and most exploitative housing in the Black Belt, especially once new construction there had ceased with the Depression and the most decrepit buildings were condemned or demolished between 1930 and 1938 but not replaced. Because of the "iron ring," displaced residents and new black migrants to Chicago could not freely search for housing elsewhere in the city. Landlords such as Dalton profited from the housing shortage they helped to create by subdividing large apartments into single-room units, which accommodated more tenants and generated more income per building, but still could not keep pace with the housing demand.[24] Wright's own historical-sociological study of migration and the black metropolis, *12 Million Black Voices*, made explicit the connections he drew in *Native Son* between Bigger's housing and his crimes, the color line and prison: "The kitchenette is our prison, our death sentence without a trial, the new form of mob violence that assaults not only the lone individual, but all of us, in its ceaseless attacks" (106). Far from simply failing to function as a home, the kitchenette instantiates the most brutal forms of the outside world's hostility. Like other types of racial violence, such as lynching, the kitchenette attacks and terrorizes an entire racial group, not only the people who inhabit one. According to Wright, Bigger is suspended between two death sentences: one for killing Mary and the other simply for living in her father's housing. The kitchenette tries and sentences Bigger before he has done anything; Mary's death is the crime that postdates and is produced by the punishment signified by the kitchenette.

Her death is directly linked to Bigger's overcrowding and desire to lay claim to more space. In his last conversation with Max, he gives one final account of his actions: "I hurt folks 'cause I felt I had to; that's all. They was crowding me too close; they wouldn't give me no room" (388). Bigger's explanation resonates not only with the kitchenette scene but also with his brief tenancy at the Daltons. His experience with the people who employ him as a chauffeur duplicates his experience of them as landlords: they give him no room. The Daltons' house provides him with some of the real walls that are missing from their housing, but the privacy of his own room is undermined by the decorations left by the previous occupant, the vent that brings voices from the kitchen below into his quarters, and, more viciously, the surreptitious searches and brutal questioning by Dalton's security chief. More urgently, Bigger accidentally smothers Mary to keep her quiet when blind Mrs. Dalton bustles into Mary's bedroom. Somebody had to go.

While driving Mary and her white communist lover, Jan Erlone, earlier in the evening, Bigger is likewise overcrowded when they push into the front seat with him in a misguided gesture of solidarity: "he was sitting between two vast and looming white walls. Never in his life had he been so close to a white woman. . . . His arms and legs were aching from being cramped into so small a space, but he dared not move. . . . [H]is moving would have called attention to himself and his black body" (68–69). Surrounding and crushing him, Jan's and especially Mary's white bodies are made to stand in for a claustrophobic city of constraints, the proscription of Bigger's physical movement but also of the broader geographical and social mobility implied by the metaphorical walls. Bigger has earlier protested that white people don't live "[o]ver across the 'line'" but "[r]ight down here in my stomach" (24). Living apart from white people is represented as living with them in the most intimate way, as Bigger articulates and literally embodies the connection between white flight and white rule.

Jan and Mary do not simply maintain spatial and racial boundaries as walls, but they encroach upon and cross them, even penetrating the boundaries that separate one racialized body from another.

Segregation in *Native Son* is never envisioned as merely the isolating effect of discrimination. This is especially evident in the manhunt for Bigger, which brings thousands of white police and vigilantes into the Black Belt; tellingly, the rights of the inhabitants are uniformly abrogated by a "blanket warrant" that allows police and vigilantes to search "every Negro home" (229). Segregation is associated with the absolute mobility of whites and the violation and invasion of public and private black space. The meaning of Mary's death as the result of encroachment on Bigger's space and his quest for more space on any terms is most intelligible in relation to the analyses of urban migration, segregation, and expansion put forth by Chicago school sociologists. Bigger's expansiveness identifies and seeks release from the particular constraints that distinguished the movement of African Americans within the city from the mobility of other groups. In an influential essay collection that set a research and methodological agenda for investigating human behavior in the city, Ernest W. Burgess studied the spatial distribution of bodies as a natural aspect of the city's "ecology."[25] He produced an ideal map, based on Chicago, that traced the movement of incoming groups from near the center of the city toward the periphery (see figure 1). Upon arrival, poor newcomers tended to cluster together by ethnicity or race, hence areas in Chicago with names such as "Little Sicily" and "Chinatown." They settled in zone II, with the worst housing and highest rates of what the sociologists called "disorganization": juvenile delinquency, illegitimacy, transiency, and the like. Where he described ethnic concentration as "segregation," he did not mean discrimination but simply separation, to which he attributed productive effects. It gave "the individuals who compose the group a place and a role in the total organization of city life" (56). Their "place" provided the individual and the community with a clearly defined, if subordinate, relation to other people and spaces in the city.

Burgess described a process of ongoing migration, however; inhabitants of the inner zone improved their fortunes, adapted or "reorganized" in line with new conditions, and exchanged the slums for nicer housing in the outer zones. Economic and social progress was always manifested as geographical advancement across urban boundaries: through the area of second settlement, inhabited by workers who had begun to adjust to urban life and sought more stable housing and neighborhoods, to a yet better class of housing in apartment buildings and single-family houses, as they rose in status, and finally to the "commuter zone," where social, economic, and geographical arrival converged. The natural trajectory of human movement was from the country to the city and then to the suburb,

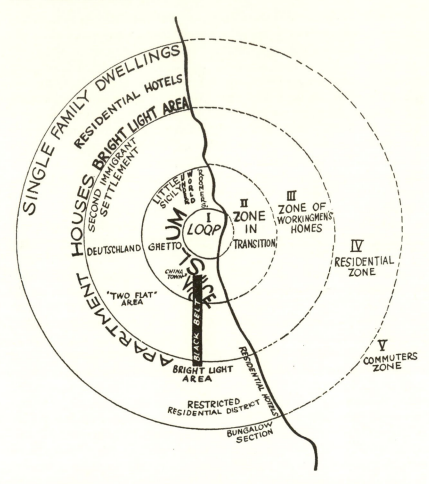

Figure 1. "Urban areas." From *The City*, ed. Park, Burgess, and McKenzie, p. 55. Copyright 1925, 1967 by The University of Chicago. All rights reserved. Reprinted with permission.

the real "Promised Land" (56) of the essay. Disorganization was the province of the slum, organization the property of the suburb.[26]

Burgess elsewhere argued that "the residential separation of white and Negro . . . is only one case among many of the workings of the process of segregation in the sorting and shifting of the different elements of population in the growth of the city."[27] The movement of African Americans through the city "appears to vary little, if at all, from [that] of other groups" (110). Their segregation was simply part of an impersonal "process," the "sorting and shifting" by color, nationality, or religion, with no particular value placed on those identities. But Burgess's own map belies his pronouncements on the neutrality and parity of segregation and mobility for African Americans. In contrast with the vague locations of the ethnic enclaves, which are marked only by their names, the stark and perfect geometry of the Black Belt emphasizes the rigidity of its boundaries. Moreover, only the Black Belt extends all the way from the deteriorated second zone into the residential fourth zone. Jews are also represented by an immigrant enclave (Deutschland) that is contiguous with and extends outside the "Ghetto" of the transitional zone but ends at the "boundary" of the fourth, which Burgess called "the home of the great middle class" ("Residential Segregation" 107). The abrupt termination of the Jewish section implies what other sociologists of urban migration argued explicitly: the farther ethnic whites moved from the center of the city, the less likely they were to remain within an area defined by ethnicity. Geographical movement through the city to the outer zones represented not merely social and economic progress but assimilation.[28]

The map is reproduced exactly in *The Negro Family in Chicago*, for which Burgess wrote the preface. Frazier endorsed Burgess's model of the economic and social distribution of population, arguing that the Black Belt was divided into seven zones of "progressive stabilization" (126). The farther south one moved from the center, the higher the rates of house ownership, his primary index of financial success and social stability, and the lower the levels of delinquency and illegitimacy. The seventh zone was the least "disorganized," inhabited by "those families who had succeeded in the struggle of city life" (101). But Frazier did not emphasize the ways in which Black Belt residents did not fit Burgess's model, that they were prevented from moving with their white counterparts into other areas of zones III and especially IV and V on Burgess's map, as money and inclination permitted.[29] Perhaps Frazier's omission is attributable to his investment in depicting both the disintegrating forces of the city upon southern migrants and the heterogeneity of the community: differences between groups within the Black Belt superseded the differences between its patterns of migration and mobility and those of other disenfranchised groups.

Wright's friend Horace Cayton confronted the differences between black and white mobility in a *Social Action* pamphlet published the same year as *Native Son* and with coauthor Drake in *Black Metropolis*. Cayton pointed out in the pamphlet that white immigrants were freer to find good jobs than were black migrants, and as the former climbed the urban economic ladder, they could progress horizontally from the slums to the "middle and upper class suburban areas surrounding the city. With the final move into these neighborhoods the adaptation to American culture is more or less complete."[30] For Cayton the melting pot was also a geographical as well as cultural and economic phenomenon, and the suburb's cultural homogeneity was an attraction, not a drawback. But African Americans were not allowed to move and thus could not melt. "Unlike all other urban residents, the Negroes' only mobility is within the boundaries of the area of 'concentration' " (11), the Black Belt and a few other small, scattered enclaves. Despite a few quibbles with Frazier's analysis of the zones, Drake and Cayton observed that within the Black Belt people tended to follow Burgess's general pattern of relocation from the center of the city outward as they grew more affluent, but they also insisted that the Black Belt diverged from the integrationist and assimilationist aspect of the pattern. Residents "are not finally absorbed in the general population" (17). Prosperous and poor alike were confined to an area whose boundaries were determined from without. Far from noting an impersonal process of "sorting and shifting" that just happened to limit one racial group to a prescribed area, the authors described at length the mechanisms designed to keep them there: the discriminatory practices of white realtors and neighborhood associations, the evolution of restrictive racial covenants, and, when other tactics failed, the bombing of houses recently occupied by blacks in "white" neighborhoods.[31]

In order to get better housing in the city, residents had to move out of their "place." The racist techniques of white property owners and realtors did not prevent the Black Belt from expanding into adjacent white areas; the pressures of extreme overcrowding periodically extended the boundaries that white people tried to maintain. Indeed, the transgression of boundaries was considered a constitutive feature of urban growth more generally. Cities were intrinsically expansive. Burgess noted that the borders of the zones were not static; as population density increased, the slums expanded by "inva[ding]" (50) the adjacent outer zone. The city grew as each zone colonized the next, which deteriorated to the level of the invader and pushed the well-off farther out: "The present boundaries of the area of deterioration were not many years ago those of the zone now inhabited by independent wage-earners, and within the memories of Chicagoans contained the residences of the 'best families' " (50–51). This is essentially Jacob Riis's argument about tenements and immigrants presented in chapter one. The putative colonization of the suburb by the city was a political process, as I discussed in relation to *Tarzan*, but flight to outlying suburbs was also imagined as an attempt to stay ahead of the physical deterioration that always threatened to follow. Drake and Cayton chronicled an analogous process within the Black Belt: "[the] 'worst' areas begin to encroach on the 'more desirable areas,' and large 'mixed' areas result. These, in turn, become gradually 'worst,' and the 'more desirable' areas begin to suffer from 'blight' and become 'mixed' " (383). The spread of deterioration in the Black Belt involved a double transgression, because middle-class black families who moved outward for better housing ultimately encountered and sometimes sought to cross the boundaries between black and white Chicago. Such crossing, when it took place, was only temporary. Where bombings or court enforcement of covenants could not dislodge unwelcome newcomers, black flight from poverty and segregation stimulated white flight from blacks. Drake and Cayton described white house owners who sold at panic prices, shrewd speculators who sold houses on contract to African Americans, who filled them with renters to make the payments, single-family houses and spacious apartments that were subdivided into kitchenettes. As we see from Drake and Cayton's map (figure 2), the contested area eventually became part of the Black Belt and subject once again to the problems of overcrowding, deterioration, and further battles over the newly reconstituted boundaries.[32]

The Depression had severely restricted the expansion of the Black Belt; Drake and Cayton noted that by 1940 it had virtually ceased to grow. *Native Son* was written during and responds to a crisis of geographical immobility. When Bigger explains to Max his reasons for killing Mary, who we should remember owned approximately $250,000 of real estate in her own right, he describes his resistance to confinement as well as overcrowding: " 'They make us stay in one little spot. . . .' 'And you didn't want to stay there?' Bigger glanced up; his lips tightened. There was a feverish pride in his bloodshot eyes. 'I *didn't*,' he said" (327). Later he reflects with satisfaction, "He had told Max . . . that he had not stayed in his place" (333). Bigger thinks of Mary's death as an attempt to force mobility out of constraint. He does not try just to protect what little room he has from the Daltons and his family; he claims the right to expand into their territory.

Under Cayton's influence, Wright elsewhere described and deplored the freedom of white people to "advance . . . upward according to [their] ability" and so to advance outward "to the spacious middle class suburbs of our American cities," from which black people were excluded.[33] But in *Native Son* he was unconcerned with the usual terrain on which the contest over urban space was thought to play itself out, whether articulated in terms of Burgess's theory of urban growth as a neutral flight from deterioration through economic and geographical progress, or of Cayton and Drake's empirical work on the growth of Black Metropolis as a failed flight from deterioration, in which economic and geographical progress are most unneutrally circumscribed by racism. The novel is not about extending to middle-class black people the privilege of mobility, the right of the affluent to choose their community and to attempt to escape from the slums and the slum dwellers. In *12 Million Black Voices*, Wright envisioned Black Belt expansion in terms of "the tide of black life, pushing

EXPANSION OF THE BLACK BELT

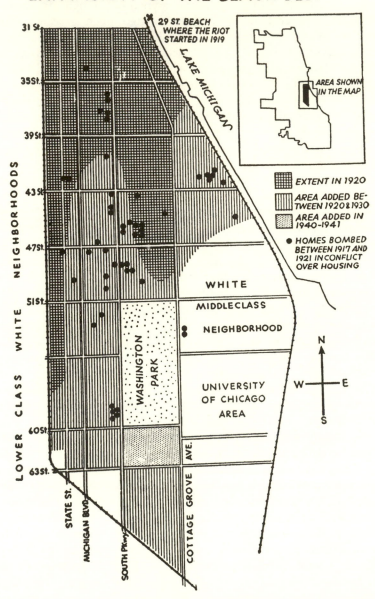

Figure 2. From Drake and Cayton, *Black Metropolis*, p. 63. Copyright 1945, 1962, 1970 by St. Clair Drake and Horace R. Cayton. All rights reserved. Reprinted by permission of the University of Chicago.

irresistibly outward" to "the border of some restricted middle-class neighborhood, and then the warfare begins anew" (112). Growth is treated as an uncontrollable force, made apparent through the inevitable metaphor of the "tide," which had become almost a cliché to describe the volume of black migration northward. *Native Son* differs from all the sociologies including Wright's own, producing an account of Bigger's mobility that is more purposeful than the tidal forces of *12 Million Black Voices*. Asserting Bigger's haunting desire to be "at home" and linking the project of homecoming to the murder of his slumlord's daughter, it insists on the expansive ambitions of those most confined by segregation's walls as it explores the essential transgression embedded for white people in the very notion of blacks in urban space.

BIGGER'S TRESPASSES

Mary's casual, patronizing interest in "how your people live," the question that represents her death sentence as the kitchenette represents Bigger's, thus stands for more than a further invasion of the psychic walls that Bigger has constructed and the physical walls that she and other white people have erected between them. As Bigger drives the couple, Mary pretends that she is a sociologist rather than a landlord: "I've long wanted to go into those houses . . . and just *see* how your people live. . . . I've been to England, France and Mexico, but I don't know how people live ten blocks from me. . . . [T]hey *must* live like we live. They're *human*. . . . There are twelve million of them. . . . They live in our country. . . . In the same city with us" (70, first two ellipses mine). Even as Mary intends to ally herself with Bigger, and as she invades his territory, she cannot help but represent his presence in Chicago as a kind of encroachment on "our" city and country, the intrusion of the stranger and alien, possibly the nonhuman, into the neighborhood. She reestablishes the boundaries even as she attempts to cross them, in sympathy if not in fact, but they are asserted only in the process of depicting her and Bigger's transgression of them.

Native Son demonstrates that white people are not constrained to regard any of the barriers established by black people, and Bigger returns the favor. He refuses to respect the "iron ring" that encircles him; he takes down white Chicago's walls. Bigger's reasons for killing Mary are too little room and not enough mobility, which signify less the desire to harm white people physically than to lay claim to white space. Even the first crime he contemplates, the plan to rob Blum's store with his friends, is understood as the rejection of his "little spot": "the robbing of Blum's would be the violation of ultimate taboo; it would be *trespassing* into territory where the full wrath of an alien white world would be turned loose upon them" (18, emphasis mine). The "symbolic challenge" the robbery poses to "the white world's rule over them" is the demand for access to the white world. Taking the property of white people is transposed into the less serious crime, from a legal standpoint, of simply *being* on their property. The State's Attorney misunderstands the significance of Bigger's act: "the central crime here" (228) is neither rape nor murder but trespassing. Or does Buckley intuit this? He argues for the death penalty, trusting that "the law is strong and gracious enough to allow all of us to sit here in this courtroom today . . . and not tremble with fear that at this very moment some half-human black ape may be climbing through the windows of our homes to rape, murder, and burn our daughters!" (373). We ought to read Buckley's false assertion that Bigger climbed in through the window as more than inflammatory oratory. Buckley cannot distinguish between Bigger's living in the Daltons' house and breaking into it. He registers an imminent threat of black people to white security as the unwarranted claim of trespass. It is not merely the safety of white women that is at stake, but the integrity of white homes.

Felonious crimes against the property and person of whites in *Native Son* originate in what is always imagined to be an unauthorized black presence. The symbolic primacy of trespassing speaks directly to the logic of Black Belt expansion. Mary's sense that Bigger is encroaching on her city is concurrent with the observation that he lives just ten blocks away. She is vaguer about their relative locations than Wright is, who situates his characters precisely on the Chicago map: the Daltons live at 4605 Drexel Boulevard, roughly ten blocks east and ten blocks south of the Thomases, at 3721 Indiana Avenue. More crucial than the exact distance between the Daltons' "palatial . . . home" (195) in Kenwood and the Thomases' cramped kitchenette is the Daltons' immediate relation to the "color line." Drexel Boulevard is only one block east of Cottage Grove Avenue, the thoroughfare that divided the Black Belt from affluent white residents of Kenwood and the neighborhood just south, Hyde Park. In 1911, fictional Hyde Park neighbors, "well-to-do, aspiring, middle-class people," shunned newcomer Jennie Gerhardt, Dreiser's unmarried, white working-class mother, who jeopardized their status and respectability.[34] By 1940, the Daltons and their real-life counterparts were subject to a rather different incursion. In 1939 a journalist described Kenwood as "a stately paradise full of fearful angels," because the mere "width of one street" separated white residents from the "envious glances" across Cottage Grove, and Kenwood's "sprawling old houses would make a fine annex to take care of Bronzeville's extra population."[35] As part of the village of Hyde Park, Kenwood had been annexed to Chicago in 1889 over the objections of residents and was now undergoing a second unwelcome process of "annexation." Mary is described in the newspapers as a "Hyde Park heiress" (194), which is technically incorrect, but the mistake expresses residual nostalgia for "the clubby little village" of yore, consolidating and uniting white neighborhoods between the Black Belt and Lake Michigan as the old suburban refuge fighting once again to keep the city at bay.[36]

According to Louis Wirth, Wright's one-time mentor in sociology, at the turn of the century Kenwood was an "aristocratic" neighborhood, "one of the richest and most beautiful suburban residential districts" of Chicago. Wirth noted in 1938 that one-third of Kenwood, the area south of 47th Street between Drexel and Dorchester Avenue, was "still an area of oak and elm-shaded streets lined with fine homes," but above "47th Street the character of the neighborhood has changed greatly, due largely to the proximity of the Black Belt." [37] If we reexamine Drake and Cayton's map of Black Belt expansion (fig. 2), we observe that the Black Belt had swept east of Cottage Grove with the curve of the "tide" (60) in the twenties, down to and just beyond 47th Street. The great unacknowledged joke of *Native Son* is that at 4605 Drexel Boulevard, one short block from Cottage Grove, the Daltons really are Bigger's neighbors; their territory is already being annexed. It makes textual as well as historical sense to think of Bigger's room at the Daltons' house as the first step toward long-term tenancy. Bigger observes of the building in which he and Bessie were to have awaited the ransom money: "dusty walls, walls almost like those of the Dalton home. . . . Some rich folks lived here once, he thought. Rich white folks. That was the way most houses on the South Side were, ornate, old, stinking; homes once of rich white people, now inhabited by Negroes or standing dark and empty with yawning black windows. He remembered that bombs had been thrown by whites into houses like these when Negroes had first moved into the South Side" (172). Despite violent resistance, rich white homes like the Daltons' eventually become poor black housing like the Thomases'.

In light of the Daltons' location, Buckley's image of Bigger breaking into the house seems also to border on nostalgia: better in through the window than through the front door. The scene where the police and vigilantes swarm into the Black Belt to apprehend Bigger is driven by the desire to catch him but also by the fantasy of putting him back in his literal "place." Bigger learns just what it means for white people to be able to "move out [of the slums] and lose themselves" (*Black Metropolis* 175) when he realizes that hiding from his captors would be easy "if he had the whole city in which to move about" (233). But he cannot "merge himself with others and . . . lose himself" (226) outside the Black Belt:

He looked at the paper and saw a black-and-white map of the South Side, around the borders of which was a shaded portion an inch deep. Under the map ran a line of small print:

Shaded portion shows area already covered by police and vigilantes in search for Negro rapist and murderer. White portion shows area yet to be searched.

He was trapped. He would have to get out of this building. But where could he go? Empty buildings would serve only as long as he stayed within the white portion of the map, and the white portion was shrinking rapidly. (230)

The map is subsequently reprinted to reflect the growing pressure of white infiltration on black space: "This time the shaded area had deepened from both the north and south, leaving a small square of white in the middle of the oblong Black Belt" (239). Here is the inverse of Drake and Cayton's map. Instead of the Black Belt advancing outward along the lines of Burgess's model of invasion and conquest, the "white belt" proceeds inward with military precision. The novel's maps restage white flight as a terrifying white return.

The maps also invert color as though to obscure the real power dynamic at work in confining African Americans to a particular region of the city. The blacker the map becomes—the closer it comes to reflecting the color of the residents—the greater their constraints. As the white on the map gradually disappears, or more precisely, as the maps' deceptive white center is overwhelmed by the advancing circle of black, white Chicago's authority in the Black Belt intensifies. It is when black seems to swallow white that white power becomes absolute; Bigger is surrounded, captured, and delivered to Buckley. Mary's death affords white Chicago the opportunity to stream into the Black Belt with the purpose of making it blacker than ever before. The maps' spatial and racial sleight of hand creates a scandalous picture of a white city engulfed by blackness, in which white authority is imagined as the defense against rather than the instigator of racial trespasses and violence.

The manhunt is a grotesque caricature of the mundane fact of segregation. Bigger only makes white power manifest in its bald attempt to erect and enforce indestructible walls, to control the Black Belt while disavowing claims to domination by verbally and visually representing white Chicago as the city under siege. Not only is Bigger immobilized by the white forces on all sides, his expansion, like that of the Black Belt, arrested. The manhunt and maps also exemplify Wright's vision of the black metropolis as a constricted city, rather than, ultimately, an expansive or even a static one. Black expansiveness is overmatched by white compression. Bigger's territory inexorably shrinks to the dimensions of a prison cell, the only place in the novel where he is not a trespasser. For Wright, a boundary is a boundary; there is little to distinguish the feeling of "living in jail" from being there. But prison paradoxically frees Bigger to experience something like a home, even though it represents exclusion at its most literal. The actual prison is significant for Bigger less as evidence of the barriers that divide him from others than as the occasion of an exhilarating and frightening release from their constraints and protection. It is the place where expansion and conquest are problematically imagined to give way to contact and community.

No Man's Land

Wright's maps articulate the techniques of constraint and domination with which white Chicago resists further encroachments on its territory by representing them as counteroffensives. But not all efforts to isolate blacks involve overt appeals to white security. Dalton's ability to reconcile his housing practices and his philanthropy at Mary's inquest requires an evasion of his own commitment to segregation by invoking black community. Max's questions and Dalton's answers at the inquest are worth reproducing at some length:

> "You are president of the Dalton Real Estate Company, are you not?"
> "Yes."
> "Your company owns the building in which the Thomas family has lived for the past three years, does it not?"
> "Well, no. My company owns the stock in a company that owns the house."
> "I see. . . . Now, Mr. Dalton, the Thomas family paid you . . ."
> "Not to *me*! They pay rent to the South Side Real Estate Company."
> "You own the controlling stock in the Dalton Real Estate Company, don't you?"
> "Why, yes."
> "And that company in turn owns the stock that controls the South Side Real Estate Company, doesn't it?"
> "Why, yes."
> "I think I can say that the Thomas family pays rent to *you*?"
> "Indirectly, yes."
> "Who formulates the policies of these two companies?"
> "Why, I do."
> "Why is it that you charge the Thomas family and other Negro families more rent for the same kind of houses than you charge whites?"
> "I don't fix the rent scales," Mr. Dalton said.
> "Who does?"
> "Why, the law of supply and demand regulates the price of houses." (302)

To rely once again on Burgess's terminology for describing the neutral distribution of racial bodies in urban space, Dalton begins by presenting himself as something like an impartial sorter and shifter, although he alleges the impersonal workings of the corporation and the market rather than the city as such. There is nothing intimate or personal about the corporation in *Native Son*. Dalton inserts two companies between himself and the Thomases; he denies that he is Bigger's landlord but finally concedes that he indirectly collects the money. On the one hand, Dalton wants to present himself as the man in charge, who formulates the companies' policies, but on the other, he professes to have nothing to do with them: "I don't fix the rent scales." Dalton's claim to agency gives way to abstract market forces over which he has no control and for which he assumes no responsibility.

As Max's pointed questions make clear, market laws are as man-made as the housing they regulate:

> "Now, Mr. Dalton, it has been said that you donate millions of dollars to educate Negroes. Why is it that you exact an exorbitant rent of eight dollars per week from the Thomas family for one unventilated, rat-infested room in which four people eat and sleep?"
> ... "Well, there's a housing shortage."
> "All over Chicago?"
> "No. Just here on the South Side."
> "You own houses in other sections of the city?"
> "Yes."
> "Then why don't you rent those houses to Negroes?"
> "Well . . . Er . . . I—I—I—don't think they'd like to live any other place."
> "Who told you that?"
> "Nobody." . . .
> "Isn't it true you *refuse* to rent houses to Negroes if those houses are in other sections of the city?"
> "Why, yes."
> "Why?"
> "Well, it's an old custom."
> "Do you think the custom is right?"
> "I didn't make the custom," Mr. Dalton said. . . . "I think that Negroes are happier when they're together."
> "Who told you *that*?"
> "Why, nobody."
> "Aren't they more profitable when they're together?"
> "I don't know what you mean."
> "Mr. Dalton, doesn't this policy of your company tend to keep Negroes on the South Side, in one area?"

"Well, it works that way. But I didn't originate . . . "

"Mr. Dalton, do you think that the terrible conditions under which the Thomas family lived in one of your houses may in some way be related to the death of your daughter?"

"I don't know what you mean." (302–4)

While it may be true that supply and demand are affected by a housing shortage, the housing shortage is in turn generated by discriminatory rental practices and the economic motivations for them. For the Chicago school sociologists, money mediated most relations between people in the city, where contacts are primarily economic rather than affectional. Money thus symbolized the impersonality that is the central fact of urban life. According to Robert Park: "It is just because we feel no personal and no sentimental attitude toward our money, such as we do toward, for example, our home, that money becomes a valuable means of exchange."[38] Impersonal dollars are usefully traded with people for whom we care nothing. Although people generally do not feel emotionally connected to individual bills, Park seems less persuasively to suggest that people are basically indifferent to whether they have money or not. But money is a "valuable means of exchange," not because it means nothing to us, but because its value is so readily recognized. Dalton is no more likely to give away all his money than he is to trade away his home. Nor should the sentimental value of the home obscure the economic value of the building that houses it. Whether rental or residential, all Dalton's properties are financially implicated in his endorsement of segregation and the difference between Bigger paying rent as a kitchenette tenant and receiving wages as a live-in servant on Drexel Boulevard.

Chicago sociologists held the impersonality of the city and the indifference of urban dwellers toward each other to be among the most traumatic psychic experiences of modern life, the antithesis of the close communal ties and casual intimacy found in villages and small towns.[39] But for African Americans, impersonality, neutrality, and indifference implied freedom from white hostility and thus could potentially be envisioned as psychic *benefits* of urban life. In *12 Million Black Voices* Wright described the southern migrant's arrival in the city in terms of a welcome respite from racial conflict in the city's temporary haven of impersonality. At first "these white men [on the trains] seem impersonal and their very neutrality reassures us—for a while. Almost against our deeper judgment, we try to force ourselves to relax, for these brisk men give no sign of what they feel. They are indifferent. O sweet and welcome indifference!" (99). Tentative freedom on public transportation becomes something of a trope in migration literature, such as in *American Hunger*, when Wright observes the self-absorption of the white man next to him and, more complexly, when the protagonist of *Invisible Man* (1952) is both freed in urban anonymity and crushed by the enormous physical and psychical presence of the large white woman who crowds him on his first subway ride in New York.[40] For Wright, indifference does not signify inadequate attention to one's personal individuality, but rather adequate inattention to racial difference. Unfortunately, "soon enough we learn that the brisk, clipped men of the North, the bosses of the buildings, are not at all *indifferent*" (*12 Million* 100). For Wright, when migrants are herded by men like Dalton off the public transportation and into extortionate Black Belt kitchenettes, the illusion of urban impersonality ends. The opposite of indifference in this instance isn't intimacy, but segregation.

If anything, then, the problem of the city is that it is *insufficiently* impersonal. Max's questions to Dalton are designed to reveal that there is nothing neutral about the city's pecuniary nexus. Dalton probably doesn't care who pays him eight dollars for the rat-infested room, as long as those people are black: no segregation, no eight dollars, perhaps only six or four. But investment in the race of the tenants is personal; that is, segregation depends upon a stake in who the tenants are even if their identity continues to be significant only at the level of the group and not as individuals. As a tenant, an employee, and an object of philanthropy (remember the Ping-Pong tables Dalton gave to the South Side Boys' Club), Bigger is targeted by Dalton precisely for who he is, which is to say, for the race to which he belongs. Put another way, what it means for Bigger's landlord to be his employer and putative benefactor as well is to establish a dense network of connections that belies the alleged randomness, superficiality, and impersonality of urban contacts. Dalton eventually acknowledges his role in the creation of the artificial housing shortage: he refuses to rent available units to African Americans elsewhere in the city. But he also denies responsibility for the policy, shifting it first to time-honored racist traditions and then to the agency of the very population most harmed by it. Dalton finds another scapegoat besides impersonal market forces in the natural affinity of African Americans for their place in the city. He suggests that they are responsible for the high rents he charges, because they could not be happy anywhere but the Black Belt. Dalton denies that segregation is about the freedom of whites to live where they please, linking it instead to the prerogatives of black community. Segregation is almost discriminatory against whites; he asserts the sentimental attachment of his black tenants to each other rather than his own attachment to profits.

Dalton's alibis shift between fanciful, incompatible commitments to urban impersonality and neutrality, and to the free choice and racial preferences of black people.[41] The latter position also informs the newspaper accounts of Bigger's resistance to communist overtures. "What a story!

. . . These Negroes want to be left alone and these reds are forcing 'em to live with 'em, see," and "Say, I'm slanting this to the primitive Negro who doesn't want to be disturbed by white civilization" (201). The reporters intend to broadcast the story of voluntary black seclusion, of *exclusivity*, the unwillingness to live with people of a different color, whether white or red. Although the account of segregation as willful isolation may seem inconsistent with the novel's emphasis on trespassing, recall that the flight from segregation was also represented as the extension of the Black Belt. The effect was not to mix the races but to replace whites with blacks. From the racist perspective, where one black settler climbs through the window, others will soon follow.

In *Tarzan* the pursuit of happiness among black people is antithetical to the happiness of whites, because it involves encroachment upon the latter's territory and homes. Bigger shatters white Chicago's dream that black happiness in the city is compatible with the sanctity of white property: enabled by segregation, antiexpansionist, a function of knowing and loving one's place. He rejects Dalton's account of his agency on behalf of segregation, claiming agency instead in the disavowal of his "little spot." He links the meaning of Mary's death to his powerful desire to "feel at home" (329), which he explains to Max means being "happy in this world" (329), not isolated from it either in church or, implicitly, in the artificial community created and enforced by Dalton. When captured, Bigger is at first despondent over what he sees as the failed project of her death: "Having been thrown by an accidental murder into a position where he had sensed a possible order and meaning in his relations with the people about him; having accepted the moral guilt and responsibility for that murder because it had made him feel free for the first time in his life; having felt in his heart some obscure need to be at home with people and having demanded ransom money to enable him to do it—having done all this and failed, he chose not to struggle any more" (255). Killing Mary provides Bigger with "a natural wall" (101) that enables him to appropriate her question about how his people live and begin to perceive the relation of his life to the lives of others. Unlike the defensive wall that divides Bigger from his family and himself, this wall is associated with the freedom to feel deeply as well as think analytically about his experience. The kidnapping scenario is significant not only because Bigger appreciates with the astuteness of the impoverished that feeling "at home" in the world is easier with money than without it, but it also contributes to the fiction that he planned to kill her, underwriting Bigger's assertion of self-direction, to use Alain Locke's phrase, upon which the possibility of belonging in the world depends.

Throughout *Native Son* Bigger rewrites accident into intention, manslaughter into murder, claiming his right to moral responsibility as a self-

determining agent. In this context, the brutal rape and murder of Bessie
Mears represents Bigger's effort to realize his conception of Mary's death.
Critics have long been troubled by Wright's insistence on Bessie's absolute
passivity and by the gratuitous violence done to her. Robyn Wiegman
reads this violence as strategically, rather than symptomatically, misogy-
nistic and links it to Bigger's feelings of violation. She argues that like
other acts of violence in the novel, the crimes against Bessie are responses
to what Bigger perceives to be the real crime of rape—of him—by white
people. In negotiating racial difference among men by violently sexualiz-
ing it, *Native Son* does not count women as "sexual and social victim[s]."[42] Bigger's own troubled relationship to white violence, however,
does not neutralize Bessie as the target of his. Rather, his excessive brutality is the vehicle by which he can free himself from victimization and
affirm his agency. That is, Bigger doesn't rape and murder Bessie so that
he can emerge as the text's lone victim; he won't have to be a victim at
all if he has an indisputable victim of his own.

Bigger's relation to Mary's death is most striking in relation to Dalton's
vision of his own criminal practices. It would be going too far to suggest
that Dalton sees himself even unconsciously as the victim of abstract
forces and ancient customs; his attitude would be more that of a fortu-
itous beneficiary. But in defending white property, Dalton comes much
closer than Bigger does to seeing himself as the protagonist of a naturalist
novel, a waif amid forces. Bigger treats an accident as though it were an
intentional act, while Dalton treats intentional acts as though they were
dictated by forces beyond his control. Bigger demands the freedom to
hold himself accountable, while Dalton disavows responsibility and
blames everything else. Bigger strives to understand his relation to Mary's
death; Dalton doesn't understand the question. Bigger's claim to agency
is tantamount to denying that he is a victim of Dalton or anyone else,
which makes pity an irrelevant, even insulting, response. "I ain't asking
nobody to be sorry for me" (330), Bigger tells his lawyer; like Wright, he
doesn't want his story to be a tragic victim's tale that "even bankers'
daughters could read and weep over and feel good about" ("How Bigger
Was Born" xxvii). Wright attributed his relentless portrait of Bigger to
the negative power of sympathy to console white readers by bringing them
into pleasurable contact with their own humanity, and thus to evade the
question of how their lives are materially connected to Bigger's. Bigger's
agency is not designed to absolve readers of their responsibility but invites
them to acknowledge it and, in contrast with Dalton, to understand the
relation of white privilege to Bigger's life and crimes.

Jan is a figure for the ideal reader who senses his own responsibility
but also withholds pity and respects Bigger's agency. Jan visits Bigger in
prison and tells him that "maybe in a certain sense, I'm the one who's

really guilty" (266), but also: "I didn't come here to feel sorry for you. I don't suppose you're so much worse off than the rest of us who get tangled up in this world" (267). Jan further entreats him: "Let me be on your side. . . . I can fight this thing with you, just like you've started it. I can come from all of those white people and stand here with you" (268). Jan's acknowledgment of his own accountability as a man who is white as well as red takes the form of an offer to cross the line, to detach himself from the white mob and "stand" with Bigger on his "side." And Bigger reads Jan's overture precisely as the voluntary erosion of a spatial boundary: "Suddenly, this white man had come up to him, flung aside the curtain and walked into the room of his life. Jan had spoken a declaration of friendship that would make other white men hate him. . . . For the first time in his life a white man became a human being to him" (268). The segregated room of the kitchenette is figuratively replaced by the integrated "room of his life." Curtains and walls are irrelevant. Jan not only expresses willingness to share his physical space but once again encroaches on it. Although Jan's entrance is an intrusion, the rhetoric of friendship works to reclaim it from the logic of trespass, as though Jan's declaration retroactively issues him an invitation.

The color line continues to lose a measure of its reality for Bigger, and the further destabilization of boundaries results in a simultaneously threatening and promising disequilibrium. When Max invites him to speak about himself, Bigger is torn between his faith in Max for "taking upon himself a thing that would make other whites hate him" (321) and the difficulty of crossing the color line: "He felt that he should have been able to meet Max halfway; but, as always, when a white man talked to him, he was caught out in No Man's Land" (321). As the World War I term for the vacant, contested, battle-scarred ground between enemy trenches, and a metaphor for Bigger's sense of dislocation, No Man's Land implies the unavailability of his usual defensive strategy—the hard veneer of masculine indifference with which he variously has kept family, friends, and white people at bay. It evokes an amorphous and alien place, or rather, placelessness, that is between and beyond the hostile white world and the familiarity of the segregated black, where boundaries are no longer certain.[43] Max goes farther than Jan; he does not enter Bigger's "room" but seeks to draw him into the open, as it were, where Bigger is suspended between boundaries and identifications.

Mary and Jan unsuccessfully attempted something of the sort the night she was killed. Their awkward effort to befriend him produced a similar experience of dislocation: "It was a shadowy region, a No Man's Land, the ground that separated the white world from the black that he stood upon. He felt naked, transparent" (67–68). Bigger felt Jan and Mary struggling and failing to extricate him and themselves from the racial categories and geographies that condition their interaction. No Man's Land marks that failure but also points the way to new identifications and affinities. Although it expresses a black vantage point on the confusions of identity and location produced by white subjects, No Man's Land is neither here nor there, black nor white. Insofar as it has a color, it would be red, the color of potential political and racial and, in this case, gender alliance. Because it is just that territory neither black nor white can claim as its own, it is immune to allegations about trespassing. The cognitive No Man's Land cannot be conquered and controlled; balanced precariously *on* the color line, as long as there is a color line, it is logically unavailable to expansion from either direction, which would only displace but never settle it.

No Man's Land opens up a beneficial but discomfiting psychological territory—"the space between" identities—from which Bigger continues to explore his relation to the world.[44] Bigger meets Max "halfway" by narrating to a white man his experiences, and in turn he receives "a recognition of his life, of his feelings, of his person that he had never encountered before" (333). With Max, as with Jan, Bigger feels as though he has emerged from a sort of racial anonymity into identity. But their acknowledgment immediately sets him to the task of producing relations, which is to say, it also points him in the direction of community:

> He stood up in the middle of the cell floor and tried to see himself in relation to other men, a thing he had always feared to try to do. . . . For the first time in his life he felt the ground beneath his feet, and he wanted it to stay there. . . . Standing trembling in his cell, he saw a dark vast fluid image rise and float; he saw a black sprawling prison full of tiny black cells in which people lived; each cell had its stone jar of water and a crust of bread and no one could go from cell to cell and there were screams and curses and yells of suffering and nobody heard them, for the walls were thick and darkness was everywhere. Why were there so many cells in the world? . . . [I]f he reached out with his hands and touched other people, reached out through these stone walls and felt other hands connected with other hearts—if he did that, would there be a reply, a shock? . . . [I]n that touch, response of recognition, there would be union, identity; there would be a supporting oneness, a wholeness which had been denied him all his life. (334–35)

The vision of a "black . . . prison" of single-room living spaces replicates the domestic topography of the Black Belt, but here Bigger sees isolation from others who share a metaphysical condition rather than enforced exclusion from others with whom he shares nothing. In prison he has a room to himself, but though solitary, he is not quite alone.[45] Isolation makes him "the equal of others" (335), and with the perception of equality comes the mutual permeability of barriers. As with No Man's Land, trespassing is again beside the point, because the issue is contact with people, not conquest of space: he wants "the ground . . . to stay there." His attention to groundedness suggests that Bigger has moved into a different psychical space from No Man's Land, one that is not beyond and between, but more generative of his ambition to feel at home with other people. Like the recognition Bigger achieved with Max and Jan, the answering touch of his fellow inmates would signify the mutual recognition of persons and is indistinguishable from connection with them. The image articulates a fantasy of tentative community that in no way compromises the sanctity of the person. Indeed, each is treated as evidence and a guarantee of the other—"union, identity," "a supporting oneness, a wholeness"—one term seeming to point to the other as an extension of itself. The mutuality of "union, identity" accounts for the seeming discrepancy in Bigger's final conversation with Max between his bold insistence on identity in and through the criminal act—"what I killed for, I *am*!" (391–92)—and the pathos of his final words that seek again to make contact with something outside the self: "Tell . . . Tell Mister . . . Tell Jan hello. . . ." (392, ellipses in original). Bigger enunciates the identity that claims recognition from and confers it on Jan; the greeting does not cancel but reinforces the commitment to "I am."

Prison is imagined to resolve the problems of both overcrowding and isolation. There is something appealing and disturbing about Bigger's meditations. Throughout the novel he has expressed a desire for belonging in the world that was incommensurate with the inferior and segregated position assigned him, and thus he refused to stay "in his place" (333). One consequence of embracing himself as a murderer and accepting moral responsibility is to make prison a place that he has in effect chosen to inhabit. It is a symbol of his agency. But here prison becomes something Bigger inhabits independent of his crimes and in virtue of his humanity. He feels provisionally at home there because it provides him with an interpretive structure that posits isolation as a fact of the human condition and transcends it through the possibility of others' responsive desire for connection. For Bigger, the cells of the prison are more meaningful in the potential for human community than as evidence of exclusion from society.

Like the Black Belt with which it is repeatedly identified, however, prison is a concrete place too imbricated in material and social conditions to sustain the abstractions of either human solitude or community. To choose at once the most extreme and logical example, men like Bigger and Dalton are certainly isolated from one another, "strangers" (325) even though they are neighbors, but the metaphorical prison fails to explain the glaring differences between Dalton's luxurious isolation in a white mansion and the stressful physical and psychological isolation that

Bigger experienced within the "tiny black cell" of the kitchenette or the prison cell from which he offers this generous view of human relations. It fails as well to address Dalton's own agency in creating and maintaining isolation. In seeking to develop a spatial understanding of human relations that moves beyond the dualism of the color line, Bigger has produced an account of provisional community that is unresponsive to the fact of segregation, to the fact that "[w]e live here and they live there." It endorses the integrative knowledge of shared suffering in adjoining cells by ignoring the material differences that distinguish real prisons and locked-in lives from existential ones. If living in the Black Belt is "just like living in jail," Bigger can imagine escaping from it only through another form of imprisonment. He belongs to the human community only in his isolation. What is so unsettling about Bigger's reflections is that they signify adjustment to his "place."[46]

In his speech for leniency, Max proposes an alternative theory of the links between Bigger's "life and fate" and "ours" (354). He aims "to show the degree of responsibility he had in these crimes" (343): "We planned the murder of Mary Dalton, and today we come to court and say: 'We had nothing to do with it!' " (363). Having accepted responsibility for his crimes, Bigger must be made to share it with those who are his co-conspirators but decidedly not his fellow prisoners. Max suggests that he shares his crimes as well with the rest of black America, who are incarcerated with him. "Multiply Bigger Thomas twelve-million times . . . and you have the psychology of the Negro people. . . . Taken collectively, they are not simply twelve million people; in reality they constitute a separate nation, stunted, stripped, and held captive *within* this nation, devoid of political, social, economic, and property rights" (364). To Max, Bigger stands in for the "nation within a nation," which is bound together materially and politically like an enormous Black Belt, the African American "city within a city" (*Black Metropolis* 12). Imprisonment figures here as a metaphor for the material inequalities of opportunity and outcome that divide its citizens from the jailer nation and also for the "unbelievably narrow limits" within which segregated residents struggle "to achieve that feeling of at-home-ness for which we once strove so ardently" (365). He reads Bigger's eruption in anger and hate as a sociologically significant expression of collective resistance to imprisonment, the prelude to "the tide of pent-up lava that will some day break loose, not in a single, blundering, accidental, individual crime, but in a wild cataract of emotion that will brook no control" (361). The substitution of "emotion" for the more obvious and admonitory *violence* identifies a population that is less interested in revolution per se than in bursting across the barriers to claim for themselves the right to the "feeling" of "home."

Like Bigger, however, Max turns to prison as the symbol of a certain kind of community. He pleads with the court to send Bigger

> to prison for life. What would prison mean to Bigger Thomas? It holds advantages for him that a life of freedom never had. . . . He would be brought for the first time within the orbit of our civilization. He would have an identity, even though it be but a number. He would have for the first time an openly designated relationship with the world. The very building in which he would spend the rest of his natural life would be the best he has ever known. Sending him to prison would be the first recognition of his personality he has ever had. . . . The other inmates would be the first men with whom he could associate on a basis of equality. Steel bars between him and the society he offended would provide a refuge from hate and fear. (369–70)

Max argues that "life" is not just a sentence but something prison would confer on Bigger. Numbers are not inimical to identity, nor are they impersonal. They clarify instead his relation to the world and to those who will be his neighbors. Max's version of prison appeals to equality by invoking Bigger's status as a prisoner among actual prisoners rather than by giving form to the human condition. Imprisonment signifies the recognition of Bigger's personality and dignity, but only because Max attends to its material reality. It is the finest housing Bigger has ever occupied, a room of his own, materially and psychologically superior to the experience of "living in jail." The prison cell offers the potential for human community *because* it is evidence of his exclusion from society. Through the plea for a life sentence, Max dramatizes the gap between the way society treats its criminals and the way it treats the African Americans it criminalizes. The dead-end choice that Max and *Native Son* hold out is between a prison of dislocation and discrimination where the Daltons mete out the terms of existence from the other side of the color line, and a prison that is a more secure barrier from white Chicago than the Black Belt, where Bigger was first separated and then seized. But even that choice is ultimately beside the point. Although Bigger could reinvent himself as Mary's murderer, an identity that the State's Attorney, the Daltons, and the screaming mob are only too eager to confer on him, he cannot compel the housing that fits the crime. In denying the plea for life, the death sentence denies yet again the appeal for a home.

AMERICANS IN PARIS

Richard Wright's spectacular success as a writer is the best evidence that a black person's fate could not be measured merely by the refractory problem of racial walls and "a general 'ceiling' upon all of his life's aspirations."[47] But his relocation to New York in the late thirties, later to Mexico and to France, where he was eventually followed by James Baldwin and Chester Himes, also indicates that even as a best-selling novelist Wright felt that he had to continue to reject and redefine his "place." In a letter to Gertrude Stein, he favorably compared France, which was still recovering economically and politically from a devastating war, to the United States, where there was plenty of food and money, but insufficient freedom to spend money freely and go where he pleased.[48] His distress at the limitations on his rights was nowhere more apparent than when he attempted to lay claim to the foremost middle-class privilege of house ownership. In 1945 he and Ellen Wright, who is white, attempted to buy a brownstone in Greenwich Village. Although no racial covenant prevented the transaction, the white owners refused to sell to an African American. The Wrights formed the Richelieu Estate Company, surreptitiously purchased the property, and moved in.[49] Dalton has been beaten at his own game; the Wrights appropriated the formal structures of corporate abstraction through which the landlord denied his discriminatory practices, in order to curtail them. The Richelieu name virtually advertises the company as a tactical political organization, one that seeks to increase power while pretending to be up to something else, and prophetically associates free access to housing with France.

After nearby residents learned who the purchasers were and before they moved in, they offered the Wrights $2,000 more than they had paid for the house ($2,500 according to Webb; double the purchase price according to Addison). Like the protagonists of Lorraine Hansberry's award-winning play *A Raisin in the Sun* (1959), who are offered a bonus by their new white "neighbors" to sell back a recently purchased house outside Chicago's Black Belt, the Wrights declined to resell. But while the play ended on moving day and with the triumphant prospect of residential freedom and "a home . . . a *home*" for the Younger family, Richard, Ellen, and their daughter were subjected in act 4 to the hostility and epithets of their so-called neighbors.[50] In "I Choose Exile," an unpublished essay, Wright described his subsequent, thwarted attempt to purchase a dream house outside the city as the event that finally drove him from the United States altogether.[51] Wright was impressed by the neutrality and indifference of nature, but he soon found that the country differed little from the city in its mindfulness of race: the white owner refused to sell his house to him. According to the essay, it was just after the failed house purchase, on the train back to New York, that he decided to move to France.

In fact, this account of the departure is inaccurate. According to biographers, Richard and Ellen left for Paris shortly after the dream house evaporated in 1946, but only for a brief visit at the invitation of the French government, for which he had already been trying to procure a passport.

They returned to the United States, intending to remain, but Wright finally chose exile, and they moved to Paris permanently in 1947. My point is not to fault Wright's memory but rather to suggest that the essay is probably true to the spirit of his European migration, if not the facts. The dream house, the material embodiment of his agency as an American, is the conceptual center of freedom in "I Choose Exile." He could not choose house ownership on his terms, in a rural/suburban region, and choosing exile was the next best thing.[52] Paris stood in for the thing he wanted, the opportunity to indulge his right as an American to live where and how he pleased, to uncouple race and place. Like Baldwin, Wright was "a kind of trans-atlantic commuter," unconventionally suspended between the native country that provided him with the materials for his literary work and the country that came much closer to making good on the democratic promises of home.[53]

A year after the Wrights' relocation the U.S. Supreme Court ruled that racial covenants were unenforceable, but the decision did not release a new tide of African Americans to the postwar development suburbs already taking shape at the fringes of American cities. William Levitt explained the decision to sell no houses to black purchasers in Levittowns: "We can solve a housing problem, or we can try to solve a racial problem. But we cannot combine the two."[54] The postwar suburb, like the Black Belt, continued to owe its particular form to the same white belief that race and community are coextensive. This belief would soon be challenged by the Hyde Park–Kenwood redevelopment project, which worked in the late 1940s and the 1950s to create "Chicago's first stable interracial community of high standards." In other words, white middle-class house owners came to realize that to keep the neighborhood white they had to accept that it would also be black; "the real difficulty was one of class," not race.[55] As long as middle-class families of both races stood shoulder to shoulder against the poor, the Daltons' former territory could be saved from the slum fate that otherwise awaited it. Not surprisingly, the proposal for an interracial middle-class alliance in Hyde Park prompted an enthusiastic reporter for the *Chicago Sun-Times* to tout the plan as "a new city answer to what the suburb is reputed to be," while a concerned critic protested that it "creates a suburban island in a sea of ghettoes," Drake and Cayton's description of the Black Belt as "an island in a big white sea" turned inside out.[56] The Hyde Park–Kenwood plan informs the novel *Peaceable Lane* (1960), by a former *Chicago Sun-Times* journalist, which congratulates itself on a similar solution to residential segregation by dramatizing the benefits of admitting a single wealthy black family into a white middle-class suburban neighborhood. The white residents organize but fail to prevent the house sale; working with their new, equally concerned, Jaguar-driving black neighbor, however, the newly "integrated" block prevents panic-selling to other, less affluent black families, retaining property values for all and keeping the "colored slums" at bay.[57] As a real-life Peaceable Lane, Hyde Park–Kenwood fortified the color line as a class line, allowing houses like the Daltons' to be enjoyed in their pristine form by a few black as well as white middle-class people, but once again checking and threatening to unleash the expansiveness of displaced people such as Bigger Thomas.

CHAPTER FIVE

Sanctimonious Suburbanites and the Postwar Novel

"The Middle Class, Alas!"

SLOAN WILSON'S *The Man in the Gray Flannel Suit* begins by asserting the protagonists' absolute hostility to the place they live, a more salient fact about them than even their identity: "By the time they had lived seven years in the little house on Greentree Avenue in Westport, Connecticut, they both detested it."[1] "They" have their reasons. The house is "too small [and] ugly" (5), and although they bought it new, linoleum, plaster, and plumbing need to be repaired or replaced. It seems as well that "they" can blame their anonymity on the house, which is "almost precisely like the houses on all sides" (5). But the problem is not that it obliterates who they are; rather, the shabby house reveals it too readily in ways that discredit and distort them:

> [T]he house had a kind of evil genius for displaying proof of their weaknesses and wiping out all traces of their strengths. The ragged lawn and weed-filled garden proclaimed to passers-by and the neighbors that Thomas R. Rath and his family disliked "working around the place" and couldn't afford to pay someone else to do it. The interior of the house was even more vengeful. In the living room there was a big dent in the plaster near the floor, with a huge crack curving up from it in the shape of a question mark. (3)

The crack followed an argument about money that ended when Tom threw an expensive vase against the wall. An attempt to repair it failed, and instead they are left with "a perpetual reminder of Betsy's moment of extravagance, Tom's moment of violence, and their inability either to fix walls properly or to pay to have them fixed" (4). The house reveals Betsy as an imperfect domestic manager and exposes them both as aspiring but failed "Do-It-Your selfers" who lack financial as well as creative resources.[2] The crack and a child's inky handprints, the individual traces that the Babbitt house lacked, personalize but also devalue the Raths' house. Far from nurturing the inhabitants, it is "a trap" (5) from which they may never escape.

As we have seen, there is nothing unusual about a twentieth-century American novel that begins by repudiating the home of its protagonists, whether "the trap" is an overcrowded and overpriced kitchenette like the Thomases' or, less convincingly, a two-story Dutch Colonial. What differentiates *Man in Gray Flannel* from the suburban novels we have encountered so far is the Raths' own immediate, unmistakable, and almost hopeless opposition to it as well. Ownership of a suburban house is treated here as a sign of economic weakness, suspended ambition, the *failure* of the American dream instead of its fruition. The Raths' failure is palpable. Although their families no longer have much money, Betsy had a modest coming-out party in Boston, and Tom's grandmother continues to live on the huge family estate in South Bay, Connecticut, where he was raised. The stereotypical development house poses a challenge to their otherwise legitimate claim to the title "Thomas R. Rath and family," which parodically evokes the kind of status that a house in the suburbs once communicated and conferred, but in the opening of *Man in Gray Flannel* only publicly disclaims.

Until the 1940s the suburbs continued to be identified primarily with affluent middle- and upper-middle-class families, where house ownership was the special, if not unique, province of the Thomas R. Raths of this country.[3] The career of Levitt and Sons is a case in point. From the prewar construction of small subdivisions on Long Island for the upper-middle-class market, the firm turned in the late forties to building inexpensive single-family houses and communities on an unprecedented scale for returning veterans and their families. The mass production of houses did not occur in the factory, as some Depression-era commentators had anticipated, but at the subdivision, where the Levitts relied on traditional materials and designs such as the Colonial and the Cape Cod, as well as a western import, the "Rancher," to attract prospective purchasers.[4] In the postwar period, mass production, along with cheap and accessible land, financial incentives for veterans and builders, and high wages meant that suburban house ownership became available to most white middle-class and many working-class families for the first time in American history.[5]

By the fifties *the suburb* popularly signified *the development*, a place of "uniform, unidentifiable houses, lined up inflexibly, at uniform distances, on uniform roads, in a treeless communal waste," "conforming," like the people who lived there, "to a common mold": the new residence of "the mass middle class."[6] Thus even the affluent town of Westport, which dates to the Colonial period and was within the suburban reaches of New York before the postwar housing boom, appears in *Man in Gray Flannel* as though it were simply a prison house of new developments and indistinguishable houses. The mass production of housing did not liberate people from residential mediocrity, as Depression-era visionaries had hoped, but made it the national standard. In "The Transients," one of several *Fortune* articles in which sections of *The Organization Man* (1956) were originally published, William H. Whyte identified postwar suburbia with the revolutionary degradation of the individualized middle-class house into an undifferentiated unit of a nationwide "dormitory":

> For a quick twinge of superiority there is nothing quite like driving past one of the new Levittown-like suburbs. To visitors from older communities, the sight of rank after rank of little boxes stretching off to infinity, one hardly distinguishable from the other, is weird. . . . If this is progress, God help us . . . 1984. But, onlookers are also likely to conclude, one must be sympathetic too, after all, it is a step up in life for the people who live there, and one should not begrudge them the opiate of TV; here, obviously is a group of anonymous beings submerged in a system they do not understand.
>
> The onlooker had better wipe the sympathy off his face. Underneath the television aerials lies a revolution. What he has seen is not the home of little cogs and drones. What he has seen is the dormitory of the next managerial class.[7]

Whyte disrupts the onlookers' comfortable conviction about the inferior beings who inhabit these houses, challenging as well their assumption about where the middle class must presumably live. What the onlookers and, by implication, the *Fortune* readers see are embryonic versions of themselves, not the factory crowd climbing a dubious ladder of success but the descent of office cohorts into the mass. Whyte notes the observers' smugness, but then indicates that they should feel neither superiority nor sympathy but perhaps something closer to self-pity. The putative erosion of class boundaries in the postwar period, or, alternatively, the celebration of a capitalist society that had made everyone middle class, is here working in a different direction. Many postwar intellectuals enthusiastically articulated a version of the claim made by *Harper's* editor Frederick Allen that "the dynamic logic of mass production" had at last fulfilled the promise of the twenties and made elites of the masses. Higher wages and lower prices had lifted "millions of families . . . from poverty or near poverty to a status where they can enjoy what has been traditionally considered a middle-class way of life" that included refrigerators, cars, and sometimes and with increasing frequency, houses.[8] For Whyte as well as for Wilson, it demonstrated that masses had been made of the elites.

The suburb of the mass middle class is to postwar sociology and literature what the slum was to the Chicago school between the world wars and to proletarian fiction of the Depression. Nelson Algren's "army of . . . homeless" was erased, first by an army of real soldiers, and later by an army of men in gray flannel suits.[9] As in the case of Wright and the Chicago school, postwar literature and sociology were not merely complementary. Postwar sociologists attended to literary representations of the phenomena they sought to describe, while novelists adopted quasi-sociological techniques in fiction dealing with the suburbs. Even novels that do not claim to be defining a new breed of postwar suburban American through characters named John and Mary Drone profess to be portraying the "typical commuter," or employ the statistical tone of social science to describe and deflate suburban activities: "Afternoon floated by, and the sun dropped low, and some five thousand automatic stoves were switched on while some five thousand wives cooked dinner for some five thousand returning husbands."[10] The preponderance of popular novels that borrow from and mimic sociology suggests the power of the assumption that the postwar suburb was producing a new kind of American and that novelists felt themselves to be actively participating in its construction and elaboration. The typical suburbanite became a way of demarcating within literary texts the massification of the middle class and also, unlike an earlier archetype such as Babbitt, of linking it to the deterioration of status and social privilege.

Tom Rath's renowned attire, as well as the house, register just these changes, and the title gestures toward Wilson's own sociological ambition to delineate an American type. According to C. Wright Mills, the wearing of street clothes on the job is an important psychological resource for the white-collar worker, the last vestige of status that has been eroded by his or her dependent and inglorious place within the corporation.[11] By the end of the third chapter, Tom grimly reflects that the gray flannel suit is "[t]he uniform of the day" (11); the symbol of his affluence is also the symbol of his subordination. Junior executive positions in large corporations, like houses in the suburbs, provide no social guarantees.

Sociologically speaking, the postwar suburb is the residential analogue of the national corporation; when Whyte analyzed "the organization," he referred to a place of residence as well as a place of work. Organization men (and in the suburb, women as well) are "the ones who have left home, spiritually as well as physically, to take the vows of organization life" (3). Whyte declined to offer "any strictures against ranch wagons, or television sets, or gray flannel suits" (11), the usual trappings of postwar conformity, because commodities are "irrelevant" (11) as anything but symptoms of the real problem: a new managerial class that considers "belonging" to be the highest personal and social good. It turns to the corporation and the suburb for a new "home," finding it through something that exacerbates the crisis—"the deep emotional security that comes from total integration with the group" (36)—rather than a private refuge that respects the individual.[12] In "The Suburban Dislocation," Riesman cited "aimlessness" rather than "conformity" as the central problem of the suburb. The suburb is designed to privilege home over work so as to pretend that the meaninglessness of modern white-collar work does not matter. The home cannot be a satisfactory alternative until work itself is rehabilitated; understanding the connection between "meaningful work" and a meaningful home is necessary to disconnect them.[13]

The material artifacts of suburban life are ultimately immaterial because the consumption of mass-produced housing and products does not create, nor abstinence resolve, the crisis caused by the bureaucratic construction of mass middle-class men. For both Riesman and Whyte the suburb replicates the homelessness it is supposed to alleviate, especially for business and professional men. Thus in *The Lonely Crowd* (1950), Riesman argued that they suffer from "the night shift" (141), what Whyte called the "business stream of consciousness" (163): the psychological labor of anxiety about work that persecutes men in their sanctuary, a phenomenon we saw briefly in *Babbitt*. Anthropologists Roy Lewis and Rosemary Stewart similarly reported that for top managers, the home is not a place of rest or refuge: "If they do not take work home in their briefcases, they almost certainly take it home in their heads."[14] In these scenarios, the postwar home is the double of the office, a site of, not a relief from, white-collar work—a castle, perhaps, but one ruled by a nervous and unhappy king.

Whyte's classic sociological description and Wilson's best-selling literary treatment of corporate-suburban culture, both published by Simon and Schuster in the midfifties, as well as the work of Mills, Riesman, and others, point to a trend that has gone largely unremarked even in recent revisionary studies that have challenged the prevailing view of the fifties as a "culture of complacence" and "consensus placidity."[15] The middle classes—particularly male members of what came to be called the professional-managerial class (PMC)—were identified as the preeminent victims of postindustrialization and suburbanization; their complacency was presumed to be the riskiest and most unwarranted.[16] "[D]islocation" was their paradigmatic postwar experience: "Insecurity, instability, and maladjustment . . . replace the security, stability, and social adjustment which have traditionally been the pillars of middle-class position in our society."[17] The postwar period arguably dislocated everyone, but that case was not really made, or rather, as the previous quotation from Allen suggests, whatever dislocation the working classes experienced was as the fortunate beneficiaries of postwar economic and social changes that were supposed to have dissolved many of the visible boundaries between social classes. But articles in popular periodicals with titles such as "The Middle Class, Alas!" and "Our Fear Ridden Middle Classes," as well as *White Collar* (1951) and *The Lonely Crowd*, argued that white-collar work now replicated or surpassed the dependent, dehumanizing, and impersonal conditions of most blue-collar labor and was no longer necessarily better paid. The salaried middle class had become "the new little people" and "the most kicked around class in this country."[18] As every white-collar worker was reinvented as the factory slave of the fifties, including and even especially the corporate manager and executive, the term *alienation* was increasingly invoked to describe the effects of white-collar work, which brings "the alienation of the wage-worker from the products of his work . . . one step nearer to its Kafka-like completion. The salaried employee does not make anything. . . . No product of craftsmanship can be his to contemplate with pleasure as it is being created and after it is made" (Mills xvi–xvii). Working only with people, paper, and symbols, all white-collar employees are alienated from their labor in a way that the factory worker handling concrete things, in however small or unconnected a way, could never be.[19]

According to Mills, white-collar workers do not realize their plight because of their paradoxical situation: they "may be at the bottom of the social world" but are "at the same time gratifyingly middle class" (xii). Hovering between a less than satisfactory postwar present and past "dreams of glory" (68), between the obscurity of the uniform and the entitlement implied by the gray flannel suit, Tom embodies the experience of middle-class dislocation. As a "fable of the 'tense and frantic' '50s," *Man in Gray Flannel* was thought successfully to impart "the panicky quality of the lives of so many of those commuters in gray flannel," even if one critic surmised that the difficulty of caring for a family on $7,000 a year "must be less than heartbreaking to the average reader."[20] The question that the question mark in the living room raises is how can they reclaim (maintain) their social privilege?

Unlike the benighted figures that populate the sociologies, whether Whyte's cheerful belonger, Riesman's "glad-hand[er]" (141), or Mills's white-collar drone, the man in the gray flannel suit and his wife are profoundly aware of and invested in their anguish. And while sociologists tended to focus on the psychological, economic, and political impotence of the new middle classes, Wilson's literary-sociological project recovers from the putative disintegration of social privilege the rewarding basis for a new middle-class identity grounded in its resistance to the institutions that are so crucial to it. The corporation and the suburb may not enable affluence, success, happiness, or any other mushy term associated with the postwar search for the elusive "good life," but in allegedly victimizing the protagonists, they offer Tom and Betsy opportunities to redefine themselves in terms of their absolute superiority to those institutions most identified with the degradation of the middle class. In *Babbitt*, Lewis portrayed feeling bad about being middle class as a constitutive feature of white middle-class identity, a feeling that made Babbitt vaguely ashamed. In *The Man in the Gray Flannel Suit*, discontent is pushed to the next level: being middle class means *denying* that they are middle class, and shame gives way to a pleasant conviction of how exceptional they are. The Raths' sense of self does not come through Tom's job or the couples' house and family or their roles as consumers. Rather, *Man in Gray Flannel* insists that they can define themselves only by repudiating their middle-classness, in what becomes a dominant fictional paradigm of white middle-class experience in the postwar period. Other people belong in a development, not us; everyone else is happy as a corporate drone, except for me. And their fundamental dissatisfaction with the suburb and the corporation proves an engine of mobility that frees them from the constraints of each. The moral of the novel is indeed, as a reviewer mused, that "the self pitying shall inherit the earth."[21] The Raths' fortunes imply a broader truth about postwar representations of the middle class. Thinking of oneself as a victim may be the necessary condition for not becoming one.

THE ANXIETY OF AFFLUENCE

The protagonist of *The Man in the Gray Flannel Suit* was billed, preposterously, as "a fairly universal figure in mid-twentieth-century America," evidence not only of exaggerat 1 claims about postwar affluence, but also of the assumption that affluence and misery are intertwined, for he is above all the man for whom suburban-corporate existence is defined as endless suffering.[22] The real trouble begins when Tom, who works for a charitable foundation, gets a great new job in public relations at the United Broadcasting Corporation, which comes with an almost 30 percent raise in salary and the chance "to buy a better house" (6). But the connection between home and work exceeds economics. The Raths' naive assumption that a nicer house will solve their problems collapses under the revelation that the home is not a shelter from the anxieties of working for a corporation but is implicated in them. Early in the novel Tom contemplates the "four completely unrelated worlds in which he lived": "the crazy, ghost-ridden world" of his well-connected but now impoverished grandmother; "the isolated" world of war; the corporate world that employs him; and "the entirely separate world populated by Betsy" and their children, "the only one of the four worlds worth a damn. There must be some way in which the four worlds were related, he thought, but it was easier to think of them as entirely divorced from one another" (26). The certainty of disconnection becomes wishful thinking by the end; it is "easier" to see them as independent because recognizing their contingency seems to involve the potential disintegration of the only one he claims to care about.

Tom is close to being right. Shortly after he gets the new job, his grandmother dies and bequeaths him no money but an old, immense, and unsalable mansion that compounds the Raths' financial difficulties because taxes must be paid on it and Edward, an aged servant, pensioned. At the same time, a more serious catastrophe occurs: an elevator operator at UBC "pop[s] up to form a connecting link" (98) between the war, the corporation, and the home. A former member of Tom's paratrooper unit, Caesar Gardella informs him that Tom's intense wartime romance while in Italy resulted in the birth of a son. While Caesar is trying to locate Maria, the cousin of his own wife, he asks Tom to think about arranging financial support. The news represents moral and emotional as well as economic burdens. Tom was married when he met Maria. In deciding the right thing to do, he must also consider if and how to tell Betsy about the affair. The delicate task of determining and fulfilling his economic and moral obligations, of putting these worlds in relation to one another, threatens the dissolution of the family.

While waiting several weeks in Italy for a transport plane, Tom and Maria, Caesar and Gina are, temporarily, "almost like a suburban community, with the men all working for the same big corporation" (91–92). Although Tom is Caesar's commanding officer, their army uniforms, girlfriends, and, on other occasions, the experience of common danger diminish social differences—they are more like equal coworkers and neighbors than officer and subordinate. At UBC, their respective uniforms reflect and exacerbate the now self-evident distinctions between the elevator operator and the junior executive. "[A]shamed that in addition to all the other strains involved in their relationship, he should find it awkward to have lunch with a man in an elevator operator's uniform" (155), Tom learns that working for the same big corporation back home does not necessarily entail community. But the question of hierarchy is more vexed than his embarrassment indicates. The reader is put in the unusual position of being asked to join an elevator operator in sympathizing for a young executive. Caesar tells Tom that he and his wife take turns working real night shifts to raise a family, but he is "not complaining. . . . Things have gone pretty good for us" (156). He offers this positive assessment of his own situation after Tom has made a less than gracious reply—"The breaks" (156)—to Caesar's expression of admiration for Tom's promising job at UBC. Tom appears to expect commiseration instead of congratulations and makes a bolder plea for sympathy when he answers Caesar's question about financial help for Maria with the lame confession, "I'm practically broke" (158).

At this point Tom has $9,000 in the bank, the exact equivalent of a year's salary at the new job. His gray flannel suit does not, he suggests, protect him from the vagaries of the economic world. Tom's anxious response to Caesar reflects his belief that corporate white-collar work is fundamentally insecure. Moreover, the work suggested by Tom's gray flannel uniform is not made more meaningful than the work signified by

Caesar's, and thus does not compensate him for its risks. As someone who spends two-thirds of the novel ghostwriting a speech for the corporation's president, Tom performs a job that might have been scripted by Mills and Riesman, producing only "a meaningless lifework" (130) that reduces him to "the shadow of another man" (250). But it is not really the nature of corporate employment or his work in particular that conditions his replies to Caesar. It is the novel's assumption that suffering is the inevitable by-product of affluence. Money is about fantastic obligations, not rewards, and always generates concerns about more money. The higher salary at UBC and every subsequent sign that his career is taking off, from the boss's kindly interest in him to a final, career-making promotion, bring a new crisis. Betsy hopes to follow through on their original plan to spend the extra money on a new house, but once the job is his, Tom deals with the good news by predicting imminent disaster: "With nine thousand a year, we could afford some life insurance. Did you ever stop and think what would happen to you if I dropped dead some morning?" (67). A raise seems almost tantamount to a death sentence; as the family's fortunes improve, they get increasingly precarious. Affluence never has the chance to become the source of the middle-class male's discontent, as in *Babbitt*, because Tom is incapable of perceiving himself to be materially well off. The more money and assets, the more claims made upon them, to the exaggerated extent that a needy young dependent materializes out of nowhere, and the Raths suddenly acquire a servant, not as a luxury but as a further financial burden.

Man in Gray Flannel legitimates a paradoxical truth for the PMC: anxiety and unhappiness are inevitable components of its professional and economic well-being. Nowhere is this more the case than for Judge Saul Bernstein, the son of poor South Bay delicatessen owners who achieved an "enormously powerful" (149) position in a "town notorious for its prejudice against Jews" (147). His secret? He hates what he does for a living. "He had grown reasonably rich, and respected, and might have been happy except for one thing: he detested justice almost as much as he detested violence or cruelty of any other kind" (148). Judges are the victims of justice in the novel, and the terrible responsibility of administering it always makes his stomach ache. But he is not simply a good judge who also happens to dislike justice; professional self-loathing is precisely what makes him so good at his work and so influential in the community, "for people had found that hating justice as he did, he dispensed it extremely well" (149). As the example of the judge indicates, it is not just that professional and financial success cause misery, but the misery that comes from disliking one's work propagates success. Prejudice in the town lingers—he and his wife continue to be excluded from social gatherings and country clubs—but the novel nonetheless insists that unhappiness and even self-loathing are stronger forces for professional success than anti-Semitism is against it.

The novel pays less attention, however, to the intrinsic dissatisfactions of the independent professional's or the young executive's work than to the uncertainty of the latter's rewards. During one crisis, Tom tries to convince himself that "[y]ou can't go on worrying all the time; it has to stop someday. You can't really believe the world is insane; you have to believe everything's going to turn out all right" (181). The cure for an insane world is money. "[A]n island of order obviously must be made of money, for one doesn't bring up children in an orderly way without money, and one doesn't even have one's meals in an orderly way, or dress in an orderly way, or think in an orderly way without money. Money is the root of all order" (182). In contrast with the perception of the fifties as an era of rampant consumerism, *Man in Gray Flannel* is less interested in purchasing power than in absolute value, what the wealthiest character pooh-poohs as the false virtue of "money as such" (227). Although the passage seems to suggest that money matters because of what it can buy, the emphasis is much more on its capacity to regularize one's life than to improve one's standard of living. The point is not that one needs money to buy food or clothing but that one can neither eat nor dress "in an orderly way" without it. Certainly the possibility of "think[ing] in an orderly way" is imagined to come from a stability that money, as solid ground beneath one's feet, provides quite apart from how or whether it is spent. The dilemma is that the young managerial class needs money to survive in an insane world, but worrying about getting the money it needs may drive it crazy.

Given the concerns about inhabiting "a lunatic world" (109) and "an insane world" (299) that pervade the text, it is hardly a coincidence that Tom's public relations work at UBC is to establish the company's president, Ralph Hopkins, as the formative influence and head of a national committee on mental health, which is represented as the most serious health problem to face the country. The corporation seeks to cure the problem for which it is held to be largely responsible. In writing about the preponderance of characters who suffer from mental illness in post-war American novels, Richard Ohmann argues that affluence and the "perceived . . . softening of class lines" obscured the social contradictions of American life, which are displaced onto or thematized in these texts as widespread images of "personal illness."[23] But in its depiction of a national mental illness crisis, *The Man in the Gray Flannel Suit* wears its social contradictions on its sleeve, although the point it makes is that not even the affluent are affluent and that mental illness is only a paycheck away.

SUBURBIA AND ITS MALCONTENTS

To metaphorize money as "an island of order in a sea of chaos" suggests that money has usurped a function more logically associated with property. The intrinsic value of money contrasts sharply with the surprising valuelessness, financially and emotionally, of houses and land. The Raths detest their house in Westport because it makes them look shabby; they despise the grandmother's house because she squandered her savings on it. It is easy to understand Tom's selfish hatred of the house that has eaten his inheritance but not his perverse failure to perceive the commercial value of the land it sits on, "twenty-three acres of the best land in South Bay" (61), a coastal town *closer* to New York than Westport, at a time of frantic suburban development. Not even an immediate offer on the property by a shifty man in a Jaguar, who turns out to be a real-estate speculator, alerts Tom to his economic good fortune. Eventually Betsy and a wily local contractor persuade him to tear down the house and subdivide, but Tom never feels anything less than gypped at his inheritance, which is simply one more false threat to his financial security.

His peculiar blindness to the land's value, however, also seems to reflect a belief that land and house ownership are not anchors anymore. Before his grandmother's death, Tom considers the changes in South Bay since the war. Tom notes that the old mansions are dilapidated, a sign that the owners are not quite so affluent as previously, but they preserve an aura of stability in contrast with the newer houses, which are so impermanent that they seem "quite capable of disappearing as quickly as they had come" (20). And yet the very presence of the new development houses renders the decaying old mansions just as vulnerable and insubstantial as decaying new houses like the Raths'. The plan to tear down the mansion and subdivide, which will further increase the economic value and property taxes of the surrounding estates, heralds their demise as the owners are forced either to sell or subdivide themselves and portends the reinvention of the town as a development suburb like Westport.

In the final chapters, when the owner of a neighboring estate protests the Raths' now public plan to build a small subdivision, what they call a "housing project" (267), it is not only selfishness and bile that leads him almost hysterically to denounce their proposal: "if we replace the big estates with housing projects, South Bay will become a slum within ten years—a slum, I tell you, a slum!" (270).[24] Slum dwellers generally cannot afford the $25,000 asking price that Tom, Betsy, and the contractor have discussed, and so the analogy looks like a fit of rhetorical excess designed to protect the sentimental value of his property by restraining its economic value. But the word *slum* was also used by enlightened writers with a different agenda to describe postwar suburban housing developments. Famed New York planner Robert Moses called the "fly-by-night subdivision," where greedy speculators provided housing but did not prepare for community needs, "the slums of tomorrow."[25] Critics reworked the metaphor of colonization, which sometimes framed responses to the perceived invasion of the suburbs by the city and its slums, as I have shown in relation to *Tarzan* and *Native Son*. Now suburbs were lambasted as "parasites" that fed off the central city but gave nothing in return; one writer noted that as a "twentieth-century urban empire," New York City was the "motherland" surrounded by five hundred suburban "colonies," but "unlike some colonies, these have not been 'exploited' by the parent city. Quite the contrary."[26] And yet their abuse of city resources did not mean that even "lovely oases in Westchester, Essex, Nassau" would remain undefiled: "Space disappears into subdivisions; the trains fill up; traffic thickens, parking in the village center becomes a nuisance; beaches are polluted; prices rise and taxes soar" (Laas 52). Perhaps the Raths' dilapidated house and unruly garden in Westport is supposed to say as much about the decline of the neighborhood as of their personal finances: "many suburban areas are beginning to show signs of blight and obsolescence—a sure indication that these areas will eventually become slums."[27] The "pretty" as well as the "fly-by-night" subdivision "could degenerate into the bungaloid slum of tomorrow" (Laas 53); suburban flight was but a preliminary step toward (sub)urban blight.

Other literary treatments of the postwar suburb are similarly preoccupied with the suburb as slum, with the deterioration of the just-completed housing stock and the transiency of the residents. The victims of "the fresh-air slums we're building around America's cities" (Keats xi) are not recent immigrants or African Americans like Bigger, however, but the white middle class that grew up in the stable, settled, residences of old "Elm Street" (49). *The Crack in the Picture Window* (1956) converts the protagonists into the middle-class equivalents of tenement dwellers. Stuck in "a house that could never be a home" (60), John and Mary Drone have nothing to console them but their status as owners. But Keats will not allow them even that, observing that the policy of low down payments builds equity very slowly and masks their actual financial relation to the house. Ownership under such conditions is not an investment but an affliction; the Drones are just the nominal slumlords of themselves. *Crack* ends with an extra mortgage, a third child on the way, and a real night shift for John, a petty government bureaucrat, as a salesman in a liquor store—a nightmare of downward mobility. For Mills, white-collar people have become beholden to corporations because they no longer own the property with which they work, while Keats indicts the development house because it enslaves the white-collar families who "own" the property in which they live.

The Drones find neither a home nor social mobility in the suburb; instead they encounter mobility of a more literal kind. Suburbanites are pioneers, once again, even as they are slum dwellers: development houses "serve only as brief campsites on life's wilderness trail" (xv). Modeled after Levittown, the "Camptown" subdivision in Charles Mergendahl's *It's Only Temporary* (1950) acknowledges shabby construction and impermanent community. Even when the suburb is classy, movement is championed for its own sake. The enterprising, executive protagonist of *Sincerely, Willis Wayde* (1955), by J. P. Marquand, the dean of popular suburban fiction, switches suburban houses and abandons businesses that are "like . . . an old home to [him]," because "[y]ou've got to keep on moving and growing. That's the American way."[28] Unlike the characters in Lewis and Cain, Wayde's allegiance to mobility is utterly incompatible with a sentimental investment in either homes or corporations. When Whyte and Riesman, respectively, called the suburb a "dormitory" and a "fraternity," they pointed to the transitoriness of suburban life as well as its communal quality.[29] As the titles *It's Only Temporary* and "The Transients" suggest, in the postwar period suburban house ownership and transiency were frequently aligned rather than opposed.

The postwar suburb exemplified the real meaning of white middle-class homelessness. In *Crack* and *It's Only Temporary*, the protagonists are represented as impotent victims of rapacious real estate speculators, government largesse, nosy neighbors, and the houses themselves. *Man in Gray Flannel* decisively translates suburban anguish into empowerment. The development suburb is a breeding ground of alienated homeowners who need only to capitalize upon their dissatisfaction to move up and out. In the first chapter, Betsy feels somewhat guilty about their resentment and tries to talk Tom and herself out of it: "I don't know what's the matter with us. . . . Your job is plenty good enough. We've got three nice kids, and lots of people would be glad to have a house like this. We shouldn't be so *discontented* all the time" (5). In noting that the house and job are good enough for others, Betsy indicates that they are not really good enough for them. But her conceit that many other people would be satisfied with what she and Tom spurn is undone by evidence of rampant discontent among their neighbors. Discontent is, in fact, the driving force of the Raths' subdivision, a place not to settle in but to escape. Family finances are openly discussed with neighbors, and people celebrate salary increases and the chance "to buy a bigger house" with "moving-out parties" (121). People are public about their ambition to leave; it is a community that rallies around its own disappearance.

Residents treat the subdivision not as "a permanent stop," but "a cross-roads where families waited until they could afford to move on to something better" (120). Maybe "lots of people" would appreciate their house, but no one who lives in one just like it does. A few residents consider the neighborhood "a desirable end of the road," but they are treated as social outcasts: "On Greentree Avenue, contentment was an object of contempt" (121). Tom and Betsy's dissatisfaction is normal and connected with the ability to get out. The concern is that they face a debilitating immobility—the prospect that "the house with the crack in the form of a question mark on the wall and the ink stains on the wallpaper was probably the end of their personal road" (6). The frightening possibility here is not that they are irrationally dissatisfied, but that they are not discontented enough.

No dissatisfaction, the example of Greentree Avenue suggests, no mobility. Discontent is crucial to the achievement and preservation of middle-class economic and social privileges. And yet the Raths are also concerned to make their discontent pay a kind of cultural dividend. When Betsy tries to console herself by saying that "lots of people" would appreciate their house, even though they do not, she is tacitly separating them from the crowd, refusing to settle for what is merely good enough for others. Thinking about their desire to move, she makes a standard complaint about suburban uniformity—"It's not fair to the children to bring them up in a neighborhood like this. . . . It's *dull*" (68)—but upon further reflection changes her mind: "It's not dull enough—it's tense and it's frantic. Or, to be honest, Tom and I are tense and frantic, and I wish to heaven I knew why" (121). As she instinctively realizes, their neighbors are indeed as tense and frantic as they, motivated by the same desire for better jobs and better houses. In revising her criticism, she denies her connection with the others. They are only dull, but she and Tom are anxious. Betsy generously concedes that "[n]o one here is evil," nor is the neighborhood "a bad place to be," and she tells herself that "[t]here's nothing wrong with"(121) the culture of Greentree Avenue, with the cocktail parties, harmless flirtations, and dreams of a farm in Vermont, but if that were really the case she wouldn't be at such pains to deny it. As in *Babbitt*, complacency is regarded as the norm that is violated by one's discontent, and in both instances, discontent is revealed to be widespread rather than peculiar. But unlike Babbitt, Betsy is as committed to the idea that discontent is a unique experience for them as she is to the feeling itself. Joel Pfister has observed that anxiety in the twentieth century becomes a kind of psychological status marker for the middle class. *Man in Gray Flannel* raises the stakes; anxiety is envisioned as a way of *distinguishing* oneself from the middle class.[30] Her condescension as well as her discontent are ways of marking her and Tom's superiority to these people who are so very much like them.

Malcontents, not mindless conformists, are the fixtures of both their housing development and postwar suburban literature more generally. In *It's Only Temporary*, Shelley and Don Cousins are renting a house and plan to move to Montana when Don has saved up enough to go into business. That their situation is "only temporary" convinces them of their superiority to their neighbors, whom they imagine to be there for life, although virtually everyone else also seeks to move, if only at first to the newer, larger houses on the other side of the development. Shelley "had been unable to fit herself into the general run of things—into the thousands of houses all the same. . . . She wanted to fit. She wanted to be like Mamie, easygoing, content, resigned" (65). Here Shelley seems to exemplify Whyte's social ethic, the belief that belonging is a "moral imperative" (437). But wishing that you could belong is also a way of unequivocally expressing that you cannot belong, that no matter how much you would like to fit into the suburb, you are simply too unconventional. The novel ends with the Cousinses still locked away in their "temporary jail" (159), now as owners, the move to Montana indefinitely, and one presumes eternally, postponed. They are, in effect, transients who will never get to move, their only solace that even if they spend the rest of their lives in Camptown, they both know that their real home is someplace else.

Betsy's and Shelley's discontent is importantly distinguished from Betty Friedan's now classic description of the fifties suburban housewife, going about her duties, "afraid to ask even of herself the silent question—'Is this all?' "[31] As imagined by male novelists, the problem is not that they are bored with the housewife's labors and jealous of their husband's interesting work in the city, the substance of Myra Babbitt's discounted complaints. They are primarily dissatisfied with the culture of the suburb rather than their conventional role within it. They perform work of a kind that is significant to them and unrelated to housework and consumption: they strive to make themselves and their husbands more meaningful than their neighbors.

But if, as I have demonstrated, discontent with the culture of conformity is not envisioned as the uniformly masculine problem that Barbara Ehrenreich has claimed, nor yet is it the woman's unique obligation.[32] In Jack Finney's classic science fiction novel, *The Body-Snatchers* (1955), the Marin County town of Santa Mira fights the construction of a new highway that would spoil its "quiet residential quality," but the desire for isolation doesn't prevent space pods from sacking the village.[33] In effect the pods supplant the highway as a vehicle of undesirable suburbanization; while the residents sleep they are replaced with affectless, conformist duplicates who immediately cease to take care of their property: "In seven blocks we haven't passed a single house with as much as the trim being repainted, not a roof, porch, or even a cracked window being repaired" (108–9). With the help of medication, Miles Bennell and Becky Driscoll fight to stay awake and to preserve their individuality. The novel also acknowledges, however, the attraction of ceasing the struggle: "the idea of sleep, of just dropping my problems and letting go; letting sleep pour through me . . . it was shocking to realize how terribly tempting the idea was" (159). For Miles, the desire to just let go, to be rid of "strain and worry" (162), to be "still Miles Bennell" (159) and yet also just like everyone else, expresses the profound appeal of a release from the tremendous burden of maintaining one's individuality in the face of constant threats to it. The suburb requires eternal and exhausting vigilance to preserve one's integrity against it.

Unlike the term *city dweller*, which designates only a place of residence, *suburbanite* implies that where you live has something to do with who you are—it purports to be an identity category. Richard Yates's *Revolutionary Road* (1961), set in 1955, concerns a suburban couple who is obsessed with just this relation between environment and essence. "Economic circumstances might force you to live in this environment, but the important thing was to keep from being contaminated. The important thing always was to remember who you were."[34] Just who are the Wheelers? It isn't exactly clear, except that we know that they are not *really* suburbanites, at least if we are to trust their self-assessment; they are just people who happen to live in a suburb. But in *Revolutionary Road*, the suburb is treated as a living space that is in constant danger of contaminating you, of turning you into something you're not—someone who belongs there. As in *The Body-Snatchers*, the suburb "destroy[s] our personalities" (29). When Frank and April Wheeler first moved there, they "wanted something out of the ordinary—a small remodeled barn or carriage house, or an old guest cottage—something with a little charm" (28), but the realtor explains that it is impossible to find that sort of thing anymore: it's just what everyone who moves there wants. They befriend a couple with whom they exchange "anecdote[s] of supreme suburban smugness" about their neighbors, "the idiots [Frank] ride[s] with on the train everyday" (60). Their conversation is dedicated to distinguishing themselves as an "embattled, dwindling, intellectual underground" (59) against the culture of the typical lawn-mowing, barbecuing, development suburbanite, but as the quotation suggests, their disaffection also makes them "suburban." *Revolutionary Road* brilliantly defines the postwar suburbanite as the antisuburbanite, whose existence is a protest against everyone else's putative conformity.

The problem of remembering "who you were" emerges in another postwar novel that helps to illuminate the difference between representations of the white and black middle class in literature of the period. The protagonist of *Invisible Man* has white-collar aspirations, and his landlady instructs him to remember his origins and his people: "Up here too many forgits. They finds a place for theyselves and forgits the ones on the bottom" (255). She is urging him not only to be "a credit to the race," but also to continue to identify with those at the bottom of the nation's economic hierarchy, once his personal ambitions have been fulfilled, rather than to remember and assert an essential superiority to a middle-class future. The feared alienation of the black middle class from the working class resonates with E. Franklin Frazier's famous, contemporaneous criticisms in *Black Bourgeoisie*. He notes the isolation of the black middle class, which is scorned by the white middle class and in turn scorns the "black masses" with whom it desperately fears being associated. Even though it has access to a rich folk culture, unlike its white counterparts, it is afraid to draw on that heritage and devotes itself instead to "fatuities" (98), primarily conspicuous consumption, through which it attempts to distinguish itself from the black working class.[35] Bob Jones, the protagonist of Chester Himes's brilliant, underrated *If He Hollers Let Him Go* (1945) notes "that look of withered body and soul" in his fiancée's mother, the wife of the most prominent black physician in Los Angeles.[36] The Wellingtons live in a segregated, upper-middle-class neighborhood that is "clean, quiet, well-bred" (49) and surround themselves with expensive furniture and rugs, while complaining how "hard" recent black migrants from the South "make it . . . for the rest of us" (52). That is, the behavior and values of recent working-class arrivals reflect badly on such people as they, who have "earn[ed] their equality" (52). Bob Jones despises their "smug and complacent" manner, willful blindness to the daily realities of racism, and the determination, shared by his social-worker fiancée, that he "join the ranks of Negro professionals" (51) and become one of "us." His job as a shipyard worker is too unambitious for the family, too inferior to his abilities, and too close to the working-class migrants whom they disdain.

Without the luxury of racial inclusion, black middle-class identity is imagined in these brief examples to find a fragile foundation in its superiority to the black working class. White middle-class identity, on the other hand, is typically represented in suburban literature of the postwar period as a disavowal of the things that would seem to make it middle class. The white middle class asserts its superiority to itself in the belief that middle-classness has been devalued. The result is not to identify with or emulate white workers—that association is part of the problem—but rather to lay claim to one's nonconformity.[37] In *Growing Up Absurd* (1960), Paul

Goodman marked the failure of the resolutely nonconformist Beat generation to achieve its goal of purposeful self-differentiation—"Their behavior is a conformity *plus royaliste que le roi*"—and that it more nearly approximated the banality of the "organized system" than challenged it.[38] Irving Howe similarly commented that the Beats were "at one with the middle-class suburbia they think they scorn."[39] Howe's description might serve just as well to describe the suburbanites themselves, except he imagines a difference between being "at one" with the suburb and really scorning it. Organization men and women spurn the suburbs as heartily as anyone else by self-consciously claiming not to "belong" to them.

In *It's Only Temporary*, Don Cousins eventually chooses to belong to the suburb and the corporation; his boss persuades him that he is "by nature, a prospective executive in a large company" and "should, for his own as well as the world's sake" (150), heed that higher calling and give up on Montana. After the work he has always ridiculed is gratefully rewarded with praise and a promotion, Frank Wheeler of *Revolutionary Road* chickens out of their plan to move to Paris and recommits himself to the belief that he and April might belong to "a world of handsome, graceful, unquestionably worthwhile men and women who had somehow managed to transcend their environment—people who had turned dull jobs to their own advantage, who had exploited the system without knuckling under to it" (217). To the end he believes in manipulation without capitulation. Cynicism shall set them free. Tom finds his only comfort in self-pity, even though *Man in Gray Flannel* is the only novel that translates discontent into actual mobility. During his commute one day, he decides that he must conform to the values of both the suburb and the corporation:

> [N]ow is the time to raise legitimate children, and make money, and dress properly, and be kind to one's wife, and admire one's boss, and learn not to worry. . . . I'm just a man in a gray flannel suit. I must keep my suit neatly pressed like anyone else, for I am a very respectable young man. . . . I will go to my new job, and I will be cheerful, and I will be industrious, and I will be matter-of-fact. I will keep my gray flannel suit spotless. I will have a sense of humor. I will have guts—I'm not the type to start crying now. (109)

If this doesn't count as crying, it's not clear what would. The passage derides most of the things that have come to be associated with the postwar worldview: the importance of family life, ambition in the corporate world, the pursuit of affluence. But it doesn't deride in order to reject; Tom's contempt is mainly reserved for himself and not the things he strives for. Neither quiescent belonging nor canny exploitation are tenable in *The Man in the Gray Flannel Suit*. The qualities of being "respectable," "cheerful," and "industrious" really just stand for the vice of selling out to the corporation.

At the end of the novel, when Tom rejects the big promotion he is offered on behalf of a quality home life, he has been presumed to speak for the suburban home that sustains the person and family over the corporation that annihilates them.[40] But in reality, Tom never risks his soul because the United Broadcasting Corporation is ultimately presented as a beneficent enterprise that never asks him to. By representing himself as the object of the corporation's malign intentions, he is able to thrive within it and distinguish himself from it. In precisely the same way that the suburb is represented as a contaminant that threatens to turn exceptional white people into unremarkable suburbanites, the corporation signifies for the Raths a moral hazard that threatens to corrupt the virtuous. And like the suburbanite who fantasizes about his or her incorruptibility, asserting cultural superiority to the suburb by repudiating it, the neophyte executive affirms his moral superiority by constructing the elaborate fiction that the corporation demands he sacrifice it. In *The Man in the Gray Flannel Suit*, the suburb and the corporation work together to offer Tom and Betsy endless confirmation of their own integrity.

PUBLIC RELATIONS AND THE PERSONALITY MARKET

In addition to the feeling of economic insecurity that accompanies his raise at UBC, Tom is plagued by moral doubts about the nature of public relations work. For Mills and Riesman, public relations is paradigmatically alienated white-collar work; it not only entails working with people and symbols rather than things but is one step further removed from material labor: it symbolizes the symbols, performing "the interpretive justification of the new powers to the underlying outsiders" (Mills 95). In contrast with advertising, public relations sells things indirectly by creating favorable images of a company, an industry, or business in general to promote "goodwill and understanding" toward them.[41] Tom cannot understand why a man as busy and powerful as the president of UBC would be interested in mental health. Is the public relations agenda, whether for UBC or for Hopkins himself, incompatible with a "sincere" desire "to do some good" (33)? Are public relations and sincerity inherently opposed?

The question of Hopkins's sincerity troubles Tom because he is already concerned about his own. At the initial interview, he chafes "at the need for hypocrisy" (13) when asked why he wants to work there. He wants only to make more money but lies about his motives: " 'The salary isn't the primary consideration with me,' Tom said, trying desperately to come up with stock answers to stock questions" (13). Being hired by the corporation means figuring out what it wants to hear, which is also paramount in the autobiography that he is asked to write as part of the application. He has one hour and no guidelines, except for a final sentence that begins "The most significant fact about me is that I . . . " (14). Tom devises several items that are true but unappealing, rejecting each in turn. The autobiography should not reveal who he is but what image of himself he can invent and how well he can sell it to the corporation; it is, in effect, an exercise in personal public relations, and, from Tom's perspective, it is basically dishonest.

The necessity of selling one's self to the corporation was one of the most lamentable aspects of white-collar work for postwar sociologists, who decried the rise of the "personality market" (Mills 225), in which people are newly required to sell themselves by marketing attractive images of themselves. Alienation from the products of one's labor was far less alarming than the alienation of the laborer from him- or herself. As one expositor of the "national character" put it in 1955, the American personality was the final frontier, "a raw material to be developed and exploited, in a manner analogous to any other raw material. . . . A person incapable of 'selling' him or herself is badly handicapped."[42] Riesman similarly argued that the bureaucratic order creates the market for a new "product": "a personality" (46). The effect of marketing the personality is to evaporate the psychical boundary between self and other. In the thirties, self-help guru Dale Carnegie famously advised readers in his *How to Win Friends and Influence People* (1936) to "get the other person's point of view and see things from his angle as well as from your own."[43] Riesman's description of other-direction identifies two changes from the earlier formulation: it is now internalized—one does not need to be told to get someone else's point of view—and the other guy's point of view is no longer adopted in addition to one's own. His angle has become your angle.

Mills also emphasized self-estrangement as one of the fundamental structural changes in the white-collar personality: "To sell himself is to turn himself into a commodity" (153). Public relations was itself used as a metaphor for understanding the change. "What began as the public and commercial relations of business have become deeply personal: there is a public-relations aspect to private relations of all sorts, including even relations with oneself" (187).[44] The neat collapse of relations with the public into public relations, which then structure one's relations with intimates and, most intimate of all, oneself, theorizes the development of a self whose very identity is collapsing with its projection.

Man in Gray Flannel refutes a fundamental premise of postwar white-collar sociology—the idea that selling an image of one's self necessarily entails the alienation of that self. Although Tom decides against giving his real reason for seeking a job at UBC, he is absolutely clear about what it is. The novel distinguishes between the image of himself he wishes to portray and the self that reflects upon and makes choices about the nature of that image. Insofar as public relations is about image, not essence, about images that are often designed to deflect attention from or conceal essences, his is a classic PR exercise. Just as UBC does not become a charitable foundation because its president dabbles in mental health, Tom does not cease to be who he is just because he decides to mislead his future employers about who he is.

But in the end, he doesn't even mislead them. Tom's autobiography comprises some basic facts that are standard for any job application but revises the only requirement: "From the point of view of the United Broadcasting Corporation, the most significant fact about me is that I am applying for a position in its public-relations department, and after an initial period of learning, I probably would do a good job. I will be glad to answer any questions which seem relevant, but after considerable thought, I have decided that I do not wish to attempt an autobiography as part of an application for a job" (17). In a sense the autobiography reveals far more than he lets on, not that he has applied for a job in public relations but that he is unwilling to market himself to attain it. Put another way, what he markets, intentionally or not, is his honest resistance to what he perceives as the corporation's demand that he market himself.

To his surprise, Tom is interviewed again and eventually gets the job. He becomes a PR man by refusing to subject himself to its operations. Honesty *is* the best policy, but he struggles throughout the novel with the conviction that honesty will get him fired. The crisis comes when he has to critique the final draft of the speech that Hopkins has rewritten, which reads exactly like an advertisement, all jingles and repetitions, ending with the slogan "Yes, our wealth depends on mental health!" (201). Tom reflects that a "few years ago" he would have told the truth about the speech but now believes that a "frank opinion often leads directly to the street" (201 2). Honesty is a luxury he cannot afford because it means unemployment and homelessness, the usual kind, or so he imagines.

This deception—about the corporation's response to honesty and his proximity to the street—allows him to invent himself as the compromised businessman, victimized by a system that demands he sell out. "I should quit if I don't like what he does, but I want to eat, and so, like a half million other guys in gray flannel suits, I'll always pretend to agree, until I get big enough to be honest without being hurt. That's not being crooked, it's just being smart" (202). But even as Tom congratulates himself on his clever manipulation of the system, he recognizes that dishonesty and cynicism take an inevitable toll on the spirit. Tom knows the truth, although he won't act upon that knowledge, and "feel[s] lousy"

(202) on behalf of his own deeper integrity. Cynicism is evidence not of a hardened character but of a character whose weakness is evidence of its moral strength. The corporate yes-man's is the soul in anguish. His anguish and good intentions enable him to experience a kind of alienated self-appreciation. When he tells Betsy, with cynical detachment, that he plans to feel out Hopkins's opinion of the speech before giving his own, she attacks him for his smug, "self-satisfied" (205) approach to the problem. She claims not to care what Tom tells him but resents his tone; it's okay to be dishonest, but you must at least honestly regret it.

Men in gray flannel are cynical about the prospect of lying to their bosses, while their wives experience "moral indignation" (207) at their husbands' equivocations. These are gendered strategies for coping with the organization, but more important is that both are represented as redemptive evidence of moral superiority in which each takes pleasure. Like Betsy, Tom does not particularly mind the indignation so much as he resents that she "enjoy[s]" it. Their way of defending themselves against the corporation, as against the suburb, is by demonstrating to themselves that they are above it. Cynicism allows the executive to capitulate to the corporation while preserving the integrity of a person who is forced to do so against his will. Moral indignation allows the executive's wife to permit him to capitulate, while reassuring herself that such tactics would be unnecessary if she were the employee; she is superior to both the corporation and her husband.

For Betsy evinces her own powerful commitment to honesty as well, the primary virtue to which domestic life must aspire. She decides that the family must be purified of the corrupting influences of postwar suburban culture. That means no more hot dogs and hamburgers—"I'm going to start making stews and casseroles and roasts and things" (73)—family readings instead of television, church on Sundays, and erect posture. The "new regime" (72) is represented not as the imposition of unnatural habits, but as the reassertion of a neglected regime that will enable them to live an honest life: "We ought to start doing the things we believe in" (74). The problem with hot dogs isn't that they are less tasty than stews, or even that they fail to embody the wifely and maternal attention of the stew, the commercial and sentimental imperatives of a Mildred Pierce, although Betsy's concern about the family's bad habits does reflect a certain insecurity about her role as its caretaker. Rather, the Raths are a stew family that has been living falsely as a hot dog family, and they must be true to their deeper nature. It is time to remember who they are. To eat hot dogs when you really ought to be eating stews is not only dishonest, self-violating, it is also crazy. She announces her plan to the family by saying that "[w]e're going to start living *sanely*" (73). Money is the "root of all order," but honesty is also crucial to the preservation of a sane life against a "lunatic world."

In their way, the Raths are as committed to battling phoniness as is Holden Caulfield, the teen icon of fifties nonconformity. A generation of early critics treated Holden as the archetypal adolescent, whose heroic rejection of the compromises of adulthood drives him "berserk."[45] In other words, honesty and sanity are ultimately opposed in *The Catcher in the Rye*; put in less universalizing terms, Holden seems to be helplessly trapped between the mental institution from which he produces his narrative and the "lunatic world" of the inexorable corporate-suburban culture of the fifties.[46] The Raths, on the other hand, are allowed to grow up and reclaim their integrity, to triumph over the forces that would corrupt them, while making honesty pay. Once Tom is rewarded for his honesty with a lucrative job, he ought to have learned that money is conveniently the compensation for one's honesty. Instead, honesty in the business world continues to be cast as the ultimate risk with no market value: Tom "can't imagine being honest and getting a raise for it" (206). Cynicism and indignation are both red herrings, however, because Tom is wrong about what the system wants and what it will pay for. He remains committed to the belief that the corporation demands he sell out, because only then does his integrity count for anything. The corporation requires no compromises, but by all means, think of yourself as refusing to compromise and get the moral credit of rebelling against the system that rewards your rebellion.

After much soul-searching, he tells Hopkins that the speech is empty and advises him to come up with some concrete solutions to mental health problems. Hopkins, too, can speak the truth. He replies that he knows nothing about mental health but realizes that Tom is right nonetheless. Hopkins knows publicity, and that is precisely the knowledge wanted to launch the campaign and solve the problem. The speech that has been selling mental health must begin to sell Hopkins. And Hopkins's appreciation of Tom's honesty convinces Tom of his good intentions: "I was completely honest with him, and I think he was with me. . . . [H]e showed me he's completely sincere about wanting to do something about mental-health problems. All this talk about his starting this committee just for a publicity build-up is a lot of nonsense" (224). It is at the moment that Hopkins decides to make the speech all about publicity that Tom decides that the committee is not about publicity. It really concerns essence, not image. The committee is perfect public relations because it is perfectly sincere.[47]

The result of the conversation is a speech that blames the public for not knowing enough about mental health. The public is the problem, but as the mediator between it and the medical profession, mass culture is the

solution. This is the novel's only representation of the mass culture industry in action, a force for good, not for profit, represented by a leader
whose commitment to social service enfolds and ennobles the industry as
a whole. It does not dupe or manipulate the public, as many commentators argued, but educates it sensibly, for its benefit.⁴⁸ It is an industry less
of mass culture than of mass communication, "whose business it is to
transmit information to the public" (240). Tom's honest efforts redeem
the corporation; it is no longer inimical to preserving the sanity of the
middle class, but crucial to it.

Once the mental health committee is launched, Hopkins decides to promote Tom to his personal assistant because of Tom's ability to "look at
things straight" (246) and "the honesty of [his] approach" (248). Tom
gives it a try but is put off by the hard work, the travel, and the prospect
of a transfer to California. Hopkins senses his resistance and asks if he
still wants to learn the business. Once again, despite all evidence to the
contrary, Tom vacillates needlessly between honesty and equivocation.
He confesses that he doesn't want to be "a big executive. I'll say it frankly:
I don't think I have the willingness to make the sacrifices. I don't want to
give up the time. I'm trying to be honest about this. I want the money.
Nobody likes money better than I do. But I'm just not the kind of guy
who can work evenings and week ends and all the rest of it forever" (277).
As William Whyte pointed out in an exasperated reading of the scene:
"The boss should be damn well ashamed of himself. As Rath implies so
strongly, when the younger men say they don't want to work too hard,
they feel that they are making a positive moral contribution as well"
(146). But the real moral contribution seems to come from Tom's commitment to being honest about not wanting to work hard, to the fantasy that
honesty is a tremendous risk even though it has served him so well in the
past. What passes for morality in the novel is simply describing how one
honestly feels in anticipation that the corporation will punish it, as though
executives really had to choose between honesty and the street.

Honesty carries the day, again, as he is rewarded with his old job in a
new and improved form. Hopkins wants to donate his mansion in South
Bay, where Tom and Betsy have moved, as a site for the new mental health
foundation: "That would be quite nice for you—you wouldn't even have
any commuting. How would you like to be director of the outfit? That
job would pay pretty well. I'd like to think I had a man with your integrity
there, and I'll be making all the major decisions" (278). Tom's previous
boss, who warned him against corporate indifference, was wrong; the
corporation is a charitable foundation after all. If you are honest, you
don't need to work very hard; you don't really need to work at all. Hon-

esty is its own responsibility, and its intrinsic value to the corporation also releases Tom from its pressures, inviting an integration of work and home.

Tom takes the invitation seriously. Mass communications in the novel is unproblematic, but personal communication is deeply fraught, and Tom decides that he must apply the lessons about honesty that he has learned in the workplace and tell Betsy the truth about his wartime affair. The point is to admit to but not regret his lapse: "Betsy, do you want me to apologize for this child?" (291) he asks incredulously. Honesty is all that counts, and Betsy accuses him of being "righteous" (292), which Tom seems to interpret as a cue. He says that Maria can't prove paternity and he can refuse support. "One more act of brutality wouldn't change the world. But I'm not going to do it. I can't do anything about the state of the world, but I can put my own life in order. . . . This is one decent thing I'm going to do, if I never do anything else, and I hope you'll help me" (293). As Betsy recognizes, Tom uses the illegitimate child to establish his moral authority at home. Caring for the illegitimate child is decent, but it has less to do with accepting responsibility for conditions he created in the world than to order his own life against its insanity.

Betsy flees the house, furious and hysterical, but when she returns a few hours later, honest communication has carried the day: "Tonight while I was driving alone, I realized for the first time what you went through in the war, and what different worlds we've been living in ever since. I'm sorry I acted like a child" (299). Tom's confession produces Betsy's apology: she is responsible for their past inadequacies as a couple; she failed to intuit that behind his suffering at work and home was the experience of war. For all her moral indignation, the worlds they have been living in aren't all that different; the suburban housewife lives out a version of the corporate husband's narrative about selling out: "All I know how to do nowadays is be responsible and dutiful and deliberately cheerful for the sake of the children. And all you know how to do is work day and night and worry" (294). By embracing Tom as the victim of the home, as well as of work and war, she enables the barriers that have separated the not-so-different worlds of husband and wife to give way. She apprehends that "[i]t's not an insane world. At least, our part of it doesn't have to be. . . . We don't have to work and worry all the time" (299). Mental health doesn't really require committees or corporations, just personal communication. Now that Tom's well-paying, effortless job as head of the mental health foundation is secure, money is no longer the "island of order," nor does worry connect seemingly disparate worlds anymore. Both yield instead to the husband's integrity.

And so, by the end of the novel, the gray flannel hero has become, in his words, "an honest man" (300). Honesty is, finally, as remunerative in the world of suburban real estate as it is in the corporate world. They have moved into the grandmother's house with the idea of tearing it down and building eighty houses on property zoned for four. The final chapter takes place in Saul Bernstein's office, where Tom has gone to arrange support for his Italian son. Thinking that Tom wants to see him about a divorce, the judge is surprised and delighted to discover that Tom is facing up to his responsibilities, has communicated them to his wife, and has her full support. "I suppose that may be a little unconventional, but to us it seems like simple justice" (303), the kind that Bernstein likes best. But Tom lets it be known that proper justice—the establishment of a permanent trust—must wait until "this housing project of ours goes through" (302). Bernstein is the deciding vote on the zoning board; if he supports the exemption, the project can go on as planned. Caring for his son is "a matter of conscience" (304), but it is also a matter of local politics. The subdivision is a moral obligation as well as a financial boon. So impressed is Bernstein with Tom's notion of "simple justice" that he offers to charge nothing for arranging child support, a pleasant bonus, but more importantly, there is no doubt that the last obstacle to the housing development has been overcome.

If bad houses can reflect poorly on their residents, then the ending of the novel just as clearly asserts that good people can reflect well on the housing they wish to build. Promoting favorable images of families, like corporations, helps to build small suburban developments as well as mass culture empires. The sociologists' solution to the problem of dislocation was "to find meaningful work for the displaced ones rather than locating still more of them in selling, public relations, and looking after each other" (*Lonely Crowd* 146), the kinds of professions with which the new middle-class worker was, according to Mills, "at home" (94). *Man in Gray Flannel* imagines instead that a public relations ethic can rebuild American middle-class life.

By turning the suburb into a family enterprise, Tom and Betsy can hope to create an environment that is as exclusive as they are. The novel ends happily, with the judge smiling out his window at a smiling Betsy, who is off with Tom for a week in Vermont. The fact that they are on the verge of temporary escape, however, suggests that their happiness still rests on an unstable foundation. It matters that the housing development is on the brink of construction and not an accomplished fact. The suburb is defined in this novel, as in many others, as an environment that must be resisted, but where resistance is what binds you most closely to it. It thus makes perfect sense that in *Man in Gray Flannel*, absolute resistance to the suburb culminates in its reproduction. And yet if discontent is the primary feature of the suburbanite, then to end with the family permanently ensconced in the suburb would be to start the cycle all over again. We do get a small hint of what is to come. After Tom and Betsy make up, he assures her that "[w]e're not going to worry any more. No matter what happens, we've got a lot to be grateful for" (301). As Betsy herself observed, they had a lot to be thankful for way back in the first chapter. Asserting one's privileges is the first step toward denying them. Of course, a great deal has changed, but it may be that some things never change, that the suburb is destined to be the place from which one tries to escape.

EPILOGUE

Same As It Ever Was (More or Less)

GIVEN THAT urban theorists, literary and cultural critics, and historians have described contemporary suburbia as the exemplary
national landscape of postmodern and postindustrial culture, it
might seem as though a study of the suburb and the twentieth-century
American novel ought to begin with literature written in the last four
decades rather than end with a few words about it. After all, suburbanization has proceeded at an astonishing rate: where in 1920 the census had
revealed that the United States was officially an urban nation, fifty years
later it found more Americans living in suburbs than in either the city or
rural areas, and by 1990 there were more suburbanites than city and rural
dwellers combined. Despite recent legislative attempts to control suburban sprawl, new developments continue to spring up on the ever expanding outskirts of metropolitan areas, in numbers that make the postwar operations of Levitt and Sons look quaint.[1]

Predictably, literary representations of the American suburb have also
flourished. As the suburb has become a dominant economic, political, and
cultural force in the lives of most Americans, it has fostered a distinctive
subgenre of American realism.[2] Novels by John Updike, Joyce Carol
Oates, Frederick Barthelme, Rick Moody, Richard Ford, and David
Gates, among others, are dedicated to charting the fluid contours of the
suburb's complex spatial and social geographies. The polymorphous suburb of condominiums, corporate headquarters, shopping malls, and office
parks, as well as traditional single-family houses, is not merely the obvious setting for much contemporary fiction but is explicitly identified and
celebrated as the central preoccupation of it. Unconstrained by region,
tales of the suburb have become a national literary specialty. The inside
jacket flap of Barthelme's *Two against One* (1988) offers the reader a
narrative of "the suburban new South that [he] has made peculiarly his
own," while a recent reprint of Joyce Carol Oates's *Expensive People*
situates its story of midwestern migrations as "her earliest portrait of
America's affluent suburbanites." Between 1992 and 1997 Moody published three novels exploring the anxieties of northeastern commuters,
housewives, and teens within a range of high and middle economic strata,
and the suburban orientation is prominently advertised on the back covers.[3] Clearly the suburb sells books as well as houses and office space.

And the critical acclaim that such novels now attract, including Pulitzer and National Book Award prizes and nominations and enthusiastic reviews, suggests that Edith Wharton's prediction of 1925 has proven exactly wrong. The suburb is understood to have contributed to the health of American letters rather than to its demise.[4]

Reviewers of novels about the suburb often rely on the rhetoric of commentary but also, more pointedly, of exposé. For example, Updike's *Couples* (1968) marshals "sociological" details to reveal "the heresies of the 'post-Pill Paradise' of suburban Massachusetts."[5] Moody has more recently been heralded as "a chronicler of the middle class for the millennium," a title that places him in the league of "Updike and Cheever," with whom he shares a talent for casting "penetrating looks under the suburban veneer."[6] Such comparisons between early and later generations abound, featuring Updike and Cheever as the putative fathers of a suburban literary tradition whose success is frequently measured by the extent to which it estranges readers from the environment they thought they knew so well. In recent literary promotion, critique has similarly become the most salient feature of commentary. Back covers claim that James Kaplan's *Two Guys from Verona: A Novel of Suburbia* (1998) "strips bare the cultural and moral universe of a suburb," and that the protagonist of Gates's *Preston Falls* "journey[s] to the dark side of suburban masculinity." These comments acknowledge and seek to tap the reader's desire for estrangement. The suburb is sold on the assumption that although millions of people choose to live there, it is the environment we love to hate.

And yet resistance to the suburb is nothing new. As *White Diaspora* has demonstrated, veneer stripping has been a mainstay of the suburban novel since the twenties. Suburbanites have long been characterized by alienation, anguish, and self-pity. The literary treatment of suburban masculinity, in other words, has never really had a bright side for contemporary novelists newly to refute. Writers since the 1960s have not invented a tradition so much as carried on and reworked the legacy of suburban homelessness that emerged so insistently in *Babbitt*. Updike's Rabbit tetralogy is a prime example. Like the predecessor whose name his echoes, Harry "Rabbit" Angstrom "is in a trap."[7] He runs. He returns. Having discovered that home and family are inescapable, he runs again, impelled by a desire for escape that is no less powerful. He returns again, and some thirteen hundred additional pages record his enduring fantasies of flight. Once his fortunes have improved and he stays put, Rabbit nonetheless rebels against the constraints of his environment. In *Rabbit Redux* (1971) he infuriates the neighbors by taking in a promiscuous white runaway and, more troubling still, a black man. Much like Babbitt's support for the striking workers, Rabbit's gesture toward open housing expresses a commitment not to the rights of the disenfranchised but to his individuality and autonomy, which are otherwise compromised by the "similar houses" of the Penn Villas developments: "the blot of black inside his house" diminishes the "intensity of duplication."[8] Penn Villas is no longer an *anywhere place*; it is "nowhere" (285). In the final novel, he runs for the last time, down south, the direction he first traveled to find the "sweet low cottonland" (*Rabbit, Run* 35) that is reminiscent of Babbitt's association of secure placement with plantations. But the paradox of being nowhere is that he has nowhere to go. Rabbit heads for the suburb we call Florida, where the houses remind him of Penn Villas and his condo "could belong to one of millions of part-time Floridians" in a state "made up of interchangeable parts."[9] The final, deathbed word of the series— "Enough" (512)—establishes the precious but obviously momentary equilibrium that evaded him even in *Rabbit Is Rich* (1981). In that novel, which has an epigraph from Babbitt's Real Estate Board address, he learned "the truth that to be rich is to be robbed, to be rich is to be poor."[10] The connection between abjection and affluence is a lesson straight out of *The Man in the Gray Flannel Suit* and reinforces the ineluctable truth of the tetralogy: Rabbit will only ever be "at Rest" when Rabbit is dead.

That Updike did not invent aimless middle-class suffering, but instead follows a general pattern established by Lewis and elaborated by Wilson and others, ought not to obscure the important differences between them as well as the eras they interpret. Babbitt and Rabbit are both trapped, but there is no mastery for Rabbit, only martyrdom. Babbitt's ambivalence toward his prosperity and his freedom to run and return without consequence are powerful testimonies to his general economic and social well-being. For the Raths the anxiety of affluence is rewarded with the financial security they seek. In *Rabbit at Rest* (1990), his daughter-in-law, who grew up in a series of rundown apartments, admires the Angstroms' large house in a fashionable suburb, while he replies in the fashion of Betsy Rath: "We ought to be grateful. But it's hard, being grateful. It seems like from the start you're put here in a kind of fix, hungry and scared, and the only way out is no good either" (174). Betsy enumerated their advantages and experienced a mild sense of guilt at their dissatisfaction, while exploiting it as evidence of an allegedly unique estrangement. By contrast Rabbit immediately dismisses gratitude as a difficult, indeed irrational, response to a basic human predicament for which, excepting death, there is no adequate protection—not Toyota dealerships, not property, not wealth, not family.

The grounds on which Rabbit refuses to appreciate his privileges resonate with some fundamental transformations in the representation of the white middle class. With the exception of the Drones in Keats's polemical *Crack in the Picture Window*, there is a striking discrepancy between dismal expectations and positive outcomes in postwar literature. (Even the death-dealing pods in *The Body-Snatchers* decide that Earth is too inhospitable and fly away.) While the middle classes of the 1950s were supposed to have been blissfully ignorant of their diminishing chances, the Raths are beleaguered in self-perception and triumphant in fact. They only *fear* falling. Scared but not hungry, they ride what in hindsight we know was a spectacular period of economic growth. Subsequently, literary and nonliterary discourses about the middle class converge in their concerns about the fatally deteriorating socioeconomic conditions of late capitalism. In the 1968 presidential election Nixon appealed to the "Forgotten American," not the nation's ill-housed, ill-clad, ill-fed castoffs invoked by Roosevelt during the Depression, but "the comfortably housed, clad, and fed who constitute the middle stratum of society."[11] In the 1970s, however, soaring inflation and housing costs, trouble in the world economy brought home by the energy crisis, and the worst recession in forty years prompted commentators to ponder the end of the age of affluence and a new middle class "squeeze."[12] Since the Reagan era the widening gap between the haves and have-nots has led to almost two decades of speculation that the middle class is "doomed," during which Nixon's forgotten American has become the vanishing American.[13] The downsizing vogue, as well as the growth of low-wage service-sector jobs, has made the expectation of a secure, well-paid position in the "organization" look like an idle dream of security rather than oppression. Moreover, middle-class Americans are popularly understood to share the analysts' sense of current crisis and pessimism about their future; anxiety has replaced complacency as the prevailing mood.[14]

In the 1970s Rabbit inhabits a panicky world, in which President Carter announces that for the first time Americans "think things are going to get worse instead of better" (*Rich* 86). "[T]he great American ride is ending" (1). "Rabbit is rich" because he sells fuel-efficient Japanese cars while the "fucking world is running out of gas" (1). But his riches, like the nation's and the world's, are ephemeral. His wife, Janice, inherited the business from her father and has been the real source of Rabbit's wealth. He is displaced in the business by his son, who embezzles over $200,000 to support a cocaine habit, and on top of that catastrophe Toyota revokes the dealership. Meanwhile, Janice's fledgling interest in real estate inspires her to pay off the debts by selling their quite valuable house in the "mature suburb" (*Rich* 409) of Penn Park, "the only place" where Rabbit "has ever felt at home" (*Rest* 427). He is not poor, but he also doesn't simply *feel* depleted. He lacks a home because he is also losing the house. Declining world resources find their counterpart in diminished personal resources. He adopts the metaphor of the Pan-Am air disaster to describe his plight: "he too is falling, helplessly falling, toward death" (*Rest* 176).

The fear of falling, and actual falling, loom large in this literature. *The Ice Storm* examines "the most congenial and superficially calm of suburbs. In the wealthiest state in the Northeast. In the most affluent country on earth" (3). It is set in 1973, before AIDS and multiplexes and genetic engineering and codependency (3–4), but during OPEC. Of course New Canaan, Connecticut, only seems like Paradise. Benjamin Hood "was full of dread. And anxiety" (7). His fears are as yet unrealized, but one senses that they are not groundless: "Overlooked for an important lunch, not copied on an important memo, not tipped off on a hot stock. . . . The phone never stirred in his office. . . . [H]e knew what was coming" (119). At the neighborhood key party he is troubled by the presence of his office rival, a younger, shrewder, more gifted man, who "wanted . . . Hood's air and water and space and pension and office" (119). Just as Rabbit frequently worries that it's "[t]oo crowded out there" (*Rich* 206), the parodic language of Darwinian struggle suggests that in the most affluent Connecticut suburbs and successful brokerage firms, there is more competition and less room than there used to be. The suburban key party, where wives select a sexual partner by fishing a set of keys from a bowl, attempts to gratify desire while eliminating the risks of male competition and loss. Husbands lose out anyway, though: Ben passes out and goes unclaimed, while even the men who are chosen appear "womanly and weak" (167) in a changing social and sexual order.

No wonder, then, that he prefers masturbation to sex. Although enigmatically described as "a falling sickness" (28), it enables Benjamin to forget that he is falling. Autoeroticism represents self-abnegation as well as self-involvement, freeing him from the burden of consciousness: "at least he didn't have to think. At least he was granted a moment without Benjamin Paul Hood and his fiscal responsibilities, without the lawn, the boat, the dog, the medical bills, credit card and utility bills, without the situation in the Mideast and in Indochina, without Kissinger and Ehrlichman or Jaworski or that Harvard asshole, Archibald Cox. Just a little peace" (28). The equation between man and financial obligations is familiar, but not the interweaving of personal and international crisis, psychical and world peace, expressed as the link between the price of utilities and the Middle East. He asserts himself in the process of forgetting himself, which is to say, he insists that the problem of being Benjamin Paul Hood is global rather than local or even national in scope. In a global economy his fortunes have passed far from the sphere of his comprehension, let alone control.[15]

Perhaps this is to suggest that Tom Rath saw the writing on the wall; considered in the long term, his paranoia begins to look premonitory, for his kind if not himself. Certainly perceiving oneself as a victim is no longer a way to prevail. In Gates's *Jernigan* the protagonist owns a "shitbox house" and claims to be "into the degradation."[16] Particularly in Gates's novels, irony about one's hostility to the suburb supplants the earnest discontent of the Raths and their postwar cohorts. Gates's male protagonists seem virtually to see themselves as part of a tradition of suburban self-loathing; they know that in disliking their environment they exemplify the condition of living there. To distinguish themselves from other suburbanites they purport to be "into" the things they despise. But in contrast with postwar cynicism, an ironic affect is not sufficient protection from forces more destabilizing than New Jersey tract houses. Peter Jernigan doesn't enjoy his ironic embrace long; when he is fired he tells himself: "Hey, you always said you were into degradation: dig it now" (75). In *The Ice Storm* as well, "[s]omething led Hood these days into degradation" (17–18). Degradation is something they choose because they have no choice.

Will Weiss, one of the guys from Verona, fears that he will fall through the floors of his $429,500 house and dreams that his new SAAB sport utility vehicle gets less gas mileage than advertised; like the houses built into the hillside of his suburban town, he is "holding on to that good life for dear life" (3). The precariousness of middle-class life is described here as the two poles between which men fluctuate: the unhappy success and the crazy loser. Will's friend Joel Gold, a schizophrenic alcoholic, works in a sandwich shop, drives a 1969 Chevy Impala, and is impervious to the kind of middle-class malaise that bothers Will. But Will's suspicion that "somehow . . . the very goodness of the good things felt oppressive" (146) turns out to be the least of his problems. A larger competitor is planning to buy his family's cardboard-box company, which would earn Will over $2 million but in a millennial disaster the stock market crashes, and he loses both the company and his job. He holes up in an apartment near the tracks, broke and divorced, subject suddenly to the same hallucinations Joel used to have. Meanwhile Joel buys the sandwich shop, stops drinking, and contemplates buying a new car. He thinks: "Happiness is actually possible now . . . but there are times, in the evenings, when he . . . wonders why" (337). For most of the novel Joel's has looked like the superior fate—paralysis over panic—but by the end their fates are meant to be seen as interchangeable. Peter Jernigan narrates his story of middle-class decline and fall from an asylum. In *Garden State* two of the suburban teens have been institutionalized. New Canaan's affluent residents share their community with a psychiatric hospital. It *is* a lunatic world.

In general, the discovery of national and global contingencies—corporate restructuring, stock markets, mergers and buyouts, OPEC, Asia—is significant primarily as a backdrop for the intricate family dramas that define the suburban novel in its contemporary form. Babbitt's family is no more relevant to his rebellion than is the standardized house; they are functionally equivalent aspects, and hence constraints, of exemplary middle-class citizenship. In the novels of the fifties, escape from the suburb is never tantamount to rejection of the family. In *Revolutionary Road* the Wheelers planned to run away to Paris *with* each other and the children, not *from* them. Furthermore, the family conflicts in the postwar novels are generated exclusively within couples rather than between parent and child. Aside from the occasional case of chicken pox or a growling stomach, for the most part children are neither seen nor heard.

After the 1950s the suburban family is the family in trauma. If the suburb and slum were once characterized by the profound differences between organization and disorganization, more recently their residents have been bound together in a sweeping "tangle of pathology."[17] In 1965 the infamous Moynihan report linked the economic and social problems of African Americans to the failure of the black family, and in particular to its matriarchal structure, a result of higher rates of divorce, separation, and desertion. Moynihan defined family stability in accordance with a white middle-class, specifically suburban, norm, which not even middle-class black families could meet because of "housing segregation" (75). Some critics challenged the report by observing that according to its own standards, "American families in general . . . are crumbling."[18] And indeed, the "highly standardized" "image" (51) of the stable suburban family to which Moynihan pointed was already seen as fractured and precarious. Five years before the report was released, articles in the *Atlantic Monthly* and *Saturday Evening Post* had complained about the suburb in remarkably similar, and similarly hysterical, terms. The commuter is an "absentee father" and the suburb a de facto "matriarchy": "Each suburban family is somehow a broken home."[19] Also in 1960 a team of social psychologists coined the phrase "Disturbia" to highlight the "emotional problems" that plagued the residents of Bergen County in New Jersey, "a typical section of American suburbia."[20] *The Split-Level Trap* noted that "the typical American," with "his shiny mass-produced house and car, his manners and mores . . . often finds that he isn't happy after all. Somewhere, something is missing" (28). Discontent is a symptom of pervasive "[s]ocial disintegration" (54), which affects all family members and the relationships between them: lonely and depressed housewives, tense and depressed husbands, unruly and depressed children. People aren't simply sad; they're screwed up. In these accounts the white middle-class suburb is the hotbed of social and domestic pathology.

While suburbs obviously do not guarantee familial perfection, just as slums do not ensure familial failure, it is possible to take the former insight too far and remythologize the suburb as the parodic antithesis of the good life, where gratification on every level is nonexistent. The suburban novel errs conspicuously in this direction. It refutes in two ways Tolstoy's famous dictum: "Happy families are all alike; every unhappy family is unhappy in its own way."[21] As a body of work, the suburban novel asserts instead that one unhappy family is a lot like the next, and there is no such thing as a happy family. Divorce, desertion, adultery, illegitimacy, domestic violence, incest, mental illness, suicide, matricide: the term "dysfunctional" is hardly adequate to address the scope of its continuous failure. The new dictum may well be *The Ice Storm*'s exasperated pronouncement: "Fucking family" (274). Family life provides little or no compensation in these novels for struggles outside of the home, as parents try to cope with their promiscuous, violent, and drug-taking children, and with their betrayals of one another, whether wife swapping in the swinging sixties and seventies or affairs both meaningless and meaningful. It messes you up, perpetuates all manner of injustices in its name—"racist bullshit and bigotry" (275)—and still you can't escape it: "fucking *family*." Moreover, women's liberation means that wives no longer are timidly discontented but loyal, like Myra Babbitt, or eager to labor outside the home entirely on its behalf, like Mildred Pierce, or devoted to keeping it "honest" and superior to the neighbors, like Betsy Rath. Women can be agents of family instability and grief; in *Rabbit Redux*, for example, it is Janice who abandons Rabbit and their son, temporarily, of course. And as a realtor, the first house she sells in *Rabbit at Rest* is her family's. Happy families of a sort are featured in one popular suburban novel, but Ira Levin's cult classic, *The Stepford Wives* (1972), suggests that the only contented housewife is a robotic housewife, and the only contented husband and children, the ones who live with the robot. Racial and religious differences among the WASP, Jewish, and African American population of this affluent suburb are trumped by male solidarity and a shared commitment to the fifties conventions of middle-class family life; husbands kill and replace their wives, in other words, out of a profound commitment to the suburban home. They don't want to run.

More critically acclaimed novels challenge the premise that suburban life is a sordid business but inevitably reinforce it. John Cheever's fantastical *Bullet Park* (1969) is about a happy family's discovery that it's really pretty miserable. Barthelme's *Natural Selection* reverses the process: a husband and father repairs his family and returns to it when he realizes that moderately happy is good enough. But his wife is immediately killed in a car crash, as though to suggest that any happiness is not only fleeting but ultimately destructive. John Updike has commented that "a person who has what he wants, a satisfied person, a content person, ceases to be a person. . . . I feel that to be a person is to be in a situation of tension."[22] Happiness is treated here as detrimental to the literary project because it kills whatever is intrinsically interesting about a character. "[A] satisfied person . . . in a sense dies" (504). The suburban novel is a particular trib-

ute to the belief that discontent is the only solution to the writer's dilemma. In a similar meditation on the writer's craft, the first-person narrator of *Expensive People* ponders the difficulty of trying to represent
paradise. The perfections of Fernwood, an old, elegant midwestern suburb, foil his descriptive talents: "we writers are better equipped to write
of the Inferno and Purgatory, as you know. Before the rare beauties of the
wealth of America a writer can do nothing" (111). The novel ends with
matricide; the solution is to treat paradise, like *The Ice Storm*'s New Canaan, as though it were purgatory. When Rabbit wonders "even if there
is a Heaven how can there be one we can stand forever" (*Rich* 163), when
Jernigan weighs the moral of "the *Twilight Zone* thing where the guy says
he's going nuts in heaven and won't they please send him to the Other
Place and this guy tells him this *is* the Other Place, nya-ha-ha-*hah*" (83),
heaven and hell threaten to become indistinguishable. Stepford is something worse than hell: the audioanimatronic technology that enables husbands to replace their wives with robots was brought to Stepford by
"Diz" Coba, so called because he developed it for Disneyland. The author
blurb in *The Stepford Wives* ominously notes that Levin "lives in New
York—after several years in suburbia," reversing the direction he had
moved—from the Satanic recesses of Manhattan out to suburban Connecticut—prior to the publication of *Rosemary's Baby* (1967). Faced with
the choice between New York City and its suburbs, between Satan and
Mickey, Levin opted for the devil.

"ANOTHER SHITTY DAY IN PARADISE" reads a bumper sticker in *Preston
Falls*. The SAAB's lament forcefully embodies the combination of undercut
conceit, beleaguerment, and self-pity that has characterized the white diaspora in the suburban novel. The bumper sticker is flagrantly immodest,
drawing our attention to the luxury car while petitioning us not to be
fooled by it. Denunciations of paradise are one of its staple pastimes and
prerogatives. As we have also seen, however, the view looks somewhat
different from the outside. In *Goodbye, Columbus* (1959), for example,
the Patimkins' overabundant, fruit-filled house stands as an icon of affluence to Neil Klugman of Newark. Neil's Aunt Gladys is surprised to find
that there are Jews living in Short Hills, but no more so than Mr. Patimkin,
of Patimkin Kitchen and Bathroom Sinks, who is unable to convey in
words "all the satisfaction and surprise he felt about the life he had managed to build for himself and his family."[23] It is the assimilated second
generation who sees the family's newfound affluence as the beginning
rather than the end of a struggle. His daughter Brenda takes their good
life for granted and has to manufacture travails—"her life, which, I was
certain, consisted to a large part of cornering the market on fabrics that
felt soft to the skin, took on the quality of a Hundred Years' War" (26).
Neil is ironic about Brenda's insensibility to her privileges but not about

the privileges themselves. What Gaugin's paintings of Tahiti are to the little boy in the library—"That's the fucking life" (37)—Short Hills is to Neil: "at dusk, rose-colored, like a Gaugin stream" (38). Without insisting that suburban life is either perfect or miserable, the narrative does not reject his reflection that "the hundred and eighty feet that the suburbs rose in altitude above Newark brought one closer to heaven" (8).

But then no novel insists upon the hellishness of the suburb more than Gloria Naylor's *Linden Hills*, which casts itself as a modern *Inferno*. Inhabited exclusively by African Americans, this affluent suburb comprises eight concentric, crescent-shaped drives. The more money and status, the farther in one lives; it is "a journey down to the lowest circle of hell."[24] Naylor endorses every stereotype of the soulless suburbanite. Indeed, no novel draws a sharper distinction between affluence and spiritual well-being. In a series of vignettes the novel tracks the miserable lives that residents lead. They forget who they are: "a memory was a small price to pay" (11) for such splendor. In a rare example of clearly coercive heteronormativity, one man violates his true homosexual identity and marries so that he can keep his job as a corporate lawyer, but what residents forget most is their race. "Linden Hills wasn't black; it was successful" (17). And successful people are unable "to transform" their houses "into that nebulous creation called a home" (227–28). In Linden Hills the experience of black homelessness is identical to what I have called the white diaspora, insofar as the suburb as such effectively makes the black middle class indistinguishable from white.

In two of the most lauded suburban novels of the 1980s and 1990s the equation of suburban affluence and anguish has been modified, by a white male character who brings to his reflections a heightened self-consciousness and a new, often insufferable, sense of his own discernment. In Ford's *The Sportswriter* (1986) and *Independence Day* (1995), narrator Frank Bascombe could not possibly take his commitment to embracing the "good life" more seriously.[25] Discontent is anathema to Frank. As numerous reviewers have noted, he is driven to celebrate the small, the ordinary, the familiar, to find and appreciate their mysteries; therein lies his heroism. He is levelheaded, plainspeaking, decent, all of which come across as the extraordinary virtues of an exceptional man.

"[M]ore complex" (121) than others, Frank has to work harder than less complicated people to take pleasure in the quotidian. His efforts are most evident in his relationship with an emergency room nurse, Vicki Arcenault, who is "happy to let the world please her in the small ways it can" (128). She lives in the Pheasant Meadow development, just outside Frank's prosperous suburban town of Haddam (modeled after Princeton). Her condo was furnished in a one-day whirlwind trip to the Miracle Furniture Mile in Paramus. Vicki made all her own choices: pastel poof-drapes, sunburst mirror, bright area rugs with abstract designs, loveseat with a horse-and-buggy print . . . and a whopper Sony. . . . Everything as reliable as the newly-wed suite in the Holiday Inn. My own house represents other aims, with its comfortable, over-stuffed entities, full magazine racks, faded orientals, creaky sills . . . evidence that does not announce a life's real quality any more eloquently than a new Barca Lounger or a Kitchen Magician, no matter what you've heard. . . . And the idea appeals to me of starting life over in such a new and genial place with an instant infusion of colorful, fresh and impersonal furnishings. (57)

Frank attempts to portray neutrally the tastes of the lower-middle class, without reverting to the kind of campy celebration—of shag rugs, synthetics, and seating units—that marks *The Ice Storm*'s commemoration of the 1970s living room. His large, prewar English Tudor, a quirky, personalized house that he settled in and furnished over time, is not a sign of a superior life, although it is impossible not to associate it here with the conviction of superior sensibilities. Sympathetic tolerance sounds a lot like condescension. On a visit to Vicki's father, "a man completely without a subtext, a literalist of the first order" (274), Frank mourns: "Wade Arcenault is a lucky man to live here, and I am, at heart, cast down to loss in its presence" (293). "Here" is a newer development of "fresh and immature" plantings and "perfectly isosceles" houses. But Wade's good fortune has little to do with where he and his wife live; rather, they are lucky to be satisfied with their unimaginative "little life" (295) of blue Ultrasuede loveseats and split-levels. Frank likes Vicki, who shares her family's taste for Ultrasuede, because she releases him from the burden of his own complexity. The novel applauds the fineness of Frank's perceptions even as they beset him. Appreciating the mysteries of his comfortable suburban existence means finding an almost unbearable pathos in virtually everything. His generally wistful assessments of his life—"not a bad one" (176); "that is good enough for me" (213); "[b]eing a man gets harder all the time" (343)—bespeak energies that are less directed toward epiphanies than toward cultivating feelings of poignant ambivalence. Frank insists on his serenity and general satisfaction with things as they are, in large measure because he is unable to distinguish between contentment and despair.

In *Independence Day* Frank continues to share his bright-side homilies—"There is no such thing as a false sense of well-being" (21)—and revel in his mixed blessings: "to the old taunt that says, 'Get a life,' I can say, 'I already have an existence, thanks' " (117). And yet the novel exposes new worries too, actual threats to that existence. Lovely Haddam is not so lovely anymore. Muggers attacked him in his neighborhood, and a woman from his office was murdered while showing a condominium. As crime, like drugs, has followed people to the suburbs: "There's a new sense of a wild world being just beyond our perimeter, an untallied apprehension among our residents" (5). The old protections are inadequate, as are the new. On a weekend trip with his son, yet another teenage suburban casualty who faces criminal charges of theft and assault, they stop at a motel where the driver of a Chevy Suburban has just been robbed and killed. As a quintessential artifact of contemporary suburban life, the sport utility vehicle embodies a dual commitment to family *and* rebellion: after I drop the kids off at soccer practice, look out, I just may go four-wheeling. It also takes the concept of defensive driving to a new level, mocking mere cars with the knowledge of just who is going to walk away from that crash. *Independence Day* deflates the driver's probable "sense of well-being"; neither suburb nor Suburban is adequate to a world of unimaginable risk.

Frank weaves this uneasiness into his account of Independence Day, which pivots on the sacrifices people are willing to make to protect themselves and their property, sacrifices that bring Americans into being. As he explains to his son, "on July 2, 1776, all the colonies on the seaboard distrusted the bejesus out of each other, were acting like separate, fierce warrior nations scared to death of falling property values and what religion their neighbors were practicing (like now), and yet still knew they needed to be happier and safer and went about doing their best to figure out how. . . . That's why they decided to band together and be independent and were willing to sacrifice some controls they'd always had in hopes of getting something better" (260–61). To achieve greater independence, and to protect property values, the colonists gave up independence from one another, renouncing sovereignty for union. According to Frank, reborn in this novel as a realtor, the United States appears to have been founded on principles analogous to those that have in the twentieth century engendered private homeowner associations and gated communities. The personal autonomy once associated with house ownership is now exchanged for the security of property and person in the autonomous community—privately taxed, governed, protected, and, increasingly, barricaded—in which residents are protected from outsiders as well as from "the potential misdeeds of one's neighbors."[26] Union is not even rhetorically inclusive. A man's home is no longer his castle, and the gated community has become the American fortress. It is hard to imagine that these new enclaves won't eventually yield a further literature of suburban victimization, in which characters mourn the spiritual hollowness of their lives while waving to the guard. As the Raths would surely remind us, gates and guards can look very much like prison.

NOTES

INTRODUCTION

1. Edith Wharton, "The Great American Novel," *Yale Review* 16 (July 1927), 653.

2. The book that put the study of American urban literature on the map is Blanche Gelfant, *The American City Novel* (Norman: Oklahoma University Press, 1954). Recent book-length studies that attest to the vigor of urban literary criticism include Dana Brand, *The Spectator and the City in Nineteenth-Century American Literature* (New York: Cambridge University Press, 1991); Charles Scruggs, *Sweet Home: Invisible Cities in the Afro-American Novel* (Baltimore: Johns Hopkins University Press, 1993); Ann Douglas, *Terrible Honesty: Mongrel Manhattan in the 1920s* (New York: Farrar, Straus and Giroux, 1995); and Carlo Rotella, *October Cities: The Redevelopment of American Literature* (Berkeley and Los Angeles: University of California Press, 1998). William Sharpe, *Unreal Cities: Urban Figuration in Wordsworth, Baudelaire, Whitman, Eliot, and Williams* (Baltimore: Johns Hopkins University Press, 1990); Hana Wirth-Nesher, *City Codes: Reading the Modern Urban Novel* (New York: Cambridge University Press, 1996); and Richard Lehan, *The City in Literature* (Berkeley and Los Angeles: University of California Press, 1998) analyze the tradition of urban writing in the United States and Europe. The wilderness, of course, has long been a crucial location in American literary studies. And when Richard Brodhead remarks that feminist critics have retrieved women regionalist writers from "a lesser suburb of the literary domain," he finds the appropriate spatial metaphor to contrast these writers' former marginalization with the flood of books and articles on regionalism that have appeared in recent years (*Cultures of Letters: Scenes of Reading and Writing in Nineteenth-Century America* [Chicago: University of Chicago Press, 1993], 143). On the topic of the suburb in American literature I have located one unpublished dissertation (Kathryn Louise Riley, "The Use of Suburbia as a Setting in the Fiction of John O'Hara, John Cheever, and John Updike," University of Maryland, 1981) and a scant handful of articles, all of which deal exclusively with post–World War II authors.

3. In *Home: A Short History of an Idea* (New York: Penguin, 1987), Witold Rybczynski presents the "idea" of home as inseparable from the interior of the house. In an essay on the value and meaning of home in American literature and culture, John Hollander deplores "[t]he common—and, unlike many common expressions, vulgar—use of 'home' as a euphemism for 'house,' " a euphemism rendered all the more objectionable by its source: it "is by and large the linguistic waste product of the American real-estate industry" ("It All Depends," in *Home: A Place in the World*, ed. Arien Mack [New York: New York University Press, 1993], 37). But the conflation of house and home isn't quite reducible to the commercial interests it serves. Hollander himself refers to examples of it in early-nine-

teenth-century poetry and an 1882 article from *Harper's Magazine* that predates by seven years the real-estate advertisement he goes on to cite. He also ignores the moral force of the nineteenth-century connection between the single-family house and the home as a sphere of family comfort, privacy, and affectional ties in domestic treatises such as Catharine Beecher, *Treatise on Domestic Economy: For the Use of Young Ladies at Home and at School* (Boston: Marsh, Capen, Lyon, and Webb, 1841) or in the spiritual guidance of minister John F. W. Ware, *Home Life: What It Is, and What It Needs* (Boston: Spencer, 1864). The conflation of house and home does pervade the real estate sections of American newspapers, but the ambition to sell houses as something more than shelters speaks to, rather than simply creates, a more widely diffused belief that houses really are more than shelters.

4. Sinclair Lewis, *Babbitt* (1922; rpt., New York: Signet, 1991), 16.

5. David Gates, *Jernigan* (New York: Vintage, 1992), 29.

6. Constance Perin, *Belonging in America: Reading between the Lines* (Madison: University of Wisconsin Press, 1988), 5. See also Perin, *Everything in Its Place: Social Order and Land Use in America* (Princeton: Princeton University Press, 1977). Perin, a sociologist, analyzes American attitudes toward house ownership, which is associated with full citizenship and its responsibilities, and toward renting, which bears the taint of second-class or dysfunctional citizenship: "Renters, Americans believe, are by nature morally deficient, unstable, and dangerous" (*Everything in Its Place*, 99). Her findings bear out the arguments of historians who have linked the evolution of the American suburban ideal from the mid-nineteenth century to an anti-urban Jeffersonian tradition that equates small property ownership and democracy. See Kenneth T. Jackson, *Crabgrass Frontier: The Suburbanization of the United States* (New York: Oxford University Press, 1985); and Margaret Marsh, *Suburban Lives* (New Brunswick, N.J.: Rutgers University Press, 1990).

7. Gwendolyn Wright, *Building the Dream: A Social History of Housing in America* (New York: Pantheon, 1981), 107; Tamara K. Hareven, "The Home and the Family in Historical Perspective," in Mack, *Home: A Place in the World*, 238.

8. Mary Corbin Sies, "The City Transformed: Nature, Technology, and the Suburban Ideal, 1877–1917," *Journal of Urban History* 14 (November 1987), 83, 86. Local studies such as Michael H. Ebner, *Creating Chicago's North Shore: A Suburban History* (Chicago: University of Chicago Press, 1988) and Carol A. O'Connor, *A Sort of Utopia: Scarsdale, 1891–1981* (Albany: State University of New York Press, 1983) also address the residents' self-conscious construction of upper-middle-class communities based on shared assumptions and values. Advances in transportation and construction made it feasible for people to translate the suburban ideal into reality. The classic study of the mechanics and motives of middle-class suburbanization in the late-nineteenth century is Sam Bass Warner, Jr., *Streetcar Suburbs: The Process of Growth in Boston, 1870–1900*, 2nd ed. (Cambridge: Harvard University Press, 1978). On the impact of transportation technologies, see also Jackson, *Crabgrass Frontier*, 87–124, 157–89.

9. Richard Ohmann, *Selling Culture: Magazines, Markets, and Class at the Turn of the Century* (London: Verso, 1996), 140, 135, 148. See pp. 118–74 for a fine account of the development of the suburb and its relation to the formation

and self-conception of a professional and managerial class (PMC) that comprised middle- and upper-level corporate managers, officials, mental workers such as writers and people in advertising, highly skilled technical workers, professionals, and their families. Stuart Blumin also addresses the importance of suburbanization to the "class awareness" of the middle class: "By the end of the century the attractive detached suburban house, set within a homogeneous neighborhood of commuting businessmen, professionals, officials, and senior clerical workers, had become one of the principal molders of middle-class life, and one of its most powerful symbols" (*The Emergence of the Middle Class: Social Experience in the American City, 1760–1900* [Cambridge: Cambridge University Press, 1989], 276). Blumin borrows the concept of *class awareness* from Anthony Giddens to describe "a common awareness and acceptance of similar attitudes and beliefs, linked to a common style of life, among the members of the class" (cited in Blumin, *Emergence of the Middle Class*, 10) that exists in the absence of anything as coherent and dependent upon notions of conflict as class consciousness, and pertains even when the reality of classes is itself denied. Ohmann argues persuasively that the suburb fostered rather more of a sense of "common purpose" and conscious class identity than Giddens and Blumin allow for, but that the PMC "did think more in terms of mobility and merit than in terms of fixed lines and antagonisms" (*Selling Culture*, 171–72). *Class awareness* is also useful in thinking about middle-classness as an identity (that exists in relation to other factors such as race and gender), because of the inevitable problems of defining the middle class, given what Burton J. Bledstein has called "its lack of structure in sociological terms and its lack of exclusiveness in financial terms" (*The Culture of Professionalism: The Middle Class and the Development of Higher Education in America* [New York: Norton, 1978], 3).

10. On rates of population growth, see Mark Foster, *From Streetcar to Superhighway: American City Planners and Urban Transportation, 1900–1940* (Philadelphia: Temple University Press, 1981), 47. On the advertisers' promotion of the suburban home, see Roland Marchand, *Advertising the American Dream: Making Way for Modernity, 1920–1940* (Berkeley and Los Angeles: University of California Press, 1985). According to Sies, by World War I a "broad consensus" ("The City Transformed," 108) had been reached about the basic principles of suburban design, especially the primacy of the single-family house on its own lot, within a relatively homogeneous community. On the commodification of the suburban ideal in the 1920s, see Marsh, *Suburban Lives*, 129–81. Marsh combines general analysis of suburban trends with community studies that indicate the satisfaction residents found in their homes and neighborhoods. Community newspapers such as the *Roland Park Review*, which I look at in chapter 1, are a useful resource for gauging the attitudes of residents toward where they live.

11. Christopher Lasch, *Haven in a Heartless World: The Family Besieged* (New York: Basic, 1977); Elaine Tyler May, *Homeward Bound: American Families in the Cold War Era* (New York: Basic Books, 1988), 24. See also Dolores Hayden, *Redesigning the American Dream: The Future of Housing, Work, and Family Life* (New York: Norton, 1984); Clifford Edward Clark Jr., *The American Family Home, 1800–1960* (Chapel Hill: University of North Carolina Press, 1986); and Stephanie Coontz, *The Way We Never Were: American Families and the Nostalgia*

Trap (New York: Basic, 1992). Some feminist historians such as Tyler May qualify the focus on suburban placement by emphasizing an at times profound tension between post–1945 domestic desires and fulfillment, for women in particular. Ready-made postwar suburban communities were frequently denounced by contemporaries as bastions of conformity. Barbara M. Kelly's study of the original Levittown analyzes the efforts of both upwardly mobile working- and lower-middle-class residents to lay claim to the houses and landscape by personalizing them in line with the needs of individual families. See *Expanding the American Dream: Building and Rebuilding Levittown* (Albany: State University of New York Press, 1993). In a study of the primarily lower-middle-class Levittown in New Jersey, Herbert J. Gans argued that residents associated living there with freedom and opportunities, not constraints. See *The Levittowners: Ways of Life and Politics in a New Suburban Community* (New York: Pantheon, 1967).

12. George Lipsitz argues that racist selling and lending practices in housing have had tremendous long-term financial consequences for African Americans and other minority groups. Most of the net worth of white people and the greater opportunities that their larger share of the financial pie makes available to them have come through property acquired in a disciminatory housing market. See *The Possessive Investment in Whiteness: How White People Profit from Identity Politics* (Philadelphia: Temple University Press, 1988). On the social costs of suburbanization, see also Michael N. Danielson, *The Politics of Exclusion* (New York: Columbia University Press, 1976); and Douglas S. Massey and Nancy A. Denton, *American Apartheid: Segregation and the Making of the Underclass* (Cambridge: Harvard University Press, 1993).

13. John R. Stilgoe, *Borderlands: Origins of the American Suburb, 1820–1939* (New Haven: Yale University Press, 1988), 2. The new optimism of academics regarding the suburbs and their forthcoming work are the subjects of a recent *New York Times* article: Iver Peterson, "Some Perched in Ivory Tower Gain Rosier View of Suburbs," December 5, 1999, sec. 1, p. 1, 43. Public opinion polls do sometimes indicate the residents' dissatisfaction with suburban life, but as discussed in American newspapers, the residents' unhappiness seems most often the result of their sense that the suburbs in which they live aren't suburban enough. Problems such as crime and congestion—traffic and the loss of open spaces—mark the undesirable encroachment of the city on places that were selected in part as a refuge from it. See Keith Erwin, "Has the Glow Worn Off Suburbia?" *Seattle Times*, June 10, 1996, A1; John Wildermuth, "Long Haul to American Dream," *San Francisco Chronicle*, March 18, 1997, A1; Don Melvin, "Growth Spoiling Suburbs," *Atlanta Journal and Constitution*, July 10, 1997, 1G; Daryl Kelley, "Suburbia Lost," *Los Angeles Times*, Valley edition, October 24, 1999, B1. (Articles were tracked through the Lexis-Nexis database, which lists the first page only).

14. Gillian Brown, *Domestic Individualism: Imagining Self in Nineteenth-Century America* (Berkeley and Los Angeles: University of California Press, 1990). See pp. 45–47 for a discussion of "sentimental possession" in relation to Stowe. On Stowe's vision of the nineteenth-century housekeeper who sympathetically identifies with her goods as the forebear of the modern consumer, see Lori Merish, "Sentimental Consumption: Harriet Beecher Stowe and the Aesthetics of Middle-

Class Ownership," *American Literary History* 8 (Spring 1996), 1–33. When the prototypical consumer of the mid-nineteenth century becomes the typical consumer of the twentieth, the self threatens to become indistinguishable from the commodities it consumes. See Jean-Christophe Agnew, "A House of Fiction: Domestic Interiors and the Commodity Aesthetic," in *Consuming Visions: Accumulation and Display of Goods in America, 1880–1920*, ed. Simon J. Bronner (New York: Norton, 1989), 135–55. For the definitive hostile analysis of the conflation of self and things in relation to advertising, see Stuart Ewen, *Captains of Consciousness: Advertising and the Social Roots of the Consumer Culture* (New York: McGraw-Hill, 1975).

15. Edgar Rice Burroughs, *Tarzan of the Apes* (serialized 1912; rpt., New York: Ballantine, 1963), 95. Recent scholars have protested that suburbs have never been as white and middle class as they have been represented to be by academics. There have been ethnic, industrial, and African American suburbs, and white working-class people have lived in some suburbs that have been misidentified as exclusively middle class. See, for example, James L. Wunsch, "The Suburban Cliché," *Journal of Social History* 28 (Spring 1995), 644–58; Robert Breugmann, "The Twenty-Three Percent Solution," *American Quarterly* 46 (March 1994), 31–34; and James Andrew Wiese, "Struggle for the Suburban Dream: African American Suburbanization since 1916" (Ph.D. diss., Columbia University, 1993). The issue is less one of historical inaccuracy, it seems to me, than of terminological nuance; that is, no historian who studies white middle-class suburbanization suggests that only this population has lived on the outskirts of cities, but the meaning of the term *suburb* has largely evolved in association with a particular way of life and opportunities that have traditionally been limited on the basis of race and class. Exclusion, as Robert Fishman reminds us in *Bourgeois Utopias: The Rise and Fall of Suburbia* (New York: Basic, 1987), is crucial to understanding the meaning of the suburb. My use of the term *suburb* to describe a low-density residential environment of largely middle-class and upper-middle-class people who live in single-family houses that they own, and from which the labor force commutes, is indebted to Jackson and Fishman.

16. Richard Wright, *Native Son* (1940; rpt., New York: Harper, 1966), 45.

17. Kenneth Warren raises a striking alternative to the primacy of placement in an essay on the diasporic imagination of Langston Hughes, which concludes by suggesting that Hughes may have been more invested in cultivating rather than resolving a crisis of identity; he did not seek to come home psychically but expressed "a desire to speak" multiple and contradictory identifications "in a single voice" ("Appeals for (Mis)recognition: Theorizing the Diaspora," in *Cultures of United States Imperialism*, ed. Amy Kaplan and Donald Pease [Durham, N.C.: Duke University Press, 1993], 405).

18. See Nina Baym, *Women's Fiction: A Guide to Novels by and about Women in America, 1820–1870* (Ithaca: Cornell University Press, 1978); and Jane Tompkins, *Sensational Designs: The Cultural Work of American Fiction, 1790–1860* (New York: Oxford University Press, 1985). Ann Douglas argues explicitly for the insignificance of domestic culture to 1920s New York in *Terrible Honesty*, which describes the banishment of the Victorian home and its grasping matriarch

(see Douglas's *The Feminization of American Culture* [New York: Knopf, 1977])
in the evolution of modernity's complex and contradictory public urban spaces.

19. See Cathy N. Davidson, "Preface: No More Separate Spheres!" *American
Literature* 70 (September 1998), 4443–63; and *The Culture of Sentiment: Race,
Gender, and Sentimentality in Nineteenth-Century America*, ed. Shirley Samuels
(New York: Oxford University Press, 1992). In "Manifest Domesticity," one of
the *American Literature* articles, Amy Kaplan observes the dual meanings of the
word *domestic* to argue that when understood with reference to the nation, it
makes sense to think of it as a concept that unites white men and women as "allies
against the alien" (582). The argument that follows focuses on white middle-
class women, however, to implicate them in the imperial project of envisioning
the nation as home through their central role as care-takers of the nation's homes.
The place of men in sentimental culture generally has attracted more scholarly
attention of late. See especially the essays in *Sentimental Men: Masculinity and
the Politics of Affect in American Culture*, ed. Mary Chapman and Glenn Hendler
(Berkeley and Los Angeles: University of California Press, 1999). The introduction is a superb analysis of the vast criticism on sentimentalism and domesticity
with an emphasis on its gender biases. Two of three essays in the section "Domestic Men" focus on bachelors; the third examines through nineteenth-century pho-
tography the affective ties between fathers and their children who have died. With
an essay on Frank Norris's *The Octopus* (1901), the collection barely crosses the
threshold of the twentieth century. Katherine V. Snyder offers a fine reading of
the bachelor's disruptive sexuality and domesticity at the turn of the century in
Bachelors, Manhood, and the Novel (Cambridge: Cambridge University Press,
1999). Brown's discussion of domestic men and male novelists similarly concentrates on bachelor characters in Hawthorne and Melville. Douglas Anderson's *A
House Divided: Domesticity and Community in American Literature* (Cambridge: Cambridge University Press, 1990) considers the place of sentimental domesticity in canonical texts of eighteenth- and nineteenth-century male writers,
but his analysis is for the most part decontextualized and divorced from particular
domestic spaces, to the point where, for example, community and domesticity are
treated as unproblematically coextensive, almost synonymous.

20. Upton Sinclair, *The Jungle* (1906; rpt., Urbana: University of Illinois Press,
1988), 172; John Steinbeck, *The Grapes of Wrath* (1939; rpt., New York: Bantam,
1955), 79; Pietro di Donato, *Christ in Concrete* (1939; rpt., New York: Signet,
1993); Ann Petry, *The Street* (1946; rpt., New York: Houghton Mifflin, 1991).

21. *The Street* is a featured text in the only essay of the *American Literature*
special issue to focus on the twentieth century. You-me Park and Gayle Wald are
concerned to demonstrate that "the subjective *value* of public and private is radically contingent upon gender, race, ethnicity, and citizenship," and they argue of
The Street in particular that it "makes obsolete conventional distinctions between
outside and inside, street and home, sacred and profane" ("Native Daughters in
the Promised Land: Gender, Race, and the Question of Separate Spheres," *American Literature* 70 [September 1998], 614, 619). With respect to *The Street* the
essay confuses, I think, the fact of housing with the felt requirements of the home.
Park and Wald usefully point out that the putative separation of home and workplace, private and public, has been fraught for immigrant and African American

domestic workers whose labors made possible middle-class white women's domesticity. But Lutie's ideal of a home is virtually indistinguishable from its middle-class associations—privacy, security, emotional comfort, independence—and is no less real for being unrealized. However fragile in her actual experience, the old and still vital distinctions between outside and in, public and private remain anything but obsolete so far as "subjective value" is concerned. Despite the novel's own skepticism about Lutie's faith in the power of self-making in a racist and sexist world, it comes rather closer to reifying the boundaries that differentiate streets from homes than dissolving them, and also reveals that her valuation of home cannot simply be written off as a "bourgeois" (617) value, a term that begs the question it claims to be resolving.

In *Urban Intersections: Meetings of Life and Literature in United States Cities* (Urbana: University of Illinois Press, 1992), Sidney Bremer contrasts the depictions of a community-minded "urban home" (133) that infuse the writings of white middle-class women, working-class, and minority writers with the alienated, "anticommunal" (4) tradition of city writing by middle-class white men. Bremer deliberately moves beyond a conception of home that is limited to the domestic interior and is thus uninterested in the enduring value placed on private houses and homes by those who also embrace the virtues of community or in a domestic tradition of male writing.

22. Lora Romero, *Home Fronts: Domesticity and Its Critics in the Antebellum United States* (Durham, N.C.: Duke University Press, 1997), 97. Romero specifically challenges the critical tendency to privilege nineteenth-century literary texts' own constructions of alienation as a uniquely male prerogative, even among critics who are unwilling to privilege the aesthetics associated with it. On the relation of the alienated and besieged male to canon formation, see Nina Baym, "Melodramas of Beset Manhood: How Theories of American Literature Exclude Women," in Baym, *Feminism and American Literary History: Essays* (New Brunswick, N.J.: Rutgers University Press, 1992), 3–18. Among historians, Marsh describes the temporary emergence of a suburban "masculine domesticity" in the Progressive era, which brought men into the home, as it were, as companionable husbands and nurturing fathers, roles they would not fulfill again to the same extent until the "togetherness"craze of the 1950s. Marsh's account distinguishes itself from the more typical insistence of historians on hypermasculine identifications at the turn of the century. See *Suburban Lives*, esp. chap. 3.

23. June Howard has recently pointed out that sentiment and domestic ideology are not simply interchangeable; however, as it describes and inscribes the profoundly self-conscious emotional connections that bind individuals to material places and to the people associated with them, "the home" is only ever meaningful with reference to sentiment and is probably the most powerful of American sentimental conventions. See "What Is Sentimentality?" *American Literary History* 11 (Spring 1999), 63–81.

24. Harriet Beecher Stowe, "The Ravages of the Carpet," in *House and Home Papers* (Boston: Ticknor and Fields, 1865), 17. Brown discusses "Ravages" as a parable of "sentimental possession," the decommoditization of household objects (*Domestic Individualism*, 46). Lynn Wardley demonstrates that Stowe's vision of the home accommodated mass-produced domestic objects; when well-

chosen and neatly arranged by the housewife, they could weigh in on the side of sentiment and aesthetics as against the market. See "Relic, Fetish, Femmage: The Aesthetics of Sentiment in the Work of Stowe," in Samuels, *The Culture of Sentiment*, 203–20. Wardley's account of Stowe squares nicely with Gwendolyn Wright's reading of the place of mass-produced objects in the middle-class home after the 1870s, when women who had individualized domestic space through handicrafts and other personal artifacts increasingly personalized rooms by filling them with commodities that they arranged in "fashionable, educational, and individualistic" ways (*Moralism and the Model Home: Domestic Architecture and Cultural Conflict in Chicago, 1873–1913* [Chicago: University of Chicago Press, 1980], 19).

25. The main problem with one full-length treatment of the home in twentieth-century American literature is its failure to rethink the home/market dichotomy. Helen Fiddyment Levy's *Fictions of the Home Place: Jewett, Cather, Glasgow, Porter, Welty, and Naylor* (Jackson: University Press of Mississippi, 1992) allows for no significant changes in the meaning or value of domesticity from the mid-nineteenth century through the twentieth century. Indebted to Baym and Tompkins, Levy valorizes feminine domesticity as an antithesis and alternative to the competitive values of the marketplace and public life; however, she does not seriously engage the questions raised by women's increasing participation in these arenas, which challenge the viability and desirability of domesticity as an alternative to women's active role in public life.

On the middle-class home as principal site of consumer address and appeal, see Marchand, *Advertising and the American Dream*, and Ohmann, *Selling Culture*. Jennifer Scanlon discusses the ways in which *Ladies' Home Journal* helped to shape and define the role of the white middle-class suburban housewife as a consumer. See *Inarticulate Longings: The "Ladies' Home Journal," Gender, and the Promises of Consumer Culture* (New York: Routledge, 1995).

26. Warren I. Susman, " 'Personality' and the Making of Twentieth-Century Culture," in Susman, *Culture as History: The Transformation of American Society in the Twentieth Century* (New York: Pantheon, 1984), 277.

27. Gary Cross, "The Suburban Weekend: Perspectives on a Vanishing Twentieth-Century Dream," in *Visions of Suburbia*, ed. Roger Silverstone (London: Routledge, 1997), 119. The "trade-off" Cross refers to addresses both middle- and working-class people, although he notes that in the United States, few working-class families were able to cash in on the promise of house ownership until after World War II. On the transition from a primarily entrepreneurial to a largely bureaucratic business structure, see Alfred D. Chandler Jr., *The Visible Hand: The Managerial Revolution in American Business* (Cambridge: Harvard University Press, Belknap Press, 1977); on its beginnings, see Blumin, *The Emergence of the Middle Class*.

28. Advertising trade journals in the 1920s stated that women transacted 85 percent of all consumer purchases. According to *Printer's Ink*, "[T]he proper study of mankind is MAN . . . but the proper study of markets is WOMAN" (cited in Michael Schudson, *Advertising, the Uneasy Persuasion: Its Dubious Impact on American Society* [New York: Basic, 1984], 173). On feminization and consumer culture, see Rachel Bowlby, *Just Looking: Consumer Culture in Dreiser, Gissing,*

and Zola (New York: Methuen, 1985); Merish, "Sentimental Consumption"; and Scanlon, *Inarticulate Longings*. See also the introduction to Christopher Breward, *The Hidden Consumer: Masculinities, Fashion, and City Life, 1860–1914* (Manchester: Manchester University Press, 1999), for a recent critique of the marginalization of men in historical and theoretical scholarship on consumer culture.

29. Stilgoe in *Borderlands* is most emphatic about the split; although his study is mainly concerned with changes in landscape through the 1920s, it nominally extends to 1939, and he proposes another volume to deal with subsequent transformations. The 1920s also function as the natural termination point of Marsh's *Suburban Lives* and Alan Gowans, *The Comfortable House: North American Suburban Architecture, 1890–1930* (Cambridge: MIT Press, 1986). "Edge City" describes the commercial and residential sprawl that characterizes newer cities in particular, especially in the Sun Belt. See Joel Garreau, *Edge City: Life on the New Frontier* (New York: Doubleday, 1991). Robert Fishman coined the term "technoburb" to describe a similar trend toward a new form of decentralized city in *Bourgeois Utopias*.

30. The Rodriguez citation is from the *Newshour with Jim Lehrer*, PBS, December 10, 1999.

31. Christopher P. Wilson, *White Collar Fictions: Class and Social Representation in American Literature, 1885–1925* (Athens: University of Georgia Press, 1992), 16, 17.

32. Review of *Mildred Pierce*, *Time* 38 (September 29, 1941), 93.

33. Harlan Paul Douglass, *The Suburban Trend* (1925; rpt., New York: Arno, 1970), 229; Stilgoe, *Borderlands*, 285.

34. Wilson, *White Collar Fictions*, 21.

35. Ruth Frankenberg, *White Women, Race Matters: The Social Construction of Whiteness* (Minneapolis: University of Minnesota Press, 1993), 196; Richard Dyer, *White* (London: Routledge, 1997), 78. The ambition of making whiteness visible, and thereby attempting to disable the ordinary processes by which white identity and privilege are co-constructed, is a preoccupation as well of the essays in *Whiteness: A Critical Reader*, ed. Mike Hill (New York: New York University Press, 1997); *Displacing Whiteness: Essays in Social and Cultural Criticism*, ed. Ruth Frankenberg (Durham, N.C.: Duke University Press, 1997); and *Race and the Subject of Masculinities*, ed. Harry Stecopoulos and Michael Uebel (Durham, N.C.: Duke University Press, 1997).

36. David Roediger, *Towards the Abolition of Whiteness* (London: Verso, 1994), 13.

37. Eric Lott, "White Like Me: Racial Cross-Dressing and the Construction of American Whiteness," in Kaplan and Pease, *Cultures of United States Imperialism*, 488. The essay explores the pleasures and perils of racial transgression for the white middle-class narrator of John Howard Griffin's *Black Like Me* (1961), which Lott addressed more extensively in relation to white working-class men in *Love and Theft: Blackface Minstrelsy and the American Working Class* (New York: Oxford University Press, 1993). In *The Possessive Investment in Whiteness*, George Lipsitz's analysis of the concrete economic and social advantages that accrue to white people is an important reminder that when it comes to property rights, the relation of white to black is not primarily one of fascination and desire.

38. Lott, "All the King's Men: Elvis Impersonators and White Working-Class Masculinity," in Stecopoulos and Uebel, *Race and the Subject of Masculinities*, 208. In the introduction to *Race Traitor*, ed. Noel Ignatiev and John Garvey (New York: Routledge, 1996), the editors similarly hope that "widespread borrowing" of black culture by whites "hints at the possibility of something larger and more powerful than fashion decisions" (3).

39. See also David Roediger, *The Wages of Whiteness: Race and the Making of the American Working Class* (London: Verso, 1991); Noel Ignatiev, *How the Irish Became White* (New York: Routledge, 1997); and *White Trash*, ed. Matt Wray and Annalee Newitz (New York: Routledge, 1997).

40. On this point see Phil Cohen, "Subcultural Conflict and Working-Class Community," in *Culture, Media, Language*, ed. Stuart Hall, Dorothy Hobson, Andrew Lane, and Paul Willis (London: Unwin Hyman, 1980), 78–87.

41. Another essay on whiteness similarly presents the entanglement of white and middle-class identities among young mixed-race women who grew up in predominantly suburban communities where they self-identified as white. The young women interviewed felt they had no cultural content until they began to identify themselves as nonwhite at college; at this point it is class that becomes invisible for both the students and the sociologist. See France Winddance Twine, "Brown-Skinned White Girls: Class, Culture, and the Construction of White Identity in Suburban Communities," in Frankenberg, *Displacing Whiteness*, 214–43.

42. Lipsitz, *The Possessive Investment in Whiteness*, 123. Lott makes a related point in "White Like Me," 482.

43. Merish, "Sentimental Consumption," 16. For particularly thoughtful explorations of the historical relation between consumption as a hegemonic way of being in and seeing the world and working- and middle-class powerlessness in the public sphere, see *The Culture of Consumption: Critical Essays in American History, 1880–1980*, ed. Richard Wightman Fox and Jackson Lears (New York: Pantheon, 1983).

44. Jackson Lears, *No Place of Grace: Antimodernism and the Transformation of American Culture, 1880–1920* (New York: Pantheon, 1981), xv.

45. David Savran, *Taking It Like a Man: White Masculinity, Masochism, and Contemporary American Culture* (Princeton: Princeton University Press, 1998), 4.

46. Homi Bhabha, "Postscript," in Silverstone, *Visions of Suburbia*, 300.

CHAPTER ONE
TARZAN, LORD OF THE SUBURBS

1. Eric Cheyfitz, *The Poetics of Imperialism: Translation and Colonization from "The Tempest" to "Tarzan"* (New York: Oxford University Press, 1991), 3–21. Page numbers are from Edgar Rice Burroughs, *Tarzan of the Apes* (New York: Ballantine, 1963).

2. Marianna Torgovnick, *Gone Primitive: Savage Intellects, Modern Lives* (Chicago: University of Chicago Press, 1990), 55.

3. See Patrick Brantlinger, *Rule of Darkness: British Literature and Imperialism, 1830–1914* (Ithaca: Cornell University Press, 1988), 232–36, for a treatment

of British "invasion-scare" stories as expressions of late-Victorian and Edwardian anxieties about the political and cultural ramifications of imperialism.

4. Cheyfitz argues that domestic issues are central to *Tarzan of the Apes* in virtue of their absence. He identifies a structural similarity between American foreign policy, which directs attention away from domestic crises and toward unresolvable international problems—"The terrorist is the demonized specter of our own homeless people"—and the novel's "politics of translation" (*Poetics of Imperialism*, 15). As Tarzan develops intellectually and becomes proficient in English, he finds it increasingly difficult to communicate in his first language, the language of the apes. Cheyfitz claims that while the problem of translation is produced by an internal division within English, it is treated as cultural superiority: "The failure of dialogue, figured as a genetic inability in the other, rather than as a problem of cultural difference, is the imperial alibi for domination" (16). Like the U.S. government, *Tarzan* manufactures conflicts between domestic/internal and foreign/other out of wholly domestic problems. I suggest that *Tarzan*'s domestic crisis is more directly linked to concerns about the security of white homes in the early-twentieth century than to the problems of the homeless in the 1980s.

5. John Higham, *Send These to Me: Immigrants in Urban America*, 2nd ed. (Baltimore: Johns Hopkins University Press, 1984), 195. During an era when differences in ethnicity were often construed as racial differences, "the great evil native white Americans associated with blacks . . . was essentially identical to what they discerned in immigrants. The evil in both cases was pollution" (195). Although the "tidal wave" of rural black migration to the cities did not begin in earnest until the First World War, "by 1900 a substantial flow had already begun" (Irwin Unger and Debi Unger, *The Vulnerable Years: The United States, 1896–1917* [New York: New York University Press, 1978], 65).

6. Adna Ferrin Weber, *The Growth of Cities in the Nineteenth Century* (1899; rpt., Ithaca: Cornell University Press, 1963), 307.

7. O. F. Cook, "Eugenics and Agriculture," *Journal of Heredity* 7 (June 1916), 253. Daniel J. Kevles has linked the eugenics movement in the United States and Britain after 1900 to "industrialization, the growth of big business, the sprawl of cities and slums, the massive migrations from the countryside and (in the United States especially) from abroad" (*In the Name of Eugenics: Genetics and the Uses of Human Heredity* [New York: Knopf, 1985], 76). Numerous articles warned of the fecundity of immigrants and the declining birthrate among native-born whites as tantamount to "race suicide." Even Theodore Roosevelt famously weighed in on the issue. See "A Letter from President Roosevelt on Race Suicide," *American Review of Reviews* 35 (May 1907), 550–51.

8. "Urban Sterilization," *Journal of Heredity* 8 (June 1917), 269. Weber by contrast advocated suburban residence for the working classes and immigrants as well, but he further acknowledged the concerns of eugenicists when he indicated that "the modern combination of city business life and rural residence" for the "superior elements" meant that "the best blood of the race is not liable to extinction" (*The Growth of Cities*, 444).

9. Edward Said, *Culture and Imperialism* (New York: Knopf, 1993), 9. Although Said focuses on British literature in this context, he uses the term *Western metropolis* also to refer to the French and American imperial enterprises. In Fred-

ric Jameson's essay on the effects of imperialism on literary form, in which *metropolis* signifies "the imperial nation-state as such" ("Modernism and Imperialism," in *Nationalism, Colonialism, and Literature,* by Terry Eagleton, Fredric Jameson, and Edward W. Said [Minneapolis: University of Minnesota Press, 1990], 65n), Said's "colonial actuality" manifests itself as colonial invisibility. Jameson suggests that only metropolitan literature counts as modernism, because it alone expresses the absence at the center of the city that defines the modernist project.

10. Alan Trachtenberg, *The Incorporation of America: Culture and Society in the Gilded Age* (New York: Hill and Wang, 1982), 114.

11. Amy Kaplan, *The Social Construction of American Realism* (Chicago: University of Chicago Press, 1988), 45.

12. Frances A. Walker, "Restriction of Immigration," *Atlantic Monthly* 77 (June 1896), 824.

13. Jacob Riis, *How the Other Half Lives: Studies among the Tenements of New York* (1890; rpt., New York: Hill and Wang, 1957), 5, 6, 22–23, 14–15.

14. See Robert A. Woods, ed., *The City Wilderness: A Settlement Study* (Boston: Houghton Mifflin, 1898), 33–57; Albert Benedict Wolfe, *The Lodging House Problem in Boston* (Boston: Houghton Mifflin, 1906), 11–19; Franklin Kline Fretz, *The Furnished Room Problem in Philadelphia* (Philadelphia, 1910), 60–66; and Sophonisba Breckinridge and Edith Abbott, "Chicago's Housing Problem," *American Journal of Sociology* 16 (1910), 289–308. Tenement housing was sought not only by immigrants but also by poor native-born migrants who arrived in cities from rural areas within the United States. In chapter 4 I examine in greater detail related theories of urban deterioration within the Chicago school of sociology.

15. Everett N. Blanke, "The Cliff-Dwellers of New York," *Cosmopolitan* 15 (July 1893), 355. In addition to the primary references, I draw here from the following secondary sources on the history of apartment buildings in the United States: John Hancock, "The Apartment House in Urban America," in *Buildings and Society: Essays on the Social Development of the Built Environment,* ed. Anthony D. King (London: Routledge, 1980), 151–89; Wright, *Building the Dream,* 135–51; Elizabeth Hawes, *New York, New York: How the Apartment House Transformed the Life of the City, 1869–1930* (New York: Knopf, 1993); Elizabeth Cromley, *Alone Together: A History of New York's Early Apartments* (Ithaca: Cornell University Press, 1990); and Dolores Hayden, *The Grand Domestic Revolution: A History of Feminist Designs for American Homes, Neighborhoods, and Cities* (Cambridge: MIT Press, 1981), 72–77, 189–95. See also David P. Handlin, *The American Home: Architecture and Society, 1815–1915* (Boston: Little, Brown, 1979), 214–31, 377–85, for a more detailed account of the range of arguments in favor of apartments than I have space for here. On the challenge that the apartment house poses to assumptions about the rigid separation of public and private spheres, urban and domestic life, in the French and British contexts, see Sharon Marcus, *Apartment Stories: City and Home in Nineteenth-Century London and Paris* (Berkeley and Los Angeles: University of California Press, 1999).

16. S. B. Young, *European Modes of Living, or The Question of Apartment Houses (French Flats)* (New York: Putnam, 1881), 1.

17. J. P. Putnam, "The Apartment-House," *American Architect and Building News* 27 (January 4, 1890), 3, 5.

18. Charlotte Perkins Gilman, "The Passing of the Home in Great American Cities," *Cosmopolitan* 38 (December 1904), 138; Marsh, *Suburban Lives*, 73. The apartment hotel was conventionally distinguished from an apartment house by its provision of communal services as well as communal spaces, most scandalously a public kitchen and dining room. Individual apartments sometimes had private kitchens as well but were also constructed without them. According to Cromley, apartment hotels were most successful and least controversial as housing for bachelors.

Gilman's own, unrealized proposal for apartment hotels included a public nursery for mothers who did not wish to devote themselves to childcare as a full-time occupation. In an illuminating reading of Gilman's feminism, Gail Bederman argues that Gilman highlighted the differences between the races to shore up her attacks on gender discrimination. The Anglo-Saxon housewife was to be freed not only to pursue her own destiny, but to further the advancement of white civilization. In this light, the apartment was for Gilman a *boon* to the white middle class, and not just to women. See *Manliness and Civilization: A Cultural History of Gender and Race in the United States, 1880–1917* (Chicago: University of Chicago Press, 1995), 121–69.

19. "Apartment Hotels in New York City," *Architectural Record* 13 (January 1903), 85.

20. "The Problem of Living in New York," *Harper's* 65 (November 1882), 924, 922, 923. In an exhaustive analysis of homeownership rates among working-class immigrants and native-born white Americans in and outside Detroit, Olivier Zunz has concluded that "homeownership at the turn of the century was neither particularly middle-class nor American" (*The Changing Face of Inequality: Urbanization, Industrial Development, and Immigrants in Detroit, 1880–1920* [Chicago: University of Chicago Press, 1982], 153).

21. Christine Terhune Herrick, "Their Experience in a Flat," *Harper's Weekly* (January 11, 1890), 30–1. The city is identified only as some place other than New York City, possibly to suggest the dangers of apartment life in urban areas generally and not simply in the most densely populated American city.

22. Wright also notes in *Building the Dream* that in 1878 a New York City court ruled that a tenement comprised "three or more families living independently under one roof," while "an apartment house contained collective services for all its residents" (140). While this created a legal distinction between apartment *hotels* and tenements, it also meant that apartment buildings that did not provide for communal services were technically defined as tenements.

23. "Apartment Life," *Independent* 54 (January 2, 1902), 11.

24. William Dean Howells, *A Hazard of New Fortunes* (1890; rpt., New York: Oxford University Press, 1990), 55.

25. Kaplan, *Social Construction of American Realism*, 12, 44.

26. Henry Blake Fuller, *The Cliff-Dwellers* (1893; rpt., Ridgewood, N.J.: Gregg Press, 1968), 244.

27. Frank Norris, *Vandover and the Brute* (1914; rpt., Lincoln: University of Nebraska Press, 1978), 179. His first novel, *Vandover* was written between 1894 and 1895 but published posthumously.

28. The specter of degeneration has also been fruitfully linked to neurasthenia, a turn-of-the-century illness that gave the stressful conditions of modern urban life scientific credibility as the cause of mental and physical breakdowns among the white middle and upper classes. See Tom Lutz, *American Nervousness: 1903* (Ithaca: Cornell University Press, 1991). On the relation of neurasthenia to white masculinity, see Bederman, *Manliness and Civilization*, 84–92.

29. Harlan Paul Douglass, *The Suburban Trend* (1925; rpt., New York: Arno, 1970), 312, 307, 308, 311.

30. "Suburban Cottages versus Flats," *Independent* 62 (March 28, 1907), 748, 749.

31. Richard Harding Davis, "Our Suburban Friends," *Harper's* 89 (June 1894), 156, 157, 156.

32. William Dean Howells, "Mrs. Johnson," in *Suburban Sketches* (1871; rpt., Salem, N.H.: Ayer, 1985), 13, 12. The stories were first published in the *Atlantic Monthly*.

33. Henry Cuyler Bunner, "The Newcomers," in *The Suburban Sage: Stray Notes and Comments on His Simple Life* (1896; rpt., Freeport, N.Y.: Books for Libraries, 1969), 139. The stories were published originally in *Puck*.

34. Bunner, "The First of It," in *Suburban Sage*, 151, 147, 155.

35. Waldon Fawcett, "Suburban Life in America," *Cosmopolitan* 35 (July 1903), 309. Writers still made efforts, however, to combat the comic stereotypes. See, for example, Francis E. Clark, "Why I Chose a Suburban Home," *Suburban Life* 4 (April 1907), 187–89.

36. "Park Hill," *Craftsman* 17 (February 1910), 575, 576.

37. Advertisement, *Chicago Tribune*, May 8, 1910, IX2.

38. "Among the Craftsmen: Suburban Houses," *Craftsman* 20 (June 1911), 72; "A Craftsman House," *Craftsman* 5 (March 1904), 584. By 1919 editor Edward Bok of the *Ladies' Home Journal*, which began offering five-dollar house plans in 1895, advocated strict architectural, hygienic, and spiritual standards for the home to a largely white middle-class female suburban readership of over 2 million. See Wright, *Building the Dream*, 164–66. Arts and Crafts describes both a style, albeit one characterized by regional and personal variations, and an attitude toward the design and creation of aesthetic objects. It involved social as well as aesthetic reform. Following Morris and Ruskin, American Arts and Crafts architects and artists wanted to make labor in the age of industrialism meaningful again and to democratize art by making it a part of everyday life. They rebelled against the cluttered ugliness of Victorianism and propounded an aesthetics based on simplicity, honesty, and utility that was perceived to be more masculine than its fussy predecessor. Historians have emphasized that Arts and Crafts had a difficult time living up to its rhetoric of democracy and individualism. The clean lines lent themselves extremely well to mass production, and the finest, handcrafted work was limited primarily to the affluent. Its widespread commercial possibilities through mass production meant that the regard for regionalism was inconsistent at best. For example, the first two houses featured in the *Craftsman* were designed for

particular localities but declared suitable for "almost any section of the United States" ("A Craftsman House, *Craftsman* 5 [February 1904], 500). Arts and Crafts eventually became "a style of life associated with the middle class" that was more oriented toward consumption than production (Eileen Boris, *Art and Labor: Ruskin, Morris, and the Craftsman Ideal in America* [Philadelphia: Temple University Press, 1986], 54). See also Elizabeth Cumming and Wendy Kaplan, *The Arts and Craft Movement* (London: Thames and Hudson, 1991); *"The Art That Is Life": The Arts and Craft Movement in America, 1875–1920*, ed. Wendy Kaplan (Boston: Little, Brown, 1987). In *No Place of Grace*, Lears focuses on the movement's hypocrisy with regard to its original social and political ambitions, which reduced it to a primarily therapeutic exercise for a demoralized middle class. See chap. 2.

39. Jane Addams, *Twenty Years at Hull-House* (1910; rpt., Urbana: University of Illinois Press, 1990), 56, 59.

40. In 1874 New York City annexed parts of Westchester County, now the Bronx; in 1898 it increased its area more than sixfold by adding more territory from Westchester County, as well as from Brooklyn (then the fourth largest city in the United States), Staten Island, and most of Queens, in what Jackson describes as "the most important municipal boundary adjustment in American history" (*Crabgrass Frontier*, 142). According to Jackson, the governor and the state legislature encouraged the expansion of New York City's boundaries to increase its base of middle-class voters and so dilute the power of Tammany Hall.

41. Theodore Roosevelt, "The Strenuous Life" (1899), in *The Strenuous Life: Essays and Addresses* (New York: Century, 1900), 8; *Daly v. Morgan* (69 Maryland Reports 461), cited in *The Government of Metropolitan Areas in the United States*, ed. Paul Studenski (1930; rpt., New York: Arno, 1974), 76, emphasis in text.

42. Dallas Lore Sharp, "The Commuter and the 'Modern Conveniences,' " *Atlantic* 106 (October 1910), 557.

43. "The Home, the Unit of the Community, and Its Surroundings," *Roland Park Review*, May 1913, 10. Fishman's description of "the middle-class suburb of privilege" (5) in *Bourgeois Utopias* informs my definition of the garden suburb, which I use to designate largely upper-middle-class residential communities designed primarily for single-family houses in an open, parklike setting.

44. Van Sweringen Co., *The Heritage of the Shakers* (Cleveland, 1923), 6. Incorporated communities could still be absorbed by neighboring cities because state governments traditionally had the authority to modify the governmental boundaries within their jurisdictions. During the early- and mid-nineteenth century, when suburbs had much to gain in terms of sewer and water services, schools, and streets, residents of outlying areas sometimes offered little or no objection to joining the city. As the middle-class movement to the suburbs gained momentum in the second half of the nineteenth century, the services that autonomous suburbs could provide for themselves began to seem better to many residents than those that the city could provide, while the emergence of something like a suburban identity also foiled efforts to merge city and suburb: "As suburban services and self-consciousness became stronger, the desire for absorption into the metropolis waned, and fewer annexations were unopposed: some took place over the objec-

tions of 90 percent of those concerned" (Jackson, *Crabgrass Frontier*, 147). Sam Bass Warner Jr. notes that after 1873 residents of Boston's suburbs no longer required or wanted to pay higher taxes for the city's basic residential services, and opponents to annexation "frankly stated that independent suburban towns could maintain native American life free from Boston's waves of incoming poor immigrants" (*Streetcar Suburbs*, 164).

45. Douglass also noted that suburbs were inhabited primarily by economically middle-class people. The rich could maintain city and country residences, and the poor could not afford housing and transportation costs (*Suburban Trend*, 95). Douglass has recently been praised for his inclusiveness, that is, for recognizing the presence of the working class, the foreign born, and African Americans in suburbs, in contrast with the narrow focus of historians on middle-class residential suburbs. See Wunsch, "The Suburban Cliché."

46. Jack London, *The Sea-Wolf* (1904; rpt., New York: Grosset and Dunlap, 1906), 25, 294. In the novel the city is associated with Van Weyden's effeteness and inadequacy—in short, with overcivilization; Wolf Larsen calls him a " 'Frisco tanglefoot" (29). London's influence on Burroughs as an adventure writer and a rancher is examined in Kevin Starr, *Material Dreams: Southern California through the 1920s* (New York: Oxford University Press, 1990), 74–76.

47. Brian V. Street points out that Tarzan's jungle upbringing "is not enough to erase generations of hereditary good breeding"; "his British heritage," not his humanity, marks his superiority to the apes (*The Savage in Literature: Representations of "Primitive" Society in English Fiction, 1858–1920* [London: Routledge, 1975], 108–9).

48. W. L. Pollard, "Outline of the Law of Zoning in the United States," *Annals of the American Academy of Political and Social Science* 155 (May 1931), 15. Although the first comprehensive zoning plan was not adopted until 1916, municipalities had passed zoning legislation since the nineteenth century. Modesto, California's discriminatory ordinance of 1885 that segregated laundries, an almost exclusively Chinese industry in California, has generally been regarded as the first recorded zoning ordinance. In 1926 the suburb of Euclid, Ohio, won its Supreme Court case to establish single-family residential areas as the highest type of land use from which other types of housing might be banned.

49. Madison Grant, *The Passing of the Great Race, or, The Racial Basis of European History* (New York: Scribner's, 1916), 79.

50. *Ordinances and Resolutions of the Mayor and City Council of Baltimore, 1910–1911* (Baltimore: King, 1911), 204.

51. Clement E. Vose, *Caucasians Only: The Supreme Court, the NAACP, and the Restrictive Covenant Cases* (Berkeley and Los Angeles: University of California Press, 1959), 4. In an interesting role reversal, the plaintiff in *Buchanan v. Warley* was a white realtor, while the defendant was the black president of the Louisville branch of the NAACP. Warley had contracted to purchase a lot in a white block so that he could back out of the arrangement on the grounds that the local ordinance forbade it. Buchanan then simply sought to enforce the contract. This strategy was adopted because the Court had shown itself only too willing since *Plessy v. Ferguson* in 1896 to uphold Jim Crow laws, and the NAACP hoped that where the Court would not intervene to protect the rights of black citizens,

it would act to preserve the rights of white property owners. *Buchanan v. Warley* is described in detail in Garrett Power, "Apartheid Baltimore Style: The Residential Segregation Ordinances of 1910–1913," *Maryland Law Review* 42 (1983), 289–323.

52. Editorial, *Roland Park Review*, April 1911, 6.

53. Joy Wheeler Dow, *American Renaissance: A Review of Domestic Architecture* (New York: Comstock, 1904), 18.

54. F. Scott Fitzgerald, *The Great Gatsby* (New York: Scribner's, 1925), 4, 107, 54.

55. David E. Tarn, "Co-operative Group Plannings," *Architectural Record* 34 (November 1913), 467–75.

56. Stilgoe, *Borderlands*, 223.

57. Olmsted Associates to Kirkland Land Company, 1906, Olmsted Associates Papers, no. 71, Library of Congress.

58. Francis H. Bulot, "Developing a Restricted Home Community," *American City* 15 (November 1916), 534.

59. Sage Foundation Homes Company, "Forest Hills Gardens," (New York, 1909), unpaginated. The "laboring man, whose wages are small" had to look elsewhere for housing outside the city.

60. Stilgoe draws an explicit contrast between uneven development of borderland areas, especially before 1916, and the controls exercised by planned residential communities, with an emphasis on the effects on the landscape. He observes that most restrictions were designed more to prevent anomalies than to exercise complete control; most house owners still wanted the freedom to shape their houses and properties to their own tastes. Stilgoe notes in passing the racial covenants at Forest Hills as part of the general project of establishing a uniform environment, but overall he has little to say about the efforts to enforce racial homogeneity in the suburbs. See *Borderlands*, 225–68.

61. Howells, "A Pedestrian Tour," in *Suburban Sketches*, 71.

62. See James F. Waesche, *Crowning the Gravelly Hill: A History of the Roland Park—Guilford—Homeland District* (Baltimore: Maclay, 1987). Warner notes that residential covenants came into "general suburban use" outside Boston toward the end of the nineteenth century. They "restricted purchasers to single-family houses, or forbade three-family or larger multiple structures. The minimum costs of houses to be erected were often established. Factories, saloons, and livery stables were almost always targets of residential covenants. . . . Set back and side yard lines limiting the placement of houses to certain positions on the lot, restrictions against fences or limits on their height, and rules governing the number and size of collateral structures were general" (*Streetcar Suburbs*, 122). The possibilities were endless. But Warner finds no evidence of covenants against racial, religious, or ethnic groups before 1900. By the 1920s restrictive covenants that applied to entire established neighborhoods in perpetuity were widespread, and not only in garden suburbs. As agreements between private parties, such covenants were held exempt from the 1917 ruling on civic segregation ordinances. In the spirit of *Buchanan v. Warley*, some state courts decided that while contracts prohibiting the occupancy of properties by nonwhites were valid, those forbidding the sale or rental of properties to them were not. In short, these courts protected

the right of white owners to profit from their real estate holdings while ensuring that white neighbors did not suffer any unpleasant consequences from the exercise of those rights. In theory, racial covenants might have been used to exclude whites from certain properties and neighborhoods; Vose demonstrates, however, that in practice they were inevitably used to protect white families and their property. Only in 1948, in *Shelley v. Kramer*, did the U.S. Supreme Court rule that racial covenants were legally unenforceable under the Fourteenth Amendment.

63. See Lott, *Love and Theft*; and Michael Rogin, *Black Face, White Noise: Jewish Immigrants in the Hollywood Melting Pot* (Berkeley and Los Angeles: University of California Press, 1996).

64. Throughout *Tarzan* the American Porters reveal aristocratic natures through an obsession with defending their honor. The plot twists in the second half of the novel hinge on their determination to fulfill obligations despite the misery that will inevitably result. Jane's father, unable to repay a ten-thousand-dollar debt to Robert Canler, whom Jane despises, promises Canler her hand in marriage to save his honor. Even after Tarzan has recovered her father's treasure, enabling him to repay the debt, Jane intends to go through with the marriage to save her own. After Canler has withdrawn his proposal, Jane promises to marry John Clayton; she soon realizes her love for Tarzan but will not break her word because, again, it would be dishonorable. Well-born Americans in the novel are more honor-bound than the English; even though they are not aristocrats in the same way that the English may be, they are determined to live by ostensibly noble values.

65. See Bederman, *Manliness and Civilization*, 219–32. Bederman's reading updates the response of an earlier generation of critics, who saw Tarzan's primitive masculinity as a pleasurable release for readers from the restrictions of civilized life. See Roderick Nash, *Wilderness and the American Mind* (New Haven: Yale University Press, 1967), 156; and James D. Hart, *The Popular Book: A History of America's Literary Taste* (Berkeley and Los Angeles: University of California Press, 1963), 219–20.

66. Advertisement, *Los Angeles Times*, October 1, 1922, V14.

67. The clause was extracted from a 1926 property deed in Tarzana.

68. The racial covenants actually preexisted Burroughs's ownership of the land, but Danton Burroughs, the author's grandson, told me in March 1994 that his grandfather did not want black residents in Tarzana. Subsequent novels demonstrate Tarzan's willingness to live with the "magnificent" Waziri tribe, whom he first befriends in *The Return of Tarzan* (serialized 1913; rpt., New York: Ballantine, 1963). In a straightforward imperial fantasy, the Waziri make him their king and become loyal subjects and domestic servants on his vast African estate. In fact, their loyalty and willing service mark their superiority to "west coast blacks" (84), like those he battles in *Tarzan of the Apes*. On Tarzan's domestication of the Waziri, see Torgovnick, *Gone Primitive*, 55–57.

69. Advertisement, *Los Angeles Times*, October 1, 1922, V14.

70. Edgar Rice Burroughs, *Tarzan and the Golden Lion* (serialized 1922; rpt., New York: Ballantine, 1963), 111.

71. Advertisement, *Los Angeles Times*, October 8, 1922, V13. His success as a writer aside, Burroughs was remarkable for his business failures, and Tarzana

was initially a flop. Burroughs's efforts were more successful the following year when he hired a real estate professional, who lured prospective buyers to the property with gimmicks such as a "great jungle barbecue" served by Elmo Lincoln, the original movie Tarzan (Irwin Porges, *Edgar Rice Burroughs: The Man Who Created Tarzan* [Provo, Utah: Brigham Young University Press, 1975], 382).

72. *Why Tarzana Lots Are the Best Buy on Ventura Boulevard* (Unpaginated pamphlet, 1920s).

CHAPTER TWO
SINCLAIR LEWIS AND THE REVOLT FROM THE SUBURB

1. Glen A. Love is particularly insistent on the "technological sublim[ity]" (75) of Zenith in *Babbitt: An American Life* (New York: Twayne, 1993). Page references to *Babbitt* are from Sinclair Lewis, *Babbitt* (New York: Signet, 1991).

2. On the architectural and ideological appeal of the Colonial revival in the suburbs, see Gowans, *The Comfortable House*, 101–65. Dutch Colonial designs feature prominently in house plan books of the period. See, for example, Sears, Roebuck and Company, *Honor-Bilt Modern Homes* (Chicago, 1922); and Architects' Small House Service Bureau, *Small Homes of Architectural Distinction* (Minneapolis, 1927). Several of the designs include sleeping porches, which Robert S. Lynd and Helen Merrell Lynd identified as a popular amenity among middle-class residents of Muncie, Indiana. See *Middletown: A Study in American Culture* (1929; rpt., New York: Harcourt, 1956), 96.

3. Lewis to Carl Van Doren (1920), in Lewis, *The Man from Main Street: Selected Essays and Other Writings, 1904–1950*, ed. Harry E. Maule and Melville H. Cane (1953; rpt., New York: Pocket Books, 1963), 135.

4. Jackson, *Crabgrass Frontier*, 163; Sies, "The City Transformed," 106. On the pace of new house construction, see Jackson, *Crabgrass Frontier*, 175; on the impact of the car and the new road construction on suburbanization, see 157–77; and Foster, *From Streetcar to Superhighway*, which also discusses the population growth-rate differential. Foster links these statistics to the "virtually unanimous" agreement among demographers that American suburbanization "intensified in the 1920s" (47). On the "new suburban advocacy" in the 1920s and "the suburban domestic ideal" as "a mass-produced commodity" (137), see also Marsh, *Suburban Lives*, 129–81, who emphasizes the force of popular and government promotion in accelerating the rush to the suburbs; and Gwendolyn Wright, *Building the Dream*, chap. 11. Advertising has been linked to suburbanization by Dolores Hayden, insofar as it "promoted the private suburban dwelling as a setting for all other purchases" (*Redesigning the American Dream*, 34). Roland Marchand similarly notes the prominence of the single-family house in periodical advertisements of the twenties; he suggests that the suburb molded advertising as much as advertising molded the suburb, in part because it shaped the advertisers, who identified the consumers for their products as people very much like themselves, a select group of affluent commuters and their wives. See *Advertising the American Dream*, 77–80. In 1917, one writer for a suburban periodical defended her decision to move to the suburbs by invoking the authority of the "most modern of all artists and all writers—the advertisers. It is not to the city-dweller that they make

their appeals. The radiators which bring warmth and happiness to father and mother and all the family are pictured as in the suburban home" ("Why Is a Suburb?" *Countryside* 24 [July 1917], 370). The writer, who touted the material and spiritual benefits of suburban life for all family members, all but directly responded to the question of her title with the answer "consumption."

5. The emphasis on the mutual exclusiveness of allegiance and rebellion is best captured in Frederick J. Hoffman's influential description of the "sensitive, humane" "anti-Babbitt" in *The Twenties: American Writing in a Postwar Decade* (New York: Viking, 1955), 367. See also Anthony Channell Hilfer, *The Revolt from the Village, 1915–1930* (Chapel Hill: University of North Carolina Press, 1969), 168–76; Mark Schorer, "Sinclair Lewis and the Method of Half-Truths," in *Sinclair Lewis: A Collection of Critical Essays*, ed. Schorer (Englewood Cliffs, N.J.: Prentice-Hall, 1962), 46–61; and Martin Light, *The Quixotic Vision of Sinclair Lewis* (West Lafayette, Ind.: Purdue University Press, 1975). Among contemporaneous critics see Robert Littell, review, *New Republic* 32 (October 4, 1922), 152; and Edmund Wilson, "Wanted—A City of the Spirit," *Vanity Fair* 21 (January 1924), 63, 94. Schorer notes in his biography that most of the contemporary criticism of *Babbitt* came from those who sympathized with its ambitions but were disappointed at Lewis's failure to identify the positive values that might point the way to the salvation of Babbitt and his country. See *Sinclair Lewis: An American Life* (New York: McGraw-Hill, 1961), 343–60. Clare Virginia Eby updates the conventional reading of the novel as a failed liberal rebellion by arguing that Babbitt specifically rejects "the duty of being manly," but is unable to resist the pressure to conform to conventional standards of masculinity ("*Babbitt* as Veblenian Critique of Manliness," *American Studies* 33–34 [1992–93], 6). In *Babbitt: An American Life*, Love locates Babbitt's humanity in the unstandardized particularity of his desires, which withstands his inability to be true to them.

6. Light, *Quixotic Vision*, 84.

7. Lewis, *Main Street* (1920; rpt., New York: Carroll and Graf, 1996), 286, 290, 390, 448. When the 1920 census revealed that for the first time a majority of Americans lived in cities, Lewis's claim in the foreword—"This is America"—was already obsolete.

8. Edith Wharton to Lewis, cited in R. W. B. Lewis, *Edith Wharton: A Biography* (1975; rpt., New York: Fromm, 1985), 435.

9. Carl Van Doren described recent literary criticisms of small town provincialism in "The Revolt from the Village: 1920," *Nation* 113 (October 12, 1921), 407–12.

10. Wilson, *White Collar Fictions*, 236.

11. Jackson Lears, *Fables of Abundance: A Cultural History of Advertising in America* (New York: Basic, 1994), 357, 352. Lears offers a more nuanced interpretation of Babbitt than do most historians, who have traditionally embraced him as the standard figure against which other people's rebellions during the rebellious 1920s were defined. As early as 1931, Frederick Allen represented Babbitt as "the arch enemy of the enlightened," the antithesis of the Jazz Age's disillusionment and iconoclasm (*Only Yesterday: An Informal History of the 1920s* [1931; rpt., New York: Harper, 1964], 161). See also Caroline F. Ware, *Greenwich Village, 1920–1930* (Boston: Houghton Mifflin, 1935); John W. Aldridge, *After the*

Lost Generation (New York: McGraw-Hill, 1951); and, most pertinently, Eliza-beth Stevenson, *Babbitts and Bohemians: The American 1920s* (New York: Mac-millan, 1967). Babbitt continues to be invoked as the figure for the devotional consumer and materialist, in and out of the twenties. See, for example, Lynn Du-menil, *The Modern Temper: American Culture and Society in the 1920s* (New York: Hill and Wang, 1995), 76; and Don Slater, *Consumer Culture and Moder-nity* (London: Polity, 1997), 13.

12. Lears, *Fables of Abundance*, 357, my emphasis.

13. Lewis, "Self-Portrait," in *Man from Main Street*, 45.

14. H. L. Mencken, "Portrait of an American Citizen," rpt. in Schorer, *Sinclair Lewis: A Collection of Critical Essays*, 20; Lewis Mumford, "The America of Sinclair Lewis," *Current History* 33 (January 1931), 531. Joel Fischer observes that the pairing of *Babbitt* and *Middletown* became commonplace in the works of later critics, in which the novel is treated as the "fictional correlative" of the sociology, which in turn adopted its style of analysis from the novel ("Sinclair Lewis and the Diagnostic Novel: *Main Street* and *Babbitt*," *Journal of American Studies* 20 [1986], 422). David C. Pugh has argued even more strongly that since the Lynds, "social scientists have fashioned their prose techniques after ones that Lewis had already used, so that now he reads (more so than in 1922) 'just like a sociology book' " ("Baedekers, Babbittry, and Baudelaire," in *Critical Essays on Sinclair Lewis*, ed. Martin Bucco [Boston: G. K. Hall, 1986], 205). The absence of any reference to Lewis in *Middletown* is striking, especially since the Lynds discuss a few stories by Sherwood Anderson, who was far less culturally signifi-cant than Lewis, to Anderson's eternal chagrin. It is tempting to read the exclusion as deliberate. It may have to do with differences in tone, despite the similarity of the "findings." The Lynds expressed their commitment to giving an impersonal, impartial assessment of Muncie, Indiana, which could be a veiled reference to Lewis's own stridency. Also, the Lynds might have chafed at directing readers to a novelist who had, in many respects, scooped them.

15. Littell, review of *Babbitt*, 152.

16. Van Wyck Brooks, "The Culture of Industrialism" (1917), rpt. in *Van Wyck Brooks: The Early Years*, ed. Claire Sprague (New York: Harper, 1968), 195; Waldo Frank, *Our America* (New York: Boni and Liveright, 1919), 23, 30.

17. Brooks, *The Wine of the Puritans* (1908), rpt. in Sprague, *Van Wyck Brooks*, 5, 6, 7.

18. See Casey Blake, "The Young Intellectuals and the Culture of Personality," *American Literary History* 1 (Fall 1989), 510–34.

19. Susan Hegeman, *Patterns for America: Modernism and the Concept of Cul-ture* (Princeton: Princeton University Press, 1999), 105.

20. Mumford, "The Wilderness of Suburbia," *New Republic* 28 (September 7, 1921), 45. In the 1920s Mumford participated in the Regional Planning Associ-ation of America, which he cofounded in 1923. He was interested in combining the best features of urban and rural life, with the help of new technologies, in communities that eschewed the extremes of the skyscraper metropolis and the residential suburb. On Mumford's work with the association and his influence as a theorist of American architecture and culture, see Donald L. Miller, *Lewis Mumford, A Life* (New York: Weidenfeld and Nicolson, 1989). Stilgoe mentions

the hostility of American intellectuals to the suburbs in the 1920s, but his analysis focuses more on their response to built environments in general, and although he addresses the hostility of intellectuals to the middle class, he does not discuss examples that pertain to the suburbanite. See *Borderlands*, 285–90.

21. Harold Stearns, preface, *Civilization in the United States: An Inquiry by Thirty Americans*, ed. Stearns (New York: Harcourt, 1922), vii.

22. Mumford, "The City," in Stearns, *Civilization in the United States*, 16, 14, 16. He emphasized plumbing and heating because they also demonstrated the profound dependence of the so-called private house on infrastructure, relations, and networks that ordinarily remained hidden: "the modern house . . . has become the nucleus of communal and domestic services with connections and filaments throughout the rest of the community" ("The American Dwelling-House," *American Mercury* 19 [April 1930], 474). See also "The Wilderness of Suburbia," 44–45.

23. Stearns, "The Intellectual Life," in *Civilization in the United States*, 145–46. Stearns comes closest in tone to the intellectuals that John Carey discusses in relation to the British suburb and suburban values in *The Intellectuals and the Masses: Pride and Prejudice among the Literary Intelligentsia, 1880–1939* (London: Faber and Faber, 1992), 46–70. The British suburb functioned as an opportunity for intellectuals to express unambiguous class superiority. In contrast with the United States, the British suburb was stereotyped as the home of underpaid clerks; it was associated with spiritual inadequacy because it also signified material insecurity.

24. Stearns, preface, iii, vii.

25. Janet Hutchison, "Building for Babbitt: The State and the Suburban Home Ideal," *Journal of Policy History* 9 (1997), 184–210; Karen Dunn-Haley, "The House that Uncle Sam Built: The Political Culture of Federal Housing Policy, 1919–1932" (Ph.D. diss., Stanford University, 1995), 95. See also Dunn-Haley, chap. 4. Hutchison documents the considerable impact of the "Own Your Own Home" agenda on middle-class suburbs and on consumption.

26. Marsh, *Suburban Lives*, 148. Marsh argues that homeownership was not a consistent suburban imperative; at the turn of the century location generally mattered more to white middle-class suburban families than ownership, although as both Sam Bass Warner Jr. (*Streetcar Suburbs*, 101) and Gwendolyn Wright (*Moralism and the Model Home*, 80) have pointed out, homeownership was nonetheless identified as an important middle-class value by the late-nineteenth century. It wasn't until the 1920s, Marsh claims, that it was again widely touted as a foundation of good citizenship, as it had been in the mid-nineteenth century, and for the first time became a crucial sign of middle-class status, especially in the burgeoning suburbs. On anti-immigrant sentiment and the racialization of American citizenship in the 1920s, see Walter Benn Michaels, *Our America: Nativism, Modernism, and Pluralism* (Durham, N.C.: Duke University Press, 1995); and Matthew Frye Jacobson, *Whiteness of a Different Color: European Immigrants and the Alchemy of Race* (Cambridge: Harvard University Press, 1998).

27. William Leach, *Land of Desire: Merchants, Power, and the Rise of a New American Culture* (New York: Pantheon, 1993), 354. See pp. 349–78 for a superb account of Hoover's active role in fostering a new corporate economy of consump-

tion, which refutes the view of Hoover as reluctant to interfere in the economy. As Commerce secretary, Hoover preached not only the virtues of house ownership and consumerism but of standardization in production. In "Standardization—Bane or Blessing," J. George Frederick called him, only partly in jest, "the Lord High Executioner of thousands of superfluous sizes, models, shapes, and kinds of American goods, and the Great Standardizer of the industrial era" (*Outlook* 145 [January 12, 1927], 50).

28. Herbert Hoover, "The Home as an Investment," *Delineator* 101 (October 1922), 17. The magazine's "Better Homes for America" program boasted the patronage of prominent government officials and business leaders, including Vice President Calvin Coolidge, who wrote the lead article. Until its demise in World War II, it sponsored model house exhibitions and contests across the country in conjunction with local chapters and chambers of commerce.

29. Hoover, foreword, John Gries, *How to Own Your Own Home* (Washington, D.C.: GPO, 1923), v. Although apartment house construction boomed in the 1920s, the apartment continued to be criticized for "fail[ing] to provide a home for its tenants," because "the home is based on privacy and individuality" (Randolph W. Sexton, *American Apartment Houses of Today* [New York, 1926], iv). On rates of apartment construction in city and suburb, see Coleman Woodbury, *Apartment House Increases and Attitudes Toward Home Ownership* (Chicago, 1931), vii. Hoover criticized the impermanence of "tenements [and] apartments," where a "man's home" was not "his castle," in his address in *The President's Conference on Home Building and Home Ownership*, 11 vols. (Washington, D. C.: GPO, 1932), 11:2.

30. Lewis, *The Job: An American Novel* (1917; rpt., Lincoln: University of Nebraska Press, 1994). The free enterpriser's decline as a major middle-class social and economic force in the twentieth century is most famously articulated by C. Wright Mills in *White Collar: The American Middle Classes* (1951; rpt., New York: Oxford University Press, 1956). Olivier Zunz positions himself against Mills in arguing for the impact that white-collar managerial employees had on the corporate workplace in *Making America Corporate, 1870–1920* (Chicago: University of Chicago Press, 1990). On the rise of the new bureaucracy from the late-nineteenth century through World War II, see also Chandler, *The Visible Hand.*

31. Jean-Christophe Agnew, "A House of Fiction: Domestic Interiors and the Commodity Aesthetic," in Bonner, *Consuming Visions*, 135. In *Advertising the American Dream*, Marchand discusses the telling transition in the early 1920s from the product to "the potential consumer" as advertising's "protagonist" (18).

32. Janice Radway, *A Feeling for Books: The Book-of-the-Month Club, Literary Taste, and Middle-Class Desire* (Chapel Hill: University of North Carolina Press, 1997), 242, 246, 244. Radway is drawing on articles about standardization in the popular press, which specifically cited Babbitt as the worst-case scenario. See, for example, Stuart Chase, "One Dead Level," *New Republic* 48 (September 29, 1926), 137–39; and Earnest Elmo Calkins, "Twin Peas in a Pod," *Atlantic Monthly* 136 (September 1925), 311–18.

33. See Cecelia Tichi, *Shifting Gears: Technology, Literature, Culture in Modernist America* (Chapel Hill: University of North Carolina Press, 1987). Tichi of-

fers the best account of Lewis's clunky prose as "the stylistic nemesis of the efficient ideals of streamlining or verbal economy" (90). On the primacy of authenticity in relation to the modern aesthetic of the machine, see also Miles Orvell, *The Real Thing: Imitation and Authenticity in American Culture, 1880–1940* (Chapel Hill: University of North Carolina Press, 1989).

34. Mark Seltzer, *Bodies and Machines* (New York: Routledge, 1992), 83. See also Walter Benn Michaels, "An American Tragedy or the Promise of American Life?" *Representations* 25 (Winter 1989), 71–98.

35. Stuart Chase and F. J. Schink, "Consumers in Wonderland," *New Republic* 48 (September 1925), 14, 12.

36. Daniel Horowitz, *The Morality of Spending: Attitudes toward the Consumer Society in America, 1875–1940* (Baltimore: Johns Hopkins University Press, 1985), 118. Through an analysis of family budget studies, he suggests that middle-class consumers in the early-twentieth century associated a rising standard of living not primarily with narcissism or massification but with refinement, culture, and comfort. On the perpetually dissatisfied consumer, see Ewen, *Captains of Consciousness*. As depicted here, Babbitt's discontent has much in common with Emile Durkheim's concept of *anomie*, in which dissatisfaction must always be an effect of an ever temporary satisfaction, because individual desires in modern society are wholly unregulated, limitless, and inherently insatiable. See *Suicide: A Study in Sociology*, trans. John A. Spaulding and George Simpson (Glencoe, Ill.: Free Press, 1951). In *Babbitt*, however, as I suggest below, dissatisfaction is also important as a mechanism of self-pitying satisfaction.

37. *Babbitt*'s cranky housewives fit the model of disaffected leisure described by Tom Lutz in " 'Sweat or Die': The Hedonization of the Work Ethic in the 1920s," *American Literary History* 8 (Summer 1996), 259–83. In light of a wide range of texts that includes Lewis's *Main Street* and *Arrowsmith* (1925), Lutz makes the case that in the 1920s the work ethic was transformed rather than abandoned, as alienation and boredom were frequently associated with leisure and seen to be resoluble only through an enjoyable indulgence in meaningful hard work.

Ruth Schwartz Cohan argues that the time women spent on housework did not decrease with the introduction of labor-saving equipment; even in prosperous households, women in the 1920s and 1930s spent roughly as much time on housework as their mothers had. See *More Work for Mother: The Ironies of Household Technology from the Open Hearth to the Microwave* (New York: Basic, 1983). In the early decades of the twentieth century, domestic scientists promoted hygienic, easy-to-clean interiors and greater efficiency for better family health and increased housewife and family satisfaction. Treating the labor of the household as a "trained profession" and a "business enterprise" might preempt discontent with the routine of housework, if the housewife could be made to feel more like a "manager" and "engineer" than an ordinary worker (C. W. Taber, *The Business of the Household* [Philadelphia: Lippincott, 1918], 1). For example, Christine Frederick, the household editor at *Ladies' Home Journal* and head of the Applecroft Home Experiment Station, argued that when managed according to Frederick Winslow Taylor's scientific principles, which had transformed labor in the factory, housework "was drudgery or degrading only if I allowed myself to think so" (*Household Engineering* [1915; rpt., Chicago: American School of Home Economics, 1920], 15). On the domestic science movement, see Susan Strasser, *Never Done: A History of American Housework* (New York: Pantheon, 1982), chap. 11; and Annegret S. Ogden, *The Great American Housewife, from Helpmate to Wage Earner, 1776–1986* (Westport, Conn.: Greenwood, 1986), 141–62.

38. See Leslie Feidler, *Love and Death in the American Novel* (New York: Criterion, 1960).

39. Daniel J. Boorstin, *The Americans: The Democratic Experience* (New York: Random House, 1973), 89, 136.

40. See especially the essays in *The City: Suggestions for the Investigation of Human Behavior in the Urban Environment*, ed. Robert Park, Ernest W. Burgess, and Robert D. McKenzie (1925; rpt., Chicago: University of Chicago Press, 1967); and Louis Wirth, "Urbanism as a Way of Life," *American Journal of Sociology* 44 (July 1938), 1–24. Park, the most famous and influential of the group, drew upon the seminal work of his mentor, the German philosopher Georg Simmel, who theorized extensively about urban alienation in "The Metropolis and Mental Life" (1903), in *The Sociology of Georg Simmel*, trans. and ed. Kurt H. Wolff (New York: Free Press, 1950), 409–24. Simmel argued that the intensity of psychical stimulation in the metropolis blunts discrimination; the metropolitan person responds intellectually rather than emotionally, and as the mind no longer distinguishes between and engages each image or contact, he or she becomes increasingly blasé. As urban life is structurally and psychologically more complex and impersonal than the village or small town, the result of its demand for extreme differentiation is indifference.

41. Wirth-Nesher, *City Codes*, 20.

42. For example, in 1922 Ethel Carpenter authored an eleven-part series called "The Complete Furnishing of the Little House," which described, among other things, her living room, where "[t]he woodwork was all white," the "serene beauty" of blue when used in combination with gray or cream-colored walls, and the virtues of mahogany ("Walls and Ceilings—The Background of Your Rooms," *Ladies' Home Journal* 39 [January 1922], 29; "Creating Color Schemes" [April 1922], 99).

43. See Marsh, *Suburban Lives*, 141–46; and Wright, *Moralism and the Model Home*, 244–46. The change from the numerous small, specialized rooms of Victorian houses to the greater openness of family living spaces was well underway in the early 1900s.

44. Richard Le Gallienne, "The Spirit of the House," *House and Garden* 41 (May 1922), 102. See also Alice Van Leer Carrick, "Housekeeping in the Little House," *Ladies' Home Journal* 39 (November 1922), 12; and Oscar Lewis, "To Buy or to Build?" *House Beautiful* 61 (January 1927), 45, 88–91. A 1945 housing survey in the *Saturday Evening Post* claimed that only 14 percent of Americans preferred to live in a "used" house or apartment. See Jackson, *Crabgrass Frontier*, 240–45; and Gwendolyn Wright, "Prescribing the Model Home," in Mack, *Home: A Place in the World*, 216–21. Until the post–World War II period, it was not unusual for prospective house owners to buy a lot from a subdivider and hire a builder or, less frequently, an architect to construct the house in which they

would live. In his own Glen Oriole development, Babbitt lays out and sells lots but seems to leave the house-building to the owners.

45. Schudson, *Advertising, the Uneasy Persuasion*, 145. On "buying [as] a form of belonging" (61), see also Christopher P. Wilson, "The Rhetoric of Consumption: Mass-Market Magazines and the Demise of the Gentle Reader, 1880–1920," in Fox and Lears, *The Culture of Consumption*, 40–64. In *Babbitt*, masculine consumption is seldom "organized as a discourse with oneself" (Jean Baudrillard, "Consumer Society," in *Selected Writings*, ed. Mark Poster [Stanford: Stanford University Press, 1988], 54). It "differentiates," as Baudrillard continues, among categories of consumers, "if it no longer isolates," without achieving "*collective solidarity*" (54–55) beyond the activity of consumption itself and its immediate psychological and social uses. On the role of goods in making and maintaining social relationships, see also Mary Douglas and Baron Isherwood, *The World of Goods* (New York: Basic, 1979). On emulation and social competition, see Thorstein Veblen, *The Theory of the Leisure Class* (1899; rpt., New York: Mentor, 1953).

46. Lewis, *Dodsworth* (New York: Harcourt, 1929), 125. The postmodern is associated with "a world where locality seems to have lost its ontological moorings" (Arjun Appadurai, "The Production of Locality," in *City at Large: Cultural Dimensions of Globalization* [Minneapolis: University of Minnesota Press, 1996], 178), and functions as a synonym for the "consumption-based . . . city" (Ruth Fincher and Jane M. Jacobs, introduction, *Cities of Difference*, ed. Fincher and Jacobs [New York: Guilford, 1998], 13). On the constitutive dislocations of postmodernism, see also David Harvey, *The Condition of Postmodernity: An Enquiry into the Origins of Cultural Change* (London: Basil Blackwell, 1989); Doreen Massey, *Space, Place, and Gender* (Cambridge: Polity Press, 1994); and Sara Blair, "Cultural Geography and the Place of the Literary," *American Literary History* 10 (Fall 1998), 544–67. The dense materiality of Babbitt's world, the ceaseless bombardment of images, slogans, and things, as well as the erosion of boundaries between places, bring to mind Fredric Jameson's observation of postmodern space as involving both "the suppression of distance . . . and the relentless saturation of any remaining voids and empty places" (*Postmodernism, or, The Cultural Logic of Late Capitalism* [Durham, N.C.: Duke University Press, 1991], 412).

47. Martha Banta, *Taylored Lives: Narrative Productions in the Age of Taylor, Veblen, and Ford* (Chicago: University of Chicago Press, 1993), 192.

48. Lewis, "Adventures in Auto-bumming—The Great American Frying Pan," *Saturday Evening Post* 192 (January 3, 1920), 62. Lewis was an avid automobile traveler, and his experiences driving cross-country in the 1910s are fictionally recorded in *Free Air* (1919; rpt., Lincoln: University of Nebraska Press, 1993), which also describes the horrors of the small-town hotel.

49. On the paid vacation, see Daniel Rodgers, *The Work Ethic in Industrial America, 1850–1920* (Chicago: University of Chicago Press, 1978), 106. On automobile tourism and accommodations, see Warren Belasco, *Americans on the Road: From Autocamp to Motel, 1910–1945* (Cambridge: MIT Press, 1979).

50. See Jackson, *Crabgrass Frontier*, 174–81.

51. For a history of the Covered Wagon and other forms of motorized housing in the United States, see Michael Aaron Rockland, *Homes on Wheels* (New Brunswick, N.J.: Rutgers University Press, 1980).

52. Wayne Franklin and Michael Steiner, introduction, *Mapping American Culture*, ed. Franklin and Steiner (Iowa City: University of Iowa Press, 1992), 4.

53. Lewis, *Work of Art* (New York: Doubleday, 1935), 451, 450, 452.

54. See, for example, "Exit Frontier Morality," *New Republic* 37 (January 2, 1924), 137–38; and Katherine Anthony, "The Family," in Stearns, *Civilization in the United States*, 319–36.

55. Although Lewis wrote five best-selling, and for the most part critically acclaimed, novels in the 1920s, the last of which, *Dodsworth*, actively defended Americans against cold Europeans, he was generally considered to have won the Nobel Prize for *Babbitt*, because it justified the European conception of the ugly American.

56. Steven Marcus, "Sinclair Lewis," in *Representations: Essays on Literature and Society* (New York: Columbia University Press, 1975), 44; Love, *Babbitt: An American Life*, 62.

57. Lewis, *The Man from Main Street*, 21, 22–23.

58. Christine Frederick, "Is Suburban Living a Delusion?" *Outlook* 148 (February 22, 1928), 240. On Frederick and domestic science, see n. 37.

59. Ethel Longworth Swift, "In Defense of Suburbia," *Outlook* 148 (April 4, 1928), 543.

60. Littell, review of *Babbitt*, 152; Edmund Wilson, "Wanted—A City of the Spirit," 63.

61. Cited in Schorer, *Sinclair Lewis: An American Life*, 298.

62. May Sinclair, review of *Babbitt*, *New York Times*, September 23, 1922, sec. 3, p. 1.

63. Mumford, *Sticks and Stones* (1925; rpt., New York: Dover, 1955), 87–88.

64. Susman, "Culture and Civilization: The Nineteen-Twenties," in *Culture as History*, 116.

65. See Wright, *Building the Dream*, 240; Jackson, *Crabgrass Frontier*, 193. Jackson writes that "the victims were often middle-class families who were experiencing impoverishment for the first time" (193).

66. Lewis Corey, *The Crisis of the Middle Class* (1935; rpt., New York: Columbia University Press, 1992), 230.

67. Alfred M. Bingham, *Insurgent America: Revolt of the Middle-Classes* (New York: Harper, 1935), 117.

68. Lewis, *It Can't Happen Here* (1935; rpt., New York: Signet, 1993), 83, 79.

69. On Lewis's recuperation of the middle class in the thirties, see James T. Jones's quirky and clever essay, "A Middle-Class Utopia: Lewis's *It Can't Happen Here*," in *Sinclair Lewis at 100: Papers Presented at a Centennial Conference* (St. Cloud, Minn.: St. Cloud University Press, 1985), 213–25.

70. Lewis, *Kingsblood Royal* (New York: Random House, 1947), 43.

71. Langston Hughes, "The Negro Artist and the Racial Mountain," *Nation* 122 (June 28, 1926), 692, 693. Schorer notes in the biography that Lewis consulted with Hughes and Walter White, head of the NAACP, who made its files available to him for preliminary research. Zora Neale Hurston dubbed the white

people who were interested in black uplift "Negrotarians," the kind of term that Lewis loved to coin. Among the Harlem Negrotarians, some "who were earnest humanitarians," and some "who were merely fascinated," David Levering Lewis identifies Sinclair Lewis as one who generated no "serious controversy about [his] loyalty" (*When Harlem Was in Vogue* [New York: Oxford University Press, 1982], 98, 99).

72. E. Franklin Frazier, "La Bourgeoisie Noire," *Modern Quarterly* 5 (1928–30), 82. Frazier does not condemn the black middle class so much as analyze it to demonstrate the heterogeneity of a population often treated as a uniform mass. His response was far more hostile in the book-length study *Black Bourgeoisie* (1955; rpt., New York: Collier, 1962).

73. See Norman Mailer, "The White Negro" (1957), rpt. in *Advertisements for Myself* (Cambridge: Harvard University Press, 1992), 337–58.

74. Among Lewis's papers at the Beinecke Library, Yale University, are some two dozen letters written in response to *Kingsblood Royal*. A remarkable few are written by white Southerners, who felt that it had opened their eyes for the first time to the reality and brutality of racial injustice and who vowed to amend their own practices and to teach their children about the equality of the races. While it is astonishing to think that Southerners needed a novel by Lewis to make racism manifest, and impossible to gauge its concrete political effects, we do know that some readers credited it with the possibility of productive social change.

75. In *Whiteness of a Different Color*, Jacobson is quite right to note that *Kingsblood Royal* both inscribes race as a black-white dichotomy and undermines such an inscription by exposing the kinds of biological confusions that permit a "white" man suddenly to discover that he is really "black." He is wrong, however, to argue that the novel is more interested in the "messiness" of biology than in "the social conventions and acts of fabrication that go into the enforcement of the racial order" (270). The climaxes of the novel, the mass firing of all black people who work in the city and the attack on the Kingsblood house, emphasize the tremendous legal, social, economic, and political consequences of racial ascription rather than the nuances of racial identity per se.

CHAPTER THREE
MILDRED PIERCE'S INTERIORS

1. James M. Cain, *Mildred Pierce* (1941; rpt., New York: Vintage, 1989), 3–4.

2. With the late-nineteenth-century Mission revival movement, white southern Californians embraced a romanticized Spanish past and tended to ignore the period of Mexican rule before the U.S. conquest. By the building boom of the 1920s Spanish Colonial had become a favorite style in residential, civic, and commercial architecture. Spanish-influenced house designs were especially popular in southern California and Florida, but ready-made house manufacturers such as Sears, Roebuck and Montgomery Ward made them available nationwide. See Merry Ovnick, *Los Angeles: The End of the Rainbow* (Los Angeles: Balcony Press, 1994), 179–97; and David Gebhard, "The Spanish Colonial Revival in Southern California (1895–1930)," *Journal of the Society of Architectural Historians* 26

(May 1967), 131–47. In *Suburban Lives* Marsh discusses the example of Palos Verdes, an affluent planned suburb that excluded Mexican Americans but mandated Spanish or "California" architecture (172–73).

Glendale was well known as a "lily white," lower-middle-class residential community, not only in the assessment of Carey McWilliams (*Southern California Country: An Island on the Land* [1946; rpt., Salt Lake City, Utah: Peregrine Smith, 1973], 328), certainly the shrewdest chronicler of California in the first half of the century, but also in its own promotional literature. See *Glendale, Your Home* (Glendale Merchants Association, 1928); and Eugene Hoy, *So This Is Glendale* (Glendale: 1939). Glendale's hostility to African Americans was such that black servants were not allowed to spend the night in their houses of employment: "No Negro sleeps overnight in our town" (cited in Ovnick, *Los Angeles*, 244). Race is virtually invisible as a suburban subject in *Mildred Pierce*, in which threats to property ownership emerge exclusively in relation to the economic crisis of the Depression. It is manifested obliquely as a residual trace in the architecture, which is as much about degraded middle-class tastes as regional ethnic origins.

3. Bruce Bliven, "Los Angeles: The City That Is Bacchanalian—in a Nice Way," *New Republic* 51 (July 13, 1927), 198; Robert M. Fogelson, *The Fragmented Metropolis: Los Angeles, 1850–1930* (1967; rpt., Berkeley and Los Angeles: University of California Press, 1993), 144–45; *Los Angeles: A Guide to the City and Its Environs* (New York: Hastings House, 1941), 6. McWilliams also declared the region of Los Angeles to be "a collection of suburbs in search of a city" (*Southern California Country*, 235). *Fragmented Metropolis* is the classic study of regional development. It links the spatial and the sociopolitical disconnection of the city and region that famously lacked a dominant physical center and unifying civic life. See pp. 63–84 for a discussion of the salient census figures on the extraordinary population growth during these years. Mexicans, who were categorized as nonwhite by the 1930 census, were the largest minority group, and the city of Los Angeles also had a sizable African American population, especially after the boom of the twenties, and a smaller Japanese American population.

Both recent and earlier accounts of the Los Angeles region often conflate "streetcar suburbs" and incorporated cities such as Glendale and Pasadena, where much of *Mildred Pierce* is set (Starr, *Material Dreams*, 84). That is, separate cities are folded into discussions of the generally suburban character of the metropolitan area. Thus without a sense of contradiction one writer could describe Glendale as a "self-contained" city in its own right and also as "the bedroom of Los Angeles" (Mel Wharton, "Nothing Stands Still in Glendale," *Southern California Business* 9 [October 1930], 12). Cain explicitly did not conceive of Glendale as a separate entity. It is described as "an endless suburb of Los Angeles, bearing the same relation to Los Angeles as Queens bears to New York" (9).

4. The reference to department store furniture is reminiscent as well of Theodore Dreiser's description of the Hurstwood residence in *Sister Carrie* (1900; rpt., New York: Norton, 1970). *Sister Carrie* has been read by Philip Fisher as a testimony to the modern city's embodiment of consumer desire: "far from being in any simple way estranged in the city, man is for the first time surrounded by himself" (*Hard Facts: Setting and Form in the American Novel* [New York: Oxford University Press, 1985], 132). Amy Kaplan identifies *Sister Carrie* and the turn-

of-the-century realist project in general with the ambition to make a disorienting urban landscape of apartments, lodging houses, and hotel rooms "inhabitable and representable" to a middle-class readership (*The Social Construction of American Realism*, 12). But Dreiser introduces an ancillary narrative of estrangement that directs the reader's attention toward the distinctly alienating artifacts of metropolitan domestic culture. Dreiser offers a brief homage to "[a] lovely home atmosphere . . . than which there is nothing more tender, nothing more delicate" (63), and then deplores its utter absence at the Hurstwoods. Before the novel chronicles the strained relations between Hurstwood and his family, it immediately links the deficiency of the home to the house's "fine" but anonymous furnishings: "There were soft rugs, rich, upholstered chairs and divans, a grand piano, a marble carving of some unknown Venus by some unknown artist, and a number of small bronzes gathered from heaven knows where, but generally sold by the large furniture houses along with everything else which goes to make the 'perfectly appointed house' " (63). Rather than helping readers to cope with and feel at home in strange places, the passage emphasizes alienation from familiar places. The depiction of the interior as a product of "the large furniture houses" already points to the disintegration of the integrity of the isolated residence. Living in "the 'perfectly appointed' house," the Hurstwoods occupy a category of dwelling that is marked by its fidelity to a shared standard, and it is, this passage suggests, in its absolute allegiance to the standard that its imperfection lies. *Sister Carrie* identifies this critique of middle-class culture with the explosive commercial and residential expansion of the metropolis, and in the following decades it is relocated in novels such as *Babbitt* and *Mildred Pierce* to the modern suburb, one of the products of such expansion, and to a broader, less refined middle-class population.

5. David Madden, introduction, *Tough Guy Writers of the Thirties*, ed. Madden (Carbondale: Southern Illinois University Press, 1968), xvii. Literary criticism of the 1930s has tended to focus on working-class writings and experience. See most recently *Radical Revisions: Rereading 1930s Culture*, ed. Bill Mullen and Sherry Lee Linkon (Urbana: University of Illinois Press, 1996). In a superb reassessment of Nathanael West's career, Jonathan Veitch draws an instructive contrast between two anticapitalist positions in literature of the 1930s: the prevailing critique of a failing production-oriented economy and West's own prescient and understudied protest against a more broadly based, superficially vibrant, consumption-oriented economy. See *American Superrealism: Nathanael West and the Politics of Representation in the 1930s* (Madison: University of Wisconsin Press, 1997). Neither category of critique accommodates *Mildred Pierce* or Cain's other important fiction of the Depression. In *The Postman Always Rings Twice* (1934) and *Double Indemnity* (1935), the vigor of capitalism is all too evident in the powerful insurance industry, which governs the novellas as impersonal and invincible legal, political, and economic agents. In the thirties, as Mike Davis has noted, literary L.A. was generally oriented around the struggles and indignation of the middle class, rather than the working class, which is perhaps why it has until recently received so little attention from literary critics interested primarily in working-class expression and experience of the Depression. See *City of Quartz: Excavating the Future of Los Angeles* (London: Verso, 1990), 36–40.

6. Siegfried Giedion, *Mechanization Takes Command* (1948; rpt., New York: Oxford University Press, 1955), 41.

7. Historians of the middle-class American suburb typically pay little attention to the 1930s, with the notable exception of New Deal government housing policies, which decreased foreclosure rates and impacted suburbanization in the postwar period (see Jackson, *Crabgrass Frontier*, 190–230). Studies of housing in the thirties tend to focus on public and working-class housing. Wright's short section on the 1930s in *Building the Dream* (220–32) thus deals with slum clearance and government housing projects. In *Borderlands* John Stilgoe notes that real estate periodicals recommended against experimenting with architectural innovations during the Depression, but he focuses on the fear that consumers would find them faddish and thus poor economic investments (283–85), rather than on the sentimental objections that I explore below.

8. *Bennett Homes: Better-Built, Ready-Cut* (1920; rpt., New York: Dover, 1993), 4. The Aladdin Company of Bay City, Michigan, began selling fully precut houses by mail in 1904. Sears entered the mail-order house business in 1909 with plans and materials and began to offer completely precut houses in 1916. By 1934 it had sold 100,000 houses. On Sears's influence on American housing, see Katherine Cole Stevenson and H. Ward Jandl, *Houses by Mail: A Guide to Houses from Sears, Roebuck and Company* (Washington, D.C.: Preservation Press, 1986). On the influence of the mail-order business in general, see Gowans, *The Comfortable House*.

9. Banta, *Taylored Lives*, 241. She argues that the placement of these factory houses signified "*the continuing attempt* to mediate between the machine and the garden" (241). See Leo Marx, *The Machine in the Garden: Technology and the Pastoral Ideal in America* (New York: Oxford University Press, 1964).

10. See Robert Schweitzer and Michael W. R. Davis, *America's Favorite Homes: Mail-Order Catalogues as a Guide to Popular Early Twentieth-Century Houses* (Detroit: Wayne State University Press, 1990). On the impact of the machine as the organic basis for authentically American design in this period, see Orvell, *The Real Thing*, 157–97.

11. Phillip Smith, "Ready-Made Houses," *Scientific American* 153 (August 1935), 69. The "prefabrication movement" in housing during the Depression is discussed in Albert Bruce and Harold Sandbank, *A History of Prefabrication* (1943; rpt., New York: Arno, 1972).

12. "Machine for Living," *Business Week* (December 15, 1934), 8.

13. Le Corbusier, *Towards a New Architecture*, trans. Frederick Etchells (1923; rpt., New York: Praeger, 1974), 12. The "House-Machine" would be "beautiful in the same way that the working tools and instruments which accompany our existence are beautiful" (12). Orvell distinguishes between Le Corbusier's "colder homage to technology, this *imitation* of the machine," and Mumford's and Frank Lloyd Wright's refusal to embrace the machine as an architectural end in itself; they believed instead in "the adaptation and humanizing of it" (179), what Mumford also called the "machine-for-*living*" (Mumford, "Machines for Living," *Fortune* 7 [February 1933], 82).

14. On the layperson's conception of functionalism in the period, see Mumford, "Machines for Living," 78–88. David A. Hounshell discusses the American

housing entrepreneurs of the thirties in *From the American System to Mass Production, 1800–1932: The Development of Manufacturing Technology in the United States* (Baltimore: Johns Hopkins University Press, 1984), 311–15. Manufacturers of prefabricated housing in the United States were for the most part businessmen less interested in the larger social and aesthetic issues of architecture and housing than in turning out efficient, low-cost, and easily assembled models that would profitably satisfy a demand for affordable and decent housing.

15. Editors of *Fortune, Housing America* (New York: Harcourt, 1932), 52; Catherine Bauer, "Slums Aren't Necessary," *American Mercury* 31 (March 1934), 303.

16. John T. Flynn, "Be It Ever So Prefabricated," *Colliers* 96 (July 13, 1935), 13; Mumford, "Mass Production and the Modern House (Part One)," *Architectural Record* 67 (January 1930), 16. Prefabricated housing was often hailed as a solution to the problem of low-income housing, but the houses of for-profit companies such as General Houses, Houses, Inc., and the Prefabricated Housing Corporation were designed both to accommodate all income levels and to grow with the family's fortunes and size. They sold basic four-room units; several additional rooms might be purchased at once or added later. See "Machine for Living," *Business Week*, 8–9.

17. Mumford, "Mass Production and the Modern House," 18, 13, 16.

18. Mumford, "Mass Production and the Modern House" (Part Two), *Architectural Record* 67 (February 1930), 110.

19. Ibid., 111.

20. Mumford, "The American Dwelling-House," *American Mercury* 19 (April 1930), 469. He spoke most often of the single-family house in these articles in recognition that it represented the American ideal of shelter.

21. Smith, "Ready-Made Houses," 69.

22. Karl Detzer, "Houses from the Factory," *American Mercury* 50 (August 1940), 434; Carl Herter, "And These You Buy Ready Made," *American Home* 15 (March 1936), 18. See also "The Ready-Made House Arrives," *New Republic* 82 (March 13, 1935), 117–19.

23. Hounshell, *From the American System to Mass Production*, 314. He referred here particularly to the designs of Gunnison Magic Homes and the Gunnison Housing Corporation, one of the best-known manufacturers, but its designs were characteristic of the industry. Prefabricators of housing also never got the price low enough to overcome the resistance of people who could afford alternatives to house-machines or to make them feasible for those who could not. Factory prefabricated housing was built during World War II for defense-industry and military housing but faded into obscurity in the postwar period, when on-site developers such as Levitt and Sons realized that it was more efficient to bring the factory to the subdivision than to haul the subdivision out of the factory.

24. Richard J. Neutra, "Homes and Housing," in *Los Angeles: Preface to a Master Plan* (Los Angeles: Pacific Southwest Academy, 1941), 196. On the "standardized 'variety' " of traditional southern California residential architecture, and the trend toward "functional modern residences," for which the Los Angeles area also became famous, see the WPA publication *Los Angeles: A Guide to the City and Its Environs*, 8. David Gebhard and Harriette von Breton, *L.A. in the 30s:*

1931–1941 (Salt Lake City, Utah: Peregrine Smith, 1975) is a superb history of the modernist architectural heritage.

25. Cain, *Double Indemnity* (1935; rpt., New York: Vintage, 1989), 3–4.

26. See especially the house of the homosexual pornographer and blackmailer Arthur Geiger in Chandler's *The Big Sleep* (1939; rpt., New York: Vintage, 1988).

27. Marchand, *Advertising the American Dream*, 125. For a clever gloss on Marchand's analysis that links the substitution of "objects for use" with "objects for art" in commodity culture and the British aestheticism of Ruskin, Morris, and Charles Eastlake, see Jonathan Freedman, *Professions of Taste: Henry James, British Aestheticism, and Commodity Culture* (Stanford, Calif.: Stanford University Press, 1990), 109–10.

28. Cain, "Paradise" (1933), in *60 Years of Journalism*, ed. Roy Hoopes (Bowling Green, Ohio: Bowling Green State University Popular Press, 1985), 167.

29. See Gwendolyn Wright, *Moralism and the Model Home*, 236.

30. See Walter Benjamin, "The Work of Art in the Age of Mechanical Reproduction," in *Illuminations*, ed. Hannah Arendt, trans. Harry Zohn (New York: Harcourt, 1968), 217–51.

31. Karen Halttunen, "From Parlor to Living Room: Domestic Space, Interior Decoration, and the Culture of Personality," in Bronner, *Consuming Visions*, 158. See also Katherine C. Grier, *Culture and Comfort: People, Parlors, and Upholstery, 1850–1930* (Rochester, N.Y.: Strong Museum, 1988), 290–91.

32. Emily Post, "The Personality of a House," *Ladies' Home Journal* 46 (May 1929), 14. The articles were expanded and republished as *The Personality of a House: The Blue Book of Home Design and Decoration* (New York: Funk and Wagnalls, 1930) and reprinted into the 1940s.

33. Dorothy Dix, " 'Is Your Home Furnished as It Should Be?' " *Better Homes and Gardens* 9 (November 1930), 35.

34. Susman, " 'Personality' and Twentieth-Century Culture," in *Culture as History*, 277.

35. Ben Davis, "Individuality as the Decorator Sees It," *California Arts and Architecture* (March 1937), 19.

36. Ibid., 40.

37. Post, "The Personality of a House," *Ladies' Home Journal* 46 (July 1929), 16.

38. Doris Suman, "Personality in the Small Home," *California Arts and Architecture* (July 1939), 17.

39. Isabel Hopkins, "Is There a Decorator in the House?" *House and Garden* 70 (October 1936), 58.

40. Ibid., 58.

41. In American literature men's good taste and excessive interest in decoration had long signified a weak, suspicious character or foreshadowed downright villainy. Think, for example, of Gilbert Osmond's exquisite taste in Henry James's *The Portrait of a Lady* (1881). One trope of the hard-boiled genre is played out when detectives of the Hammett-Chandler school barely conceal their disgust at weak-chinned men in mauve dressing gowns, lounging amid the calculated clutter of art and bibelots. Most memorably, Arthur Geiger is engulfed by the excesses

of his interior in *The Big Sleep*. Monty is heterosexual, but he has a semi-incestuous affair with Veda, by now his stepdaughter, and eventually runs off with her. If Monty's social class were not enough to authenticate his good taste, then at least in the hard-boiled tradition, his perversion would be.

42. William Marling, *The American Roman Noir: Hammett, Cain, and Chandler* (Athens: University of Georgia Press, 1995), ix. The analysis of Cain includes *The Postman Always Rings Twice* and *Double Indemnity* but omits *Mildred Pierce*.

43. See Eli Zaretsky, *Capitalism, the Family, and Personal Life* (New York: Harper, 1976), 24.

44. Loss of status, embodied here in the transition from housewife to waitress, was a particular source of anxiety for the middle-class during the Depression. See Glen H. Elder, *Children of the Great Depression: Social Change in Life Experience* (Chicago: University of Chicago Press, 1974).

45. In *The Woman Who Waits* (Boston: R.G. Badger, 1920), sociologist Frances Donovan discussed the identification of waitresses with loose women, which prevailed, according to Dorothy Sue Cobble, through much of the first half of the twentieth century. Cobble describes the efforts of state legislatures to ban tipping on democratic and moral grounds and relates assumptions about the waitress's sexual behavior to her significance as "part of the consumption exchange" (*Dishing It Out: Waitresses and Their Unions in the Twentieth Century* [Urbana: University of Illinois Press, 1991], 45).

46. See Susan Ware, *Holding Their Own: American Women in the 1930s* (Boston: Twayne, 1982), 21–53; Lynn Y. Weiner, *From Working Girl to Working Mother: The Female Labor Force in the United States, 1820–1980* (Chapel Hill: University of North Carolina Press, 1985), 100–110; and Peter G. Filene, *Him/Her/Self: Sex Roles in Modern America*, 2nd ed. (Baltimore: Johns Hopkins University Press, 1986), 148–61. In 1930 women made up 22 percent of the American workforce and 25 percent by 1940. Alice Kessler-Harris argues that despite various federal and state efforts to legislate against married women workers (particularly in the years 1931–32 and 1937–39) and more informal attempts to shame women in general back into the home, the 1930s accelerated the placement of women in the workforce but also affirmed their segregation into jobs according to sex. See *Out to Work: A History of Wage-Earning Women in the United States* (New York: Oxford University Press, 1982), 250–72. According to Nancy Cott, most apologists for working women in the Depression emphasized the difficult circumstances faced by many women and their families rather than a feminist agenda. See *The Grounding of Modern Feminism* (New Haven: Yale University Press, 1987), 180–211.

47. Margaret Collins, "Career, Limited," *Scribner's* 102 (October 1937), 45.

48. Lynd and Lynd, *Middletown in Transition* (New York: Harcourt, Brace, 1937), 178.

49. Dorothy Sabin Butler, "Men against Women," *Forum* 94 (August 1935), 80, 82.

50. Charlotte Muret, "Marriage as a Career," *Harper's* 173 (August 1936), 253.

51. Butler, "Men against Women," 82. Butler argued that women had "emotional balance" that was destroyed when they found employment, but only because discrimination forced them to become like men to succeed. If men ceased to resist their presence in the workforce, women could function successfully both as workers and as "women." As consumers, women were also reputed to be hard, and the victims once again were men. Most famously, in Philip Wylie's hysterical attack, men as producers had "the ulcers and colitis," while women whose only worry was to spend the money men made had "the guts of a bear" (*Generation of Vipers* [1942; rpt., New York: Farrar and Rinehart, 1946], 189).

52. Paula Rabinowitz, *Labor and Desire: Women's Revolutionary Fiction in Depression America* (Chapel Hill: University of North Carolina Press, 1991), 37.

53. Review of *Mildred Pierce*, *Sacramento Bee* (November 22, 1941), from the *Mildred Pierce* clippings file, James M. Cain papers, Library of Congress.

54. On domestic science literature, see chap. 2, n. 37.

55. Leonard Reaume, "Fine Points about Subdividing," *Los Angeles Realtor* (May 1929), 10. A. K. Moore, "Subdividers to Sell Must Build," *National Real Estate Journal* (May 1929), 21–28, dates the first uses of model homes to 1921–22.

56. It might seem reasonable to assume that Cain wants to blame Veda's ambition and monstrous selfishness on Mildred. If she had never gone into business but had stayed home and taken care of her, Veda would have turned out all right. (This is the point that feminist film critics have made about the 1945 Warner Bros. movie.) But the novel refuses to blame Mildred for Veda's character and conduct. The genetic account of Veda's nasty disposition has to do with her career rather than with Mildred's. In a preposterous twist, Veda is discovered and becomes rich and famous as a coloratura soprano. Her Italian music teacher, Mr. Treviso, explains to Mildred that her daughter's nature is a function of her musical talent: "Dees girl, she is coloratura, inside, outside, all over, even a bones is coloratura. First, must know all a rich pipple. No rich, no good. . . . All coloratura, they got, 'ow you say?—da *gimmies*. Always take, never give. . . . I tell you, is snake, is bitch, is coloratura" (250, 253). Because Veda was a coloratura before she ever sang a note, her temperament is as natural as her voice. Mildred doesn't quite get it: " 'She's a wonderful girl.' 'No—is a wonderful singer. . . . Da girl is lousy. She is a bitch' " (252). Even if this explanation is a bit thin, it is worth noting that of the dozens of reviews of *Mildred Pierce* in the James M. Cain papers at the Library of Congress, not one blames Mildred or her career for her daughter's nasty disposition.

57. See David Laidler, *Fabricating the Keynesian Revolution: Studies of the Inter-War Literature on Money, the Cycle, and Unemployment* (Cambridge: Cambridge University Press, 1999), esp. 206–12; 225–28, for an overview of American and British economists' opinions on underconsumption as an explanatory model of economic crisis.

58. *Mildred Pierce* resembles *Imitation of Life* (1933), Fannie Hurst's tale of a widow who builds an international restaurant empire based in Manhattan, but really wants only to create a suburban home for her daughter. As Lauren Berlant has pointed out in an essay on Hurst's novel and the films it inspired, Bea Pullman's entrance into the labor market and success in business requires an evolving

process of white female disembodiment and abstraction. First, as B. Pullman, she hides behind her husband's ambiguous professional identity to carry on his work after he dies. Later, she exploits the profound overembodiment of the enormous Delilah Johnson, a Mammy figure who enters Bea's private service, but offers up a good waffle recipe and, more importantly, her powerful image to become "the prosthetic public body" of the Pullman corporation and the white woman who runs it ("National Brands/National Body: *Imitation of Life*," in *Comparative American Identities: Race, Sex, and Nationality in the Modern Text*, ed. Hortense J. Spillers [New York: Routledge, 1991], 119). Mildred Pierce, Inc., by contrast, insists upon an intimate link between female entrepreneur and capitalist public sphere. As Mildred Pierce, Inc., the woman who sells the consolations of home cannily exploits cultural assumptions about gender to authenticate her product.

59. Cited in Madden, *Tough Guy Writers of the Thirties*, xx.

60. Bethany Ogden, "Hard-Boiled Ideology," *Critical Quarterly* 34 (Spring 1992), 75.

61. Edmund Wilson, *The Boys in the Back Room: Notes on California Novelists* (San Francisco: Colt Press, 1941), 11.

62. Harold Strauss, "A Six-Minute Egg," *New York Times Book Review* (February 18, 1937), 8.

63. David Geherin, *The American Private Eye: The Image in Fiction* (New York: Frederick Ungar, 1985), 22. Even when a masculine protagonist of hardboiled fiction is seen to register the "temptations of what a patriarchal-oedipal culture encodes as the feminine—sensation, disorder, and play—" in Fred Pfeil's reading of Philip Marlowe in *The Big Sleep*, the character opens himself to everything *but* emotion: Chandler, like Dashiell Hammett, refuses "to ascribe any affective or emotional response directly to their heroes, who presumably both go on functioning without feeling" (*White Guys: Studies in Postmodern Domination and Difference* [London: Verso, 1995], 116).

64. Joyce Carol Oates makes a version of this point when she suggests that an overwritten passage of *Postman*, in which Frank describes kissing Cora as "like being in church," is an example of Cain's craftsmanship: "This is precisely what Frank Chambers would think and he would express it in just that way, knowing none of the uses of rhetoric or the ways by which conceits of passionate and spiritual love are devised" ("Man under Sentence of Death: The Novels of James M. Cain," in Madden, *Tough Guy Writers*, 118). In other words, the passage exemplifies Frank's faulty writing and sentiment, not Cain's.

65. The slogan comes from an advertisement for the novel that appeared in the *New York Times Book Review* (September 25, 1941), 23.

CHAPTER FOUR
NATIVE SON'S TRESPASSES

1. "Watching Jungle Gangsters Fight and Feast," *Literary Digest* 108 (March 7, 1931), 32. On the making of *Tarzan the Ape Man* and Burroughs's response to the Weissmuller series, see Glenn Essoe, *Tarzan of the Movies* (Secaucus, N.J.: Citadel, 1968). Page references to *Native Son* are from Richard Wright, *Native Son* (New York: Harper, 1966).

2. Mass culture represents for Bigger an idealized coordination of "self-ab-straction and self-realization," tendencies that Michael Warner has defined as the acute contradictions of the contemporary public sphere ("The Mass Public and the Mass Subject," in *Habermas and the Public Sphere*, ed. Craig Calhoun [Cambridge: MIT Press, 1992], 399). At issue in most debates about the public sphere are the possibility and terms of equal access or "participatory parity," and not the benefits of participation, which are typically interrogated in relation to mass culture (Nancy Fraser, "Rethinking the Public Sphere: A Contribution to the Critique of Actually Existing Democracy," in Calhoun, *Habermas and the Public Sphere*, 122). The term *mass culture* has fallen somewhat out of favor, in part because it implies, in the Frankfurt School tradition, something one does not participate in but is manipulated by, or it at the least posits undifferentiated consumers who passively respond to its products in the same way. *Popular culture* is imagined to describe a more productive relationship between product and consumer and among consumers; according to Thomas Strychacz, it "provides a real, lived, and shared sense of being-in-the-world" (*Modernism, Mass Culture, and Professionalism* [Cambridge: Cambridge University Press, 1993], 10). For Bigger, movies, newspapers, and magazines identify only other people's actual experience of "being-in-the-world" and never his own. Even when Bigger picks up the newspaper and reads all about himself, the effect is to provide further evidence of his isolation. For example, the phrase "sex crime" "excluded him utterly from the world" (228); its power to do so derives from his preexisting exclusion. Lauren Berlant has recently denounced the sentimental lure of mass culture, which binds citizens to the nation through "pain alliances" and tricks them into identifying public and political problems as private and personal traumas ("Poor Eliza," *American Literature* 70 [September 1998], 636). In *Native Son*, mass culture does not appease or derail but rather stimulates Bigger's desire for citizenship in a public world, while also dramatizing its own inevitable failure to fulfill that fantasy. As a newspaper headline, Bigger's story underscores the political effects and possibilities behind what seem to be his private desires.

3. St. Clair Drake and Horace R. Cayton, *Black Metropolis: A Study of Negro Life in a Northern City* (1945; rpt., Chicago: University of Chicago Press, 1993), 12, 602.

4. Bigger's formulation implies the substitutability of the languages of geography and of race, as Samira Kawash recently argues about the logic of racial boundaries: the power of the color line not only to enforce but to create racial difference. See *Dislocating the Color Line: Identity, Hybridity, and Singularity in African-American Literature* (Stanford, Calif.: Stanford University Press, 1997), 1–22.

5. Wright, "How Bigger Was Born" (1940), rpt. in *Native Son*, xvi.

6. James Baldwin, "Many Thousands Gone," in *Notes of a Native Son* (Boston: Beacon, 1955), 41. Ross Pudaloff argues that Bigger can understand himself and his world only through the lens of mass culture, but Pudaloff wrongly treats mass culture as an end in itself. See "Celebrity as Identity: Richard Wright, *Native Son*, and Mass Culture," *Studies in American Fiction* 11 (Spring 1983), 3–18. Charles Scruggs claims that mass culture mediates and, in effect, distorts (rather than illuminates) Bigger's desire for community and his conception of the "ideal city" (*Sweet Home*, 92). Critics have also seized upon Wright's misogyny, which

is linked to the brutal rape and murder of Bigger's girlfriend, Bessie Mears, and the negative depiction of women as resigned and passive enforcers of the white status quo. See, for example, Trudier Harris, "Native Sons and Foreign Daughters," in *New Essays on "Native Son,"* ed. Keneth Kinnamon (Cambridge: Cambridge University Press, 1990), 63–84; and Alan France, "Misogyny and Appropriation in Wright's *Native Son,*" *Modern Fiction Studies* 34 (Autumn 1988), 413–23. On the construction of Hurston as an alternative to Wright, see Carla Cappetti, *Writing Chicago: Modernism, Ethnography, and the Novel* (New York: Columbia University Press, 1993), chap. 8.

7. Houston A. Baker Jr., *Long Black Song: Essays in Black American Literature and Culture* (Charlottesville: University Press of Virginia, 1972), 133; Baker, "Richard Wright and the Dynamics of Place in Afro-American Literature," in Kinnamon, *New Essays on "Native Son,"* 111. In the latter essay Baker draws upon the work of cultural geographer Yi-Fu Tuan to argue that the "security and stability" associated with the comforting boundaries of "place" are undone when segregation renders those boundaries meaningless with respect to the inhabitants' "human agency" (87). According to Baker, in Wright's *12 Million Black Voices* (1941) the fact of "placelessness" (92) generates "a distinctive folk culture" (93) in the South, but as in *Native Son,* the North gives rise only to an interracial network of class interests that excludes black women, who are dismissed as the "ahistorical remnant of folk culture" (101). Thus Wright's misogyny is also the vehicle for his devaluation of black culture. By contrast, Caren Irr argues that *Native Son* associates "confining spaces" in the city with folk culture, and that Wright "struggle[s] to reclaim" "the space of African American culture" by acting as a literary mediator between it and communism (*The Suburb of Dissent: Cultural Politics in the United States and Canada during the 1930s* [Durham, N.C.: Duke University Press, 1998], 131, 129). Like Baker, even when Irr deals with concrete places in the novel, the discussion of space is abstract and important primarily as a way of talking about culture, by which it is finally replaced: "urban culture . . . is a social formation more recognizable by its linguistic practice than its location" (132).

8. "How Bigger Was Born," xi, xxi, xix. The critique of structuralism is prevalent among more recent critics but not universal. Scruggs notes that to expect Wright to depict Bigger's girlfriend, Bessie Mears, "as an empowered black woman, or as a woman connected to a vital black community, is to ignore Wright's judgment about the effects of a racist social structure on relations between Afro-American women and men" (*Sweet Home,* 257n). George Kent acknowledges the limitations of Wright's position while crediting him with moving toward the end of pure structuralism; Wright's assaults on "white definitions" enabled "our growing ability to ignore them" (*Blackness and the Adventure of Western Culture* [Chicago: Third World Press, 1972], 80).

9. See Cappetti, *Writing Chicago,* esp. chap. 9.

10. Cappetti is especially interesting on the reciprocities between Chicago sociology and literature. Sociologists drew upon the work of such urban novelists as Theodore Dreiser and Emile Zola, as well as Wright; Wright, Nelson Algren, and James T. Farrell were influenced by sociological theories of urbanization and community studies. *Native Son* broadly established Wright's credentials as a sociologi-

cal writer. Bigger was soon invoked as a new "type" in studies of racism and its effects by sociologists and anthropologists such as Gunnar Myrdal (*An American Dilemma: The Negro Problem in Modern Democracy* [New York: Harper, 1944]) and Hortense Powdermaker ("The Channeling of Negro Aggression by the Cultural Process," *American Journal of Sociology* 48 [May 1943], 750–58). Wright wrote the introduction to Drake and Cayton's classic sociology of African Americans in Chicago, *Black Metropolis*, in which he illuminated the connections between his methodology and conclusions in *Native Son* and the sociologists'. Wright's readings in sociology, his tutorial with Louis Wirth, a prominent sociologist at the University of Chicago, and his friendship with Cayton also contributed to his own impressionistic historical-sociological study, *12 Million Black Voices: A Folk History of the Negro in the United States* (1941; rpt., New York: Arno, 1969).

11. "Iron Ring in Housing," *Crisis* (July 1940), 205.

12. Arnold R. Hirsch, *Making the Second Ghetto: Race and Housing in Chicago, 1940–1960* (1983; rpt., Chicago: University of Chicago Press, 1998), 52.

13. Nelson Algren, "Remembering Richard Wright," in *Twentieth-Century Interpretations of "Native Son": A Collection of Critical Essays*, ed. Houston A. Baker, Jr. (Englewood Cliffs, N.J.: Prentice-Hall, 1972), 115.

14. Robert Bone describes a black literary Renaissance in Chicago of the thirties, anchored by Wright, that rivaled the significance of Harlem's in "Richard Wright and the Chicago Renaissance," *Calaloo* 9 (Fall–Winter 1986), 446–68.

15. Sidney H. Bremer, "Home in Harlem, New York: Lessons from the Harlem Renaissance Writers," *PMLA* 105 (January 1990), 47; Ann Douglas, *Terrible Honesty*, 312. Baker stresses the international and transtemporal force of the Harlem community in *Modernism and the Harlem Renaissance* (Chicago: University of Chicago Press, 1989). See also Donald B. Gibson's euphoric description in "The Harlem Renaissance City: It's Multi-Illusionary Dimension," in *The City in African-American Literature*, ed. Yoshinobu Hakutani and Robert Butler (Madison, N.J.: Fairleigh Dickinson University Press, 1995), 37–49.

16. Alain Locke, "The New Negro," in *The New Negro*, ed. Locke (1925; rpt., New York: Atheneum, 1992), 4. See Scruggs, *Sweet Home*, 54–58.

17. E. Franklin Frazier, "La Bourgeoisie Noire," 78. The title suggests how foreign the notion of a black middle class would be to many of his white readers. Frazier also contributed an article on the black middle class of Durham to *The New Negro*, and his sociologics of black family life likewise emphasize class differentiation. See *The Negro Family in Chicago* (Chicago: University of Chicago Press, 1932); and *The Negro Family in the United States* (1939; rpt., rev. and abridg., Chicago: University of Chicago Press, 1966). Mary Esteve notes that African Americans have historically undergone "a sort of compulsory anonymity" as members of a race rather than individuals, and in the Harlem Renaissance it was specifically the undifferentiated (i.e., working-class) masses rather than the race per se that were unassimilable to the rhetoric of individuality ("Nella Larsen's 'Moving Mosaic': Harlem, Crowds, and Anonymity," *American Literary History* 9 [Summer 1997], 270). Citing Johnson's "Harlem: The Culture Capital," she observes that "the assertion of black individuality" was equated with "the emergence of a middle class" (271).

18. David Levering Lewis refers to statistics including the census and medical data to argue that "the evidence that Harlem was becoming a slum, even as Charles Johnson and Alain Locke arranged the coming-out party of the arts, is persuasive" (*When Harlem Was in Vogue*, 108). Whereas James Weldon Johnson claimed that "Negro Harlem is practically owned by Negroes" (308), Lewis notes that whites owned over 80 percent of its wealth (109).

19. Claude McKay, " 'Segregation' in Harlem?" *Column Review* (December 1941), 5.

20. Barbara Johnson, "The Re[a]d and the Black," in *Richard Wright's "Native Son,"* ed. Harold Bloom (New York: Chelsea, 1988), 115. See Wright, "Blueprint for Negro Writing," *New Challenge* 2 (Fall 1937), 53–65.

21. It is not the case, as Trudier Harris has argued, that Wright blames black women for Bigger's problems. Although "the pressure of family life . . . is one of the motivating factors in Bigger's later behavior" (65), Wright faults overcrowding and its toll upon natural bonds of affection rather than blaming the family. Harris is right to observe that Wright cannot envision black women actively protesting their oppression; whether through alcohol or the church, they simply resign themselves to it. Discontent, in the active, political sense, is the prerogative of men, as Baker likewise notes in "The Dynamics of Place."

22. Frazier, *The Negro Family in the United States*, 326–27. Five years later Gunnar Myrdal mobilized the metaphors of walls and prisons to describe the fact and effects of discrimination throughout *An American Dilemma*.

23. See "The Iron Ring in Housing," 205, 210. Loren Miller, a celebrated Los Angeles attorney who argued cases against racial segregation, also invoked the "iron ring" (15) in Bernard Sheil and Miller, *Racial Restrictive Covenants* (Chicago, 1946). Drake and Cayton similarly used "iron bands" (*Black Metropolis*, 714) to describe the barriers around the Black Belt.

24. See Drake and Cayton, *Black Metropolis*, 576–77. Both sociologists and later historians note that there was less segregation in housing, public facilities, and business establishments in Chicago before World War I, but racial tensions and restrictions mounted as large numbers of black migrants from the South came to Chicago during and after the war. See William Tuttle, *Race Riot: Chicago in the Red Summer of 1919* (New York: Atheneum, 1972); and Allan H. Spear, *Black Chicago: The Making of the Negro Ghetto, 1890–1920* (Chicago: University of Chicago Press, 1967). The African American population in Chicago more than doubled between 1910 and 1920, from 44,103 to 109,458, and again between 1920 and 1930, when it increased to 233,903. During the Depression the black population increased by another 20 percent. As boundaries hardened at the time of the race riots of 1919, according to Drake and Cayton, "[t]he sudden influx of Negroes into Chicago immediately resolved itself into a struggle for living space" (*Black Metropolis*, 61).

25. Ernest W. Burgess, "The Growth of the City: An Introduction to a Research Project," in Park, Burgess, and McKenzie, *The City*, 47–62.

26. In effect, Burgess's geographical narrative of race and ethnicity in the city mapped the social theory of race relations provided by his colleague Robert Park. Park posited a universal race relations cycle: two races (or ethnic groups) establish contact, through migration or colonization; contact produces conflict as they com-

pete for resources. Conflict yields to accommodation, or social equilibrium, in a stable, if unequal, social order. Finally there is assimilation, the cultural and physical merging of the races. See the essays collected in Park, *Race and Culture* (Glencoe, Ill.: Free Press, 1950). For a concise summary and critique of Park's theories and field studies of race relations, see Stanford M. Lyman, *The Black American in Sociological Thought: A Failure in Perspective* (New York: Capricorn, 1973), 27–70.

It is important to stress that disorganization was not intrinsically pathological for Chicago school sociologists. It signified a process of adjustment to new conditions that led many to reorganization—house ownership, financial security, a stable family structure—and individual, family, and collective health. See Anthony M. Platt, *E. Franklin Frazier Reconsidered* (New Brunswick, N.J.: Rutgers University Press, 1991), esp. 137–44.

27. Ernest W. Burgess, "Residential Segregation in American Cities," *Annals of the American Academy of Political and Social Sciences* 140 (November 1928), 105.

28. See Louis Wirth, *The Ghetto* (1928; rpt., Chicago: University of Chicago Press, 1956). Wirth noted that more than other white ethnics in Chicago, Jews who left the area of original Jewish settlement and moved into areas less defined by ethnic or religious ties continued to cherish it as a symbol of Jewish community life. Recent work suggests that suburban house ownership in the post–World War II period helped Jews and other Southern and Eastern Europeans to gain acceptance as "whites" within the American mainstream. See Karen Brodkin, *How Jews Became White Folks and What That Says about Race in America* (New Brunswick, N.J.: Rutgers University Press, 1998). George Lipsitz writes in a similar vein: "The suburbs helped turn Euro-Americans into 'whites' who could live near each other and intermarry with relatively little difficulty" (*The Possessive Investment in Whiteness*, 7). In *Making a New Deal: Industrial Workers in Chicago, 1919–1939* (Cambridge: Cambridge University Press, 1990), Lizabeth Cohen implicitly argues against the Chicago school model when she points out that white ethnic workers in Chicago between the wars did not abandon their communities when they first moved from the old immigrant neighborhoods, but brought their institutions, shops, and services with them. In *The Changing Face of Inequality*, Olivier Zunz insists that Detroit did not follow the Chicago school's model of spatial assimilation. See 41–47. Their cases are convincing, but I am less interested in the accuracy of the sociological model than in its pervasiveness, and its influence on Wright's thinking about the racial geography of the modern metropolis.

29. See also Frazier, *The Negro Family in the United States*, where he argues with Burgess that black housing patterns followed those of "other racial and cultural groups" (233).

30. Cayton, "Negro Housing in Chicago," *Social Action* 6 (April 15, 1940), 6. In "Struggle for the Suburban Dream," James Andrew Wiese examines the evolution of African American suburbs and their meaning for the people who lived there. Before World War II, northern black suburbs were not enclaves of the affluent but of working-class families, such as the section inhabited by domestic workers in Evanston, or the industrial suburbs outside Detroit, or the communi-

ties that developed on the periphery of cities where rural migrants could find small-scale farming opportunities. By 1955, black movement to the suburb became more like white, that is, a middle-class rather than a largely working-class phenomenon, but only in the 1960s did the income of black suburbanites equal the income of black city dwellers. Wiese persuasively argues that despite the poverty of most of these suburbs before World War II, the African Americans who moved there generally did so for the same reason that affluent white people moved to suburbs: to find a better life. Wiese notes that among historians these suburbs have traditionally not counted, and that to deny that black communities are suburban because they are not white and middle class "is to deny that poor and black residents of the United States are capable of creating something which is both fully their own and fully American" (50). This may be partly true, but he ignores that American historians of the last two decades have hardly celebrated the suburb's self-determination and the equation between house ownership and American-ness. And given the hostility that the suburb has generated among intellectuals, not regarding these communities as suburban is also to do them a kind of service.

31. Drake and Cayton calculated that by 1930, 75 percent of all residential property in the city was covered by legal agreements between property owners not to sell or rent to African Americans in white neighborhoods. "Iron Ring of Housing" estimated the number at 80 percent in 1940.

32. See also Hirsch, *Making the Second Ghetto*, esp. chap. 1.

33. Wright, "The Negro and Parkway Community House" (Chicago, 1941), unpaginated. Cayton was the community center's director. See also *12 Million Black Voices*, 100–104.

34. Theodore Dreiser, *Jennie Gerhardt* (1911; rpt., Philadelphia: University of Pennsylvania Press, 1992), 257. The unexpurgated edition of the novel, from which the passage is taken, dwells far more on the pretensions and social climbing of Jennie's neighbors than did the edition brought out by Harpers in 1911.

35. Henry Connor, "Your Neighborhood: Kenwood," *Chicago Tribune*, December 24, 1939, 5-M. The Kenwood article is unique in a series called "Your Neighborhood" that ran in the *Tribune* during 1939–40. The articles touted the residential charms of a variety of Chicago communities, from exclusive suburbs such as Beverly to working- and lower-middle-class areas such as Auburn Park. Where communities experienced some form of white ethnic conflict, the articles inevitably applauded the ability of different groups to "live in harmony" (Carl W. Larsen, "Your Neighborhood: Lawndale," July 30, 1939, 7-M). By contrast, the black-white racial tensions in Kenwood are represented as irresolvable unless the barriers that separate it from the Black Belt are maintained. Connor described the strategy of Alderman Abraham Cohen to persuade white owners of property across the line "to improve and modernize" it. By making "the Negro section itself a better place to live," the landlords might keep black people from "moving into their community." The purpose of these articles, to advertise the attractions of Chicago and keep people from moving out of the city, is evident when they are considered alongside another *Tribune* series in 1939 on towns and suburbs outside Chicago's municipal boundaries, which were uniformly disparaged by the reporters. See the Western Suburbs clippings file, *Chicago Tribune*, Chicago Historical Society (CHS).

36. Eleanor Graff, "Hyde Park Once Rustic Retreat for City Elite" *Chicago Tribune*, July 7, 1929, unpaginated photocopy, Hyde Park clippings file, CHS. The now separate communities of Kenwood, Oakland, and Hyde Park formerly constituted the village of Hyde Park, which was annexed to Chicago in 1889 as part of a much larger territorial increase on the South Side that extended to the blue-collar communities of South Chicago and Pullman. According to an article written for the fiftieth anniversary of the annexation, a large majority of Hyde Park residents voted against joining Chicago, but the "sweating, beer-drinking immigrants" in the more densely populated, working-class townships voted so overwhelmingly in favor that an absolute majority for annexation was achieved among all residents in the disputed territory. See Elinor Shlifer, "The Annexation," *Hyde Park Herald*, July 27, 1939, 3.

37. Louis Wirth and Margaret Furez, eds., *Local Community Fact Book* (Chicago, 1939), Kenwood entry, unpaginated. By 1918, the Kenwood and Hyde Park Property Owners' Association had shifted its attention from civic improvements such as better streets and lighting to the mission to "make Hyde Park white" (Spear, *Black Chicago*, 210).

38. Robert Park, "The City," in Park, Burgess, and McKenzie, *The City*, 16–17. Park's mentor was Georg Simmel, who influentially theorized about the relation between money and the city in "The Metropolis and Mental Life."

39. See especially Park, "The City," 1–46; and Louis Wirth, "Urbanism as a Way of Life," *American Journal of Sociology* 44 (July 1938), 1–24.

40. Wright, *American Hunger* (1977; rpt., New York: Harper, 1983), 3; Ralph Ellison, *Invisible Man* (1952; rpt., New York: Vintage, 1989), 158.

41. In *An American Dilemma* Myrdal was particularly struck by the willingness of white Americans to hold absolutely inconsistent beliefs to defend their advantages. He also remarked that he had "heard few comments made so frequently and with so much emphasis and so many illustrations as the one that 'Negroes are happiest among themselves' and that 'Negroes really don't want white company but prefer to be among their own race' " (575).

42. Robyn Wiegman, *American Anatomies: Theorizing Race and Gender* (Durham, N.C.: Duke University Press, 1995), 103.

43. On the "debilitating" "protection" of the color line's "invisible walls," see Kenneth B. Clark, *Dark Ghetto: Dilemmas of Social Power* (New York: Harper, 1965), 19.

44. No Man's Land is aligned with what Paul Gilroy calls "the space between" national and racial identities, which racist thinking has declared to be mutually exclusive in relation to black Europeans (*The Black Atlantic: Modernity and Double Consciousness* [Cambridge: Harvard University Press, 1993], 1). On Wright's own ambitious intellectual project to enlarge his identifications and "achieve the deracinated freedom of modernity," see Ross Posnock, *Color and Culture: Black Writers and the Making of the Modern Intellectual* (Cambridge: Harvard University Press, 1998), 64.

45. In one scene twelve people, including his family, friends, and the Daltons, impossibly meet in Bigger's cell, his privacy more compromised by overcrowding than ever before. But by the end of the novel, Bigger is more the master of his limited domain. For example, he tells his family to stay away, and they do. He

also stops the visits of a black preacher and makes a white priest "stand away from him" (382).

46. Barbara Foley's reading of the end focuses on Bigger's "I am" as an exclusive commitment to individual identity at the expense of a developed political consciousness. See *Radical Representations: Politics and Form in United States Proletarian Fiction, 1929–1941* (Durham, N.C.: Duke University Press, 1993), 334. But Bigger's actual commitments are more complex. He sees himself as an autonomous *and* integral part of the human community, an identification that may achieve productive political effects when we see him addressing Max and a rehabilitated Jan, but is intolerable when it lets Dalton off the hook.

47. Wright, "How Jim Crow Feels," *Negro Digest* (January 1947), 53.

48. See Wright to Gertrude Stein (March 15, 1946), James Weldon Johnson Collection, Beinecke Library, Yale University. I have had to paraphrase the letter and the essay, "I Choose Exile," below, because I was unable to get permission from the Wright estate to cite these materials.

49. See Michel Fabre, *The Unfinished Quest of Richard Wright*, 2nd ed. (1973; rpt., Urbana: University of Illinois Press, 1993), 275–76; Constance Webb, *Richard Wright: A Biography* (New York: Putnam's, 1968), 239; and Gayle Addison, *Richard Wright: Ordeal of a Native Son* (Garden City, N.Y.: Doubleday, 1980), 175–76. The substance of the story is the same in all three accounts, although details vary.

50. Lorraine Hansberry, *A Raisin in the Sun* (New York: Random House, 1959), 77. Not all kitchenette operators were white; the playwright's father, Carl Hansberry, made a small fortune converting larger Black Belt flats into single-room units. In 1938 he tried to escape the overcrowding and deterioration that his housing practices had helped to bring about by moving to Washington Park, but the family was evicted by the State Supreme Court, who ruled that the property was covered by a restrictive covenant prohibiting nonwhite residence. The case, *Hansberry v. Lee*, went to the U.S. Supreme Court, which ruled in favor of Hansberry's right to occupy the house but did not decide to ban restrictive covenants altogether. The "Iron Ring of Housing" article is about the Hansberry case. See Anne Cheney, *Lorraine Hansberry* (Boston: Twayne, 1984).

In the play, Lena Younger uses part of a $10,000 insurance check she receives after her husband's death to place a down payment on a house in Clybourne Park, a fictional neighborhood in or near Chicago. Walter Lee Younger, Lena's son, is a chauffeur, like Bigger, but he has a concrete "dream" (80) of entrepreneurship, which is defeated after he steals what is left of Lena's insurance money for a business venture and his partner runs off with it. The climax of the play comes when Walter decides to recover the down payment for the house plus the bonus offered by the neighborhood association, but at the last minute changes his mind, and the play ends with Lena's proud reflection that Walter has "come into his manhood" (130). The "home" as such is important only to the Younger women; the house matters to Walter because it grounds a masculine identity that ultimately doesn't differentiate between forms of property ownership, businesses or residences. Bigger's actions are by contrast explicitly linked to his powerful desire to "feel at home" (329), which is gendered male, insofar as it is expressed through the direct challenge to one's place that *Native Son* imagines black women to be incapable of making.

51. See Wright, "I Choose Exile," undated essay, James Weldon Johnson Collection, Beinecke Library, Yale University.

52. Fabre puts the house in Vermont, while "I Choose Exile" locates it in Connecticut, a state that suggests a more immediate commuting distance to New York.

53. *Conversations with James Baldwin*, ed. Fred L. Standley and Louis H. Pratt (Jackson: University of Mississippi Press, 1989), 15.

54. Cited in Jackson, *Crabgrass Frontier*, 241.

55. Julia Abrahamson, *A Neighborhood Finds Itself* (New York: Harper, 1959), 246, 321. Abrahamson was on the board of directors of the Hyde Park–Kenwood Community Conference, which formed in the late forties to control deterioration and helped to plan the clearance and redevelopment of the area between 53rd and 57th, Woodlawn to Lake Park in the 1950s. Hyde Park–Kenwood was the first community in which the land clearance powers of a public agency were directed to a neighborhood that was still largely in good shape. Although one-third of the families displaced by the clearance program qualified for public housing, virtually all of the rebuilt housing was designed for middle-income families. Under pressure from a Catholic group, the plan was finally amended to include 120 scattered-site public housing units, but only twelve family units for the poor (excluding accommodations for the elderly) were ever built. Its interracial ambition meant that whites were strongly encouraged to move into blocks and particular apartment buildings that housed African Americans, but there was no effort to move black people into blocks that were inhabited mainly by whites. See also Devereux Bowly, Jr., *The Poorhouse: Subsidized Housing in Chicago, 1895–1976* (Carbondale: Southern Illinois University Press, 1978), and Hirsch, *Making the Second Ghetto*, 135–70. Hirsch is particularly interesting on the role of the University of Chicago in the redevelopment. He argues that the part played by the Community Conference was in fact quite limited; the university was the power behind the plan and used urban renewal "to restructure and control its neighborhood" (137). On the changing social and economic landscape of the African American South Side and environs during the period, see also Nicholas Lemann, *The Promised Land: The Great Black Migration and How It Changed America* (New York: Knopf, 1991).

56. Ruth Moore, "New Kind of Urban Living Will Appear in Hyde Park," *Chicago Sun-Times*, January 27, 1957; Dale Pontins, letter to the editor, *Chicago Daily News*, March 22, 1958, both Hyde Park clippings file, CHS.

57. Keith Wheeler, *Peaceable Lane* (New York: Simon and Schuster, 1960), 126.

CHAPTER FIVE
SANCTIMONIOUS SUBURBANITES AND THE POSTWAR NOVEL

1. Sloan Wilson, *The Man in the Gray Flannel Suit* (New York: Simon and Schuster, 1955), 3.

2. Steven M. Gelber describes house maintenance projects in the fifties, "a virtual obligation for the suburban homeowner," as an antidote to the erosion of

masculinity in the white-collar workplace ("Do-It-Yourself: Constructing, Repairing and Maintaining Domestic Masculinity," *American Quarterly* 49 [March 1997], 89). In the passage, Betsy's failure to fix it herself is almost as telling as Tom's, and the emphasis on the lack of money as well as talent suggests that the problem is more one of the family's social status than of Tom's masculine identity. In the sixties Albert Roland examined the home improvement craze in light of David Riesman's theory of "other-directed" social character and concluded that it was "predominantly a social phenomenon focusing on relationships among people, not between the craftsman and his materials" ("Do-It-Yourself: A Walden for the Millions?" in *The American Culture: Approaches to the Study of the United States*, ed. Hennig Cohen [New York: Houghton Mifflin, 1968], 277, 280). See David Riesman, with Nathan Glazer and Reuel Denney, *The Lonely Crowd: A Study of the Changing American Character* (1950; rpt., New Haven: Yale University Press, 1961). Read together, these essays say as much about the interpretive frameworks of their times as they do about Do-It-Yourself.

3. "The costliness in time and money of movement to and from the city, the economy of the multifamily type of urban dwelling and the greater availability for the poor of low rental housing in the extensive deteriorated areas of cities put the advantages of suburban life beyond the economic reach of the majority. Choice of residence as between city and suburb is virtually limited to the most highly paid types of labor and to the upper middle classes" (H. Paul Douglass, "Suburbs," *Encyclopaedia of the Social Sciences* [New York: Macmillan, 1934], 434).

4. On Levitt and Sons and Levittown, see Herbert J. Gans, *The Levittowners*, 3–21. The Levitts ultimately built more than 140,000 houses in the United States and helped to transform the construction industry from small-scale enterprises to a mass manufacturing process. Part of their genius as developers was in depersonalizing the labor that went into the house, through a human assembly line of carpenters, electricians, and painters, who moved from lot to lot, rather than the houses themselves.

5. The increase in single-family house ownership from 1946 to 1956 surpassed the increase of the preceding 150 years; by 1960, 31 of 44 million American families owned their own house. In 1950, the suburban growth rate was ten times that of central cities, and by 1955, subdivisions accounted for more than 75 percent of new housing in metropolitan areas, the majority of which was constructed by only 10 percent of the firms. See Stephanie Coontz, *The Way We Never Were*, 24–25; Jackson, *Crabgrass Frontier*, 238, 233; and Peter Rowe, *Making a Middle Landscape* (Cambridge: MIT Press, 1991), 3–4. The federal government underwrote suburbanization through the veterans' mortgage guarantee program (created in 1944 as part of the GI Bill of Rights package) and the Housing Act of 1949, which offered builders and bankers substantial financial incentives to undertake large residential developments. Government lending practices meanwhile discouraged building and renovation in city neighborhoods, leaving even financially well off African Americans, who were still discriminated against in the suburbs, with a deteriorating housing stock. See Jackson, *Crabgrass Frontier*, 203–18, 231–45; and Wright, *Building the Dream*, 240–61, for analyses of postwar changes in house construction, housing policy, and ownership.

6. Lewis Mumford, *The City in History: Its Origins, Its Transformations, and Its Prospects* (New York: Harcourt, 1961), 486; Scott Donaldson, *The Suburban Myth* (New York: Columbia University Press, 1969), 60. In 1958 Gans moved to the New Jersey Levittown precisely to test the unexamined assumption among intellectuals and the media that the postwar suburb was creating "a new set of Americans, as mass produced as the houses they live in" (xv–xvi). He found that what critics called "conformity" was a way of coping with social heterogeneity and potential class conflict in a community whose residents ranged from skilled workers at the peak of earning power to young executives and professionals at the beginning of their careers.

7. William H. Whyte Jr., "The Transients," *Fortune* 47 (May 1953), 113, first ellipses mine. Unless otherwise noted, further quotations of Whyte are from *The Organization Man* (New York: Anchor, 1957).

8. Frederick Allen, *The Big Change: America Transforms Itself, 1900–1950* (New York: Harper, 1952), 112, 213. George Lipsitz has found that "a well-integrated capitalism" indeed replaced "the primacy of production" with "the primacy of consumption" among postwar workers; class consciousness migrated from their identities as laborers to their identities as consumers, through which they appropriated, remade, and created a new social context for mass-marketed commodities (*Rainbow at Midnight: Labor and Culture in the 1940s* [Urbana: University of Illinois Press, 1994], 264, 265).

9. Nelson Algren, *Men in Boots* (1935; rpt., New York: Thunder's Mouth, 1987), 103.

10. Max Shulman, *Rally Round the Flag, Boys!* (Garden City, N.Y.: Doubleday, 1954), 23; Charles Mergendahl, *It's Only Temporary* (Garden City, N.Y.: Doubleday, 1950), 56. John and Mary Drone are the protagonists of John Keats, *The Crack in the Picture Window* (Boston: Houghton Mifflin, 1957), a satiric portrait of development life that combines sociological observations on community composition, statistics on the economics and politics of suburbanization, and a fictional portrait of the Drone family. David Karp, *Leave Me Alone* (New York: Knopf, 1957) begins each chapter with an epigraph from a clumsy, jargon-filled, fictional sociology about the new conformists of the suburbs, which the novel then dramatizes. The situation of more serious literary fiction is different; for example, John Cheever is so committed to not defining a typical suburbanite that the inhabitants become almost monotonous because each is so glaringly unique. See *"The Housebreaker of Shady Hill" and Other Stories* (New York: Harper, 1953). A. C. Spectorsky's *The Exurbanites* (Philadelphia: Lippincott, 1955) is a sociology that experiments with impressionistic prose, interspersing the examination of particular enclaves on the periphery of metropolitan areas with vignettes about fictional housewives and their husbands. It echoes *It's Only Temporary*'s loose technique of recording a random number of people engaged in the same activity, such as a story that was told 190 times on a particular Friday night (192). Spectorsky's use of the word *exurban* to describe the postwar decentralization of affluent culture workers in New York suggests the extent to which the word *suburb* had been tainted by the rise of new developments and inhabitants. Gans noted in the preface to *The Levittowners* that sociology was a maligned discipline for being at once too technical and impersonal (in the Talcott Parsons tradition) and

for "usurping the novelist's function" (xv). Women's postwar literature about the suburb followed a different course. Popular "housewife writers" such as Jean Kerr, Shirley Jackson (when she was not tackling gothic fiction), and Margaret Halsey published humorous accounts of their own lives as homemakers. Whereas much of the fiction by men sought to create a typical portrait of suburban life, semi-autobiographical texts by women who were also paid writers of national renown were by definition strikingly anomalous. On women's writing about the suburbs, see Nancy Walker, "Humor and Gender Roles: the 'Funny' Feminism of the Post–World War II Suburbs," *American Quarterly* 37 (Spring 1985), 98–113.

11. C. Wright Mills, *White Collar*, 74.

12. There is a certain affinity between Whyte's account of the organization man and Christopher Newfield's reading of Emersonian liberalism, a creed that articulates the collapse of both individual autonomy and public (democratic) control and insists that one's freedom is enhanced rather than sacrificed by their loss. See *The Emerson Effect: Individualism and Submission in America* (Chicago: University of Chicago Press, 1996). Newfield argues that Emerson's particular contribution to a prevailing American liberal discourse was to generate the appropriate affective response; he "develops the political sensibility" that makes private and public submission to an abstract "law" of "unity and inclusion" (38) "*feel OK*" (4). *The Organization Man* similarly describes a level of organizational fealty that subsumes the individual to the group but simultaneously "converts what would seem in other times a bill of no rights into a restatement of individualism" (6). Whyte also asserts that his most important discovery about the organization is the emergence of a "Social Ethic," which not only allows submission or "belonging" to "feel OK" but guides people with the force of a moral imperative: "it is right to be that way" (439). In contrast with Newfield, Whyte is concerned more about the fate of the individual than about the political effects of the new allegiances, but he imagines a quasi-political alternative to the organization in an ideal balance between "the individual's rights against society" and "the individual's obligations to society" (443).

13. Riesman, "The Suburban Dislocation," *Annals of the American Academy of Political and Social Science* 314 (Fall 1957), 142, 144. In *The Lonely Crowd*, Riesman argued for satisfying leisure as a solution to meaningless work but rejected that position in "The Suburban Dislocation" and in the preface to the 1961 edition of *Lonely Crowd*: "we soon realized that the burden put on leisure itself cannot rescue work, but fails with it, and can only be meaningful for most men if work is meaningful" (xlv).

14. Roy Lewis and Rosemary Stewart, *The Managers: A New Examination of the English, German, and American Executive* (1958; rpt., New York: Mentor, 1961), 122. Historians have commonly talked of the fifties suburb as a comparatively stable refuge for men and have generated forceful arguments about the political and personal ramifications of suburbanization and the gender inequities it has entailed. See Tyler May, *Homeward Bound*; Hayden, *Redesigning the American Dream*; and Clark, *The American Family Home*. Christopher Lasch argues that the American house as isolated refuge "came close to realization" only in the postwar suburb, which attempted to preserve it not only from the workplace but "from outside influences of any kind" ("The Sexual Division of Labor," in *Women*

and the Common Life: Love, Marriage, and Feminism, ed. Elisabeth Lasch-Quinn [New York: Norton, 1997], 105). Gelber ("Do-It-Yourself") shows that men made a place for themselves in the fifties home by performing physical labor on the house, whereas Coontz discusses the father's more active presence in family life within a home that was otherwise gendered female.

15. Joel Foreman, introduction, *The Other Fifties: Interrogating Midcentury American Icons*, ed. Foreman (Urbana: University of Illinois Press, 1997), 1. See also the essays in *Recasting America: Culture and Politics in the Cold War*, ed. Lary May (Chicago: University of Chicago Press, 1989).

16. See Barbara Ehrenreich and John Ehrenreich, "The Professional-Managerial Class," in *Between Labor and Capital*, ed. Pat Walker (Boston: South End Press, 1979), 5–45. In *Fear of Falling: The Inner Life of the Middle Class* (New York: Harper, 1989), Barbara Ehrenreich explores the relationship between the increasing anxiety of the PMC and its retreat from liberalism after the sixties. In her account, the PMC became fearful when it rediscovered poor people after the affluence and complacency of the fifties; that is, it was only after the PMC began to think of themselves *"as an elite"* (10) that it became particularly self-protective. I want to suggest that its defensiveness became intelligible earlier, when places such as the corporation and the suburb were perceived to threaten its status. Foreman notes that the stereotypical portraits of the fifties "appear as histories of victimization" (3), but he is referring to the situation of outsiders such as gays and lesbians, communists, ethnic and racial minorities, and women. The essays in *The Other Fifties* focus on popular culture's subversive attacks on the decade's white middle-class norms to produce new "histories of nascent rebellion and liberation" (3–4). Jackson Lears demystifies the monolithic conception of "a homogenized, asphyxiating[,] dominant," postwar white-collar and consumer culture and examines the role that intellectuals played in its development and circulation. Lears describes the PMC as a Gramscian "hegemonic historical bloc" that ascribed to a whole period and population its own interests, experiences, and perspectives, but he doesn't consider how and why this bloc explicitly cast itself as the losers in postwar economic and social transformations ("A Matter of Taste: Corporate Cultural Hegemony in a Mass-Consumption Society," in May, *Recasting America*, 47, 50).

17. Leo M. Cherne, "The Future of the Middle Class," *Atlantic Monthly* 173 (June 1944), 75, 76. Published before the war's end, it warned middle-class Americans about the anticipated postwar effects of the wartime concentration of industry, their increased dependence upon big business for employment, and the resultant decline in social status and psychological satisfaction. In *White Collar*, Mills amplified these arguments in his discussion of the shift from a society of "free enterprisers" who owned and actively managed the property with which they worked to a society of salaried employees, who did not and never would own that property. Although he was describing a process that had begun in the late-nineteenth century, and was a focus of business commentaries in the twenties, his study conveys a sense of the dramatic transformation of the American business landscape in the forties, when wartime industrial expansion disproportionately benefited the largest and wealthiest corporations. For details of corporate wartime growth, see John Blair et al., *Economic Concentration and World War II*, Report

of the Smaller War Plants Corporation to the U.S. Senate Special Committee to Study Problems of American Small Business (Washington, D.C.: GPO, 1946). The consolidation of resources and assets among the largest American corporations continued in the postwar period, as noted in Alfred D. Chandler Jr., *The Visible Hand*, 482–83. Chandler argues that modern business practice, characterized by "many distinct operating units and management by a hierarchy of salaried executives" (1), "had reached . . . maturity in the United States by the 1920s" (483), but the years after World War II "mark[ed] its triumph" (477).

18. Mills, *White Collar*, xviii; Dorothy Thompson, "Our Fear-Ridden Middle Classes," *Ladies' Home Journal* 67 (February 1951), 12. Thompson began the article with the story of a magazine editor who was laid off twice in five years before deciding to enter "the workingmen's end of the publication business" (11) as a printer, where he makes the same money and enjoys more job security and less stress. She considered the fate of democracy to be dependent upon improved conditions for the middle class; in words befitting the former wife of Sinclair Lewis, she warned her readers: "it can happen here" (12). See also C. Harley Grattan, "The Middle Class, Alas!" *Harper's* 202 (February 1951), 39–47. Mary McCarthy demonstrated just how muddled the conception of class in the United States had become: "Class barriers disappear or become porous; the factory worker is an economic aristocrat in comparison to the middle-class clerk" ("Mlle Gulliver en Amérique," *Reporter* [January 22, 1952], 36). A Hartford businessman assured *Business Week* in 1956, the year that nonmanual jobs first outnumbered manual jobs: "You talk about monotony on an assembly line, that's nothing compared with the stultifying effect of these big insurance offices" ("Aiming at White-Collar Target," *Business Week* [May 12, 1956], 170). The article was one of several that ran in *Business Week* and *Fortune* describing attempts to unionize white-collar workers whose salaries trailed those of skilled craftsmen and foremen. The difficulty, according to these journals, was that status as a white-collar worker seemed to depend upon not belonging to a union, and he or she was more likely to identify with management than with labor.

19. For Mills, alienation is a general trend in white-collar work that affects a range of different, and differently rewarded, occupations: lawyers, doctors, intellectuals, as well as executives, clerks, salespeople, and secretaries. As hard as it may be to swallow that executives and the office staff who do their bidding are victimized in quantitatively and qualitatively comparable ways, Riesman and Whyte asserted the *superior* suffering of the executive/managerial cadre. For Riesman, managers are the people rewarded for talent in their field with a promotion that "*forced [them] to leave it*" and who become "alienated from [their] craft" (129, 130). The targets of Whyte's censure and sympathy are not the clerks who "only work for The Organization," but those who "*belong* to it as well," the new "elite" from which will come "most of the first and second echelons of our leadership" (3). In a shrewd dissent, John Kenneth Galbraith called the tendency in sociology to conflate very different kinds of work "one of the oldest and most effective obfuscations in the field of social science" and noted the incursion of this view into the workplace: "The president of the corporation is pleased to think that his handsomely appointed office is the scene of the same kind of toil as the assembly line" (*The Affluent Society* [New York: Mentor, 1958], 263, 264).

20. Review, *Time* 66 (July 18, 1955), 102; review, *New York Times*, July 17, 1955, sec. 7, p. 18; Gerald Weales, review, *Commonweal* 62 (August 26, 1955), 525. The average reader to whom Weales refers is of *Collier's*, where the novel was serialized.

21. Gerald Weales, review, 526.

22. Quotation from book jacket.

23. Richard Ohmann, *Politics of Letters* (Middletown, Conn.: Wesleyan University Press, 1987), 82, 83. Ohmann focuses upon novels written between 1960 and 1975.

24. Although *housing project* has almost always signified multiple group housing, with a general implication of inferiority and often the taint of public funding, it also appears a few times as a synonym for *housing development* in popular postwar periodical and newspaper articles about the suburbs, when the writer was neutral (see Harry Henderson, "The Mass-Produced Suburbs," *Harper's* 207 {November 1953], 25–32, and [December 1953], 80–85), and also critical (see Sidonie M. Gruenberg, "Homogenized Children of the New Suburbia," *New York Times Magazine* [September 19, 1954], 14, 42, 47). *Housing project* is the term of choice to signify a housing development in *Man in Gray Flannel*, perhaps to endorse the view of the Raths' neighbor. Gruenberg at one point distinguishes between suburban development for the mass middle class and "publicly initiated housing projects" (14), as though to draw an unflattering comparison between private commercial development and government funded housing for the poor.

25. Robert Moses, "Build and Be Damned," *Atlantic Monthly* 186 (December 1950), 41.

26. William Zeckendorf, "Cities versus Suburbs," *Atlantic Monthly* 190 (July 1952), 24; William Laas, "The Suburbs Are Strangling the City," *New York Times Magazine* (June 18, 1950), 22.

27. Edgar Hanford, "Surprised in the Suburbs," *American Mercury* 81 (September 1955), 70.

28. J. P. Marquand, *Sincerely, Willis Wayde* (Boston: Little, Brown, 1955), 444.

29. Whyte, "The Transients," 113; Riesman, "The Suburban Dislocation," 134. Mergendahl also makes the fraternity comparison (*It's Only Temporary*, 122), which is distinguished from Keats's attack on the suburb as an unnatural matriarchy, with men present merely as "overnight lodgers or casual weekend guests" (60).

30. See Joel Pfister, "On Conceptualizing the Cultural History of Emotional and Psychological Life in America," in *Inventing the Psychological: Toward a Cultural History of Emotional Life in America*, ed. Pfister and Nancy Schnog (New Haven: Yale University Press, 1997), 17–59.

31. Betty Friedan, *The Feminine Mystique* (1963; rpt., New York: Dell, 1984), 15.

32. See Barbara Ehrenreich, *The Hearts of Men: American Dreams and the Flight from Commitment* (New York: Anchor, 1983). She claims that " 'conformity' became the code word for male discontent" (30). Shulman's comic novel *Rally Round the Flag, Boys!* does assume that discontent is prototypically, indeed, universally, suburban and male. The protagonist is introduced as "a typical commuter of Putnam's Landing, Connecticut, which is to say that he was between 35

and 40 in age, married, the father of three children, the owner of a house, a first mortgage, a second mortgage, a gray-flannel suit, a bald spot, and a vague feeling of discontent" (23). His discontent is stimulated by his wife's passionate attachment to the round of community activities, through her absolute contentment with suburban life. I have come across one fifties novel in which the male protagonist is genuinely different from the other suburbanites he loathes. But the hero of Karp's *Leave Me Alone* hates everyone; the difference is that "those he had detested in New York he had managed to avoid" (186), while he is thrown together with undesirables more often in the suburb. He presumes his superiority to everyone in the novel, including his wife, who likewise resisted New Yorkers but has found a home in the suburbs.

33. Jack Finney, *The Body-Snatchers* (1955; rpt., Boston: Gregg Press, 1976), 105. In *Class in Suburbia* (Englewood Cliffs, N.J.: Prentice-Hall, 1963), sociologist William M. Dobriner used the term "sacked village" for an established town that becomes a "reluctant suburb" when it is "invaded by suburbanites" (127), who are more economically mobile than the older residents.

34. Richard Yates, *Revolutionary Road* (1961; rpt., New York: Vintage, 1989), 20.

35. Kevin K. Gaines observes that the "emphasis on class differentiation as race progress" led many black elites to distinguish themselves "as bourgeois agents of civilization, from the presumably undeveloped black majority" (*Uplifting the Race: Black Leadership, Politics, and Culture in the Twentieth Century* [Chapel Hill: University of North Carolina Press, 1996], 2). In "Harlem on Our Minds," *Critical Inquiry* 24 (Autumn 1997), Henry Louis Gates Jr. argues that "[t]he black middle class defines itself by consumption" (6) and against the history of racism, and calls for an African American literature that is more sensitive to the dynamics of class: "one is forced to wonder where *this* generation's Bigger Thomas is" (12).

36. Chester Himes, *If He Hollers Let Him Go* (1945; rpt., New York: Thunder's Mouth Press, 1986), 49.

37. The quest for nonconformity among the white middle class had a racial component as well. In "The White Negro" (1957) Norman Mailer famously suggested that black men were intrinsically nonconformist and thus an attractive and liberating remedy for the boredom of being a white male. Andrew Hoberek argues that the fascination of white middle-class men with black men did not merely signify either a crisis of masculinity, resistance to the organization's seeming stranglehold on individuality, or attraction to the racial other. More importantly, it masked the organization man's fear of a postwar future as proletarianized as the black worker's: "Behind the white (-collar) desire to become black is the fear that one already *is*" ("Race Man, Organization Man, *Invisible Man*," *Modern Language Quarterly* 59 [March 1998], 116). Thus the white middle class's sense of itself is not threatened by the existence of a black middle class but by a homogenized and universal working-class blackness that seems, fantastically, to be in a position analogous to it.

38. Paul Goodman, review of *On the Road*, rpt. in *Growing Up Absurd* (New York: Vintage, 1960), 281. The mainstream co-optation of a nonconformist resistance to mass society reached an apotheosis in the 1960s, according to Thomas

Frank. In *The Conquest of Cool* (Chicago: University of Chicago Press, 1997), he describes the rise of hip marketing strategies that mirrored, rather than rejected, the decade's countercultural tendencies, as Madison Avenue wooed all those alienated, gray-flannel consumers.

39. Irving Howe, "Mass Society and Postmodern Fiction," in *Decline of the New* (New York: Harcourt, 1970), 205. Subsequent scholarship on the fifties has sought to restore the context in which the Beat philosophy could be understood as a meaningful, if not wholly unproblematic, attack on mainstream American culture. See Andrew Ross, *No Respect: Intellectuals and Popular Culture* (New York: Routledge, 1989); and Thomas Schaub, *American Fiction in the Cold War* (Madison: University of Wisconsin Press, 1991).

40. See Elizabeth Long, *The American Dream and the Popular Novel* (Boston: Routledge and Kegan Paul, 1985), 82–88. Long's account is echoed in Tyler May, *Homeward Bound*; and David Halberstam, *The Fifties* (New York: Villard Books, 1993). Long's analysis of popular fiction after World War II demonstrates a shift from the old-fashioned, entrepreneurial hero, who conquered best-seller lists as the nation sought a return to normalcy in the midforties, to a "corporate-suburban" (82) hero that tried to integrate his activities in the business world with the requirements of home and family. *Man in Gray Flannel* is the only novel that she examines in detail (Long is trained as a sociologist rather than as a literary critic), because it exemplifies the later trend she describes.

41. Shirley Harrison, *Public Relations: An Introduction* (London: Routledge, 1995), 12. See also Stuart Ewen, *PR! A Social History of Spin* (New York: Basic, 1996); and Roland Marchand, *Creating the Corporate Soul: The Rise of Public Relations and Corporate Imagery in Big Business* (Berkeley and Los Angeles: University of California Press, 1998). According to Marchand, American corporations took particular pride in "the healthy recuperation of their corporate images" (358) during World War II, when wartime service became a staple of national advertising, and public opinion polls revealed that national corporations were viewed quite favorably by the public, an advantage that American business eagerly pressed into the postwar period.

42. Geoffrey Gorer, *The Americans: A Study in National Character* (1948; rpt., London: Cresset Press, 1955), 104, 105.

43. Dale Carnegie, *How to Win Friends and Influence People* (1936; rpt., New York: Pocket Books, 1948), 45. Carnegie argued that only a lifetime of rigorous self-policing could prevent people from neglecting to consider the perspective of other people. He rejected the idea that he advocated techniques in manipulating others on the grounds that simple manipulation would fail. His "psychology" could not be applied "mechanically": some people "will try to boost the other man's ego, not through genuine, real appreciation, but through flattery and insincerity. And their technique won't work" (212). If one has trained oneself to be genuinely interested in other people, then one's interest is sincere.

44. Like the Chicago school sociologists, Mills drew upon the insights of German sociologist Georg Simmel, who theorized the effect of transient contacts and the replacement of personal relations with pecuniary relations on the modern metropolitan psyche in "The Metropolis and Mental Life." Mills similarly argued that face-to-face business contacts maintain the illusion of personal relationships

in the white-collar world; in reality, physical proximity masks social and psychological distance. By turning his analysis toward the new middle classes in particular, Mills gives Simmel's reflections on the modern psyche a class inflection that they originally lacked.

45. Arthur Heiserman and James E. Miller Jr., "J. D. Salinger: Some Crazy Cliff," in *Salinger's "Catcher in the Rye": Clamor vs. Criticism*, ed. Harold P. Simonson and Philip E. Hager (Boston: D. C. Heath, 1963), 76. The early criticism, which has been extensively analyzed by Carol and Richard Ohmann, often compares Holden to Huckleberry Finn, celebrating their shared commitment to "the right of the nonconformist to assert his nonconformity" (Charles Kaplan, "Holden and Huck: The Odysseys of Youth," in *If You Really Want to Know: A "Catcher" Casebook*, ed. Malcolm S. Marsden [Chicago: Scott, Foresman, 1963], 132). See Ohmann and Ohmann, "Reviewers, Critics, and *The Catcher in the Rye*," *Critical Inquiry* 3 (Fall 1976), 15–37.

46. According to Leerom Medavoi, the word *phony* is Holden's and "the novel's master signifier for critique," of commodity culture in general, for Medavoi, and of class hierarchy and privilege, for the Ohmanns (Medavoi, "Democracy, Capitalism, and American Literature: The Cold War Construction of J. D. Salinger's Paperback Hero," in Foreman, *The Other Fifties*, 277). Medavoi makes a powerful case that the disenchanted youth in *Catcher* opens up a safe space for the representation and valorization of the immature, naive liberal, whose postwar demise Schaub traces in *American Fiction of the Cold War*. Medavoi offers his analysis of Holden's resistance to hierarchy, exchange, commodities, and capitalism as a "progressive reading" (278) of the novel. But surely, as social critique, a novel about a rich kid spending money with both hands as he complains about all the phonies sounds suspiciously complacent. *Catcher* is as dishonest in its fashion as *Man in Gray Flannel*; Tom at least entertains the idea of his own phoniness.

47. The words *honesty* and *sincerity*, which appear in the novel with incredible frequency, often appear to be used interchangeably but do not share precisely the same connotations. *Sincerity* suggests a slight remove from honesty, the recognition or representation, and possibly the exploitation (Hopkins might believe in mental health *and* in public relations) of one's honest beliefs or commitments and is thus the term more closely identified with public relations in the novel. Sincerity is directed outward, and while one can be honest with one's self, it makes no sense to say that one is sincere with one's self. Tom's concerns about his relation to the corporation are always cast in terms of honesty, which works to redeem public relations and the corporation. Note even here that Tom is honest, while Hopkins is only sincere. For an account of American naturalist literature and the tension between sincerity and "cynical commercialism" that *Man in Gray Flannel* specifically erodes, see Christopher P. Wilson, "American Literary Naturalism and the Problem of Sincerity," *American Literature* 54 (December 1982), 511–27.

48. See, for example, the largely skeptical essays in *Mass Culture: The Popular Arts in America*, ed. Bernard Rosenberg and David Manning White (Glencoe, Ill.: Free Press, 1957); and "The Culture Industry: Enlightenment as Mass Deception," in Max Horkheimer and Theodor W. Adorno, *The Dialectic of Enlightenment*, trans. John Cumming (New York: Continuum, 1988).

EPILOGUE
SAME AS IT EVER WAS (MORE OR LESS)

1. The census data are discussed in Jackson, *Crabgrass Frontier*, and Jackson, "America's Rush to Suburbia," op-ed, *New York Times*, June 9, 1996, sec. 1, p. 15. In 1999, 240 antisprawl initiatives appeared on ballots nationwide. See Richard Lacayo, "The Brawl over Sprawl," *Time* 153 (March 22, 1999), 44–48. The term *postmodern suburb* has been proposed to describe the functional differences between more traditional residential suburbs and contemporary postindustrial suburbs, where most new nonresidential construction and job opportunities are located. See William Sharpe and Leonard Wallock, "Contextualizing Suburbia," *American Quarterly* 46 (March 1994), 55–61. See also Brian Jarvis, *Postmodern Cartographies* (New York: St. Martin's Press, 1998); and Fishman, *Bourgeois Utopias*, chap. 7. Joel Garreau speaks of the new "Edge City," which has "more jobs than bedrooms," with an enthusiasm that would make Babbitt blush (*Edge City*, 7). Critics of suburban sprawl attack its inefficiency and environmental costs as well as its ugliness. See Philip Langdon, *A Better Place to Live: Reshaping the American Suburb* (Amherst: University of Massachusetts Press, 1994); James Kunstler, *The Geography of Nowhere: The Rise and Fall of America's Man-Made Landscape* (New York: Simon and Schuster, 1993); and Andres Duany, Elizabeth Plater-Zyberk, and Jeff Speck, *Suburban Nation: The Rise of Sprawl and the Decline of the American Dream* (New York: North Point Press, 2000).

2. The influence of suburbanization is felt not only by those who live in suburbs but also by those who have been excluded for economic reasons or because of discrimination. Suburban residents "are the most heavily subsidized of our citizens," and much of the cost of these subsidies is borne by the urban poor, who receive no tax breaks or only paltry deductions as renters, and who lose valuable tax revenues when higher-income families leave the city for the suburbs (Jackson, foreword, *Suburbia Re-examined*, ed. Barbara M. Kelly [Westport, Conn.: Greenwood Press, 1989], xil). Massey and Denton argue in *American Apartheid* that segregation is the most important "structural factor" in "the perpetuation of black poverty in the U.S." (9). While segregation is not merely an urban/suburban problem, the authors note that high rates of black suburbanization are deceiving because much of it is accounted for by poor, declining, largely black-inhabited cities just outside of central northern cities and by the South, where blacks have long been excluded from central cities.

3. Frederick Barthelme, *Two against One* (New York: Weidenfeld and Nicolson, 1988); Joyce Carol Oates, *Expensive People* (1968; rpt., New York: Book-of-the-Month Club, 1992). See also Rick Moody, *Garden State* (1992; rpt., Boston: Little, Brown, 1997); Moody, *The Ice Storm* (New York: Warner, 1995); and Moody, *Purple America* (Boston: Little, Brown, 1997).

4. Readers of Ford, Moody, and Gates paperbacks are treated to glowing excerpts of reviews before they reach the title page. Updike's *Rabbit Is Rich* (1981) and *Rabbit at Rest* (1990) and Ford's *Independence Day* (1995) won Pulitzers, while Gates's first novel, *Jernigan* (1991), was nominated. *Expensive People* was a finalist for the National Book Award, as was *Rabbit at Rest*.

5. Richard Locke, review of *Couples* and *Rabbit Redux*, *New York Times Book Review*, November 14, 1971, 2.

6. Janet Burroway, review of *Purple America*, *New York Times Book Review*, April 27, 1997, 7; Gary Williams, review of *Purple America*, *Rocky Mountain News*, cited in *Purple America*. See also James Kaplan, *Two Guys from Verona* (New York: Grove, 1998); and David Gates, *Preston Falls* (New York: Vintage, 1998).

7. John Updike, *Rabbit, Run* (1960; rpt., New York: Fawcett Crest, 1991), 20.

8. Updike, *Rabbit Redux* (New York: Knopf, 1971), 223.

9. Updike, *Rabbit at Rest* (New York: Knopf, 1990), 32, 173.

10. Updike, *Rabbit Is Rich* (1981; rpt., New York: Ballantine, 1996), 339.

11. Kenneth Crawford, "Middle-Class Revolt," *Newsweek* 72 (November 18, 1968), 52. See also "The Forgotten?" *Nation* 207 (September 23, 1968), 259–60.

12. See, for example, "Squeeze on America's Middle Class," *U.S. News and World Report* 77 (October 14, 1974), 42–44; and "The Squeeze on the Middle Class," *Business Week* (March 10, 1975), 52–60.

13. Barbara Ehrenreich, "Is the Middle Class Doomed?" *New York Times Magazine* (September 7, 1986), 44. See also Robert Kuttner, "The Declining Middle," *Atlantic Monthly* 252 (July 1983), 60–64; George J. Church, "Are You Better Off?" *Time* 132 (October 10, 1988), 28–30; Mark Levinson, "Living on the Edge," *Newsweek* 118 (November 4, 1991), 22–25; Jack Beatty, "Who Speaks for the Middle Class?" *Atlantic Monthly* 273 (May 1994), 65–66; Jolie Solomon, "Are You Anxious? You're Not Alone," *Newsweek* 125 (January 30, 1995), 42; John Cassidy, "Who Killed the Middle Class?" *New Yorker* 71 (October 16, 1995), 113–14; and Andrew Hacker, "Meet the Median Family," *Time* 147 (January 29, 1996), 41–43.

14. See, for example, Katherine S. Newman, *Declining Fortunes: The Withering of the American Dream* (New York: Basic, 1993); and Wallace C. Peterson, *Silent Depression: The Fate of the American Dream* (New York: Norton, 1994).

15. In *Manhood in America: A Cultural History* (New York: Free Press, 1996), Michael S. Kimmel notes the erosion of many of "the structural foundations of traditional [American] manhood" (298) since the 1970s: economic independence, national autonomy, social and geographical mobility, and dominance within the family. Perceiving himself victimized on all counts, Benjamin Hood exemplifies Kimmel's theory that manhood "is less about the drive for domination and more about the fear of others dominating us" (6).

16. David Gates, *Jernigan* (New York: Vintage, 1992), 29.

17. Daniel Patrick Moynihan, *The Negro Family: The Case for National Action* (1965); rpt. in *The Moynihan Report and the Politics of Controversy*, ed. Lee Rainwater and William L. Yancey (Cambridge: MIT Press, 1967), 76.

18. William Ryan, "Savage Discovery: The Moynihan Report," *Nation* 201 (November 22, 1965), 382. Ryan's point was not that the American family was in fact crumbling, but rather that the report used statistics in misleading and irresponsible ways. He objected above all to its insistence that "the weaknesses and defects of the Negro" (380) accounted for inequality between the races. In "Negro Family: Reflections on the Moynihan Report," *Commonweal* 83 (October 15, 1965), Herbert J. Gans became the first sociologist to suggest that what looked

like family instability was really "the most positive adaptations to the economic conditions which negroes must endure" (49). See also the accounts of the controversy in Rainwater and Yancey, *Moynihan Report.*

19. Peter Wyden, "Suburbia's Coddled Kids," *Saturday Evening Post* 233 (October 8, 1960), 44; John Keats, "Compulsive Suburbia," *Atlantic Monthly* 205 (April 1960), 47.

20. Richard E. Gordon, Katherine K. Gordon, and Max Gunther, *The Split-Level Trap* (New York: Bernard Geis, 1960), 7.

21. Leo Tolstoy, *Anna Karenina*, trans. Constance Garnett (1877; rpt., New York: Modern Library, 1993), 3.

22. John Updike, *Picked-Up Pieces* (New York: Knopf, 1975), 504. These remarks are made with reference to the putative contentment of Piet Hanema at the end of *Couples* (New York: Knopf, 1968). Piet has married his mistress, left Tarbox, and gone to work as a federal construction inspector. But the final sentence— "The Hanemas live in Lexington, where, gradually, among people like themselves, they have been accepted, as another couple" (458)—suggests circularity rather than progress, and the endurance of "the couple" as the primary social unit does not bode well for marital or family satisfaction.

23. Philip Roth, *Goodbye, Columbus* (1959; rpt., Boston: Houghton Mifflin, 1989), 94.

24. Gloria Naylor, *Linden Hills* (New York: Penguin, 1985), back cover.

25. Richard Ford, *The Sportswriter* (1986; rpt., New York: Vintage, 1995), 3. See also Ford, *Independence Day* (New York: Vintage, 1996).

26. Evan McKenzie, *Privatopia: Homeowner Associations and the Rise of Residential Private Government* (New Haven: Yale University Press, 1994), 14. Edward J. Blakely and Mary Gail Snyder estimate that in 1997 there were as many as 20,000 gated communities with over three million units, and their popularity is growing in all regions and price ranges. See *Fortress America* (Washington, D.C.: Brookings Institution, 1997). Found in urban as well as suburban areas, they "enhance and harden the suburbanness of the suburbs, and they attempt to suburbanize the city" (11).

INDEX

Abrahamson, Julia, 217n.55
Addams, Jane, 29–30
Agnew, Jean-Christophe, 54
Algren, Nelson, 103, 135, 210n.10
alienation. *See* homelessness
Allen, Frederick, 135, 137, 192n.11
Anderson, Douglas, 178n.19
Anderson, Sherwood, 64, 193n.14
apartment buildings, 24–25, 27–28, 35, 184n.15, 185n.18, 195n.29; compared to tenements, 25–26, 27, 185n.22
Appadurai, Arjun, 198n.46
architecture: Colonial, 44, 134, 191n.2; critiques of middle-class domestic, 80–82; and mass production, 80, 134, 204n.14; Spanish, 200–201n.2
Arts and Crafts movement, 29, 32, 186–87n.38

Babbitt (Lewis): community of consumption in, 61–64, 198n.45; desire for home in, 47, 52, 59–60, 62–63, 66; discontent in, 16, 46–48, 52–53, 57–60, 67–68, 75, 146, 196n.36; homelessness in, 4–5, 46–47, 52, 56–57, 60, 62, 66, 68, 70, 76, 83; male affect in, 47, 59–60, 63; middle-class aesthetics in, 52, 54–55, 56; political content of, 46, 47, 66–67, 70; and the Rabbit novels, 161–62; and race, 17–18, 45, 59–60, 74–75; and self-consciousness, 67, 69–70; self-pity in, 48, 58, 67–68, 138; in sociology, 15, 47, 48, 65, 136, 193n.14; standardization in, 45–46, 54–57, 60–63, 165–66; suburb in, 6, 13, 18, 44–47, 56–57, 59, 61–62, 67–70, 74–75, 202n.4; white-collar work in, 47, 53, 137; white middle-class identity in, 7, 45–48, 57–58, 67–68, 71, 138
bachelors, 10, 178n.19
Baker, Houston A., Jr., 101, 210n.7, 211n.15, 212n.21
Baldwin, James, 130, 131
Baltimore, Md., 30, 35–36

Banta, Martha, 64, 79, 203n.9
Barthelme, Frederick, 4, 14, 160; *Natural Selection*, 7, 167; *Two against One*, 160
Baudrillard, Jean, 198n.45
Bauer, Catherine, 80
Baym, Nina, 9, 11, 180n.25
Beat generation, 150
Bederman, Gail, 41, 185n. 18, 186n.28
Benjamin, Walter, 84
Berlant, Lauren, 207–8n.58, 209n.2
"Better Homes for America" campaign, 134, 186n.28
Bhabha, Homi, 19
Bingham, Alfred, 71
black middle class: in Chicago, 105–6, 111–13, 131–32; compared to black working class, 149, 211n.17, 224n.35; compared to white middle class, 18, 72–73, 111–12, 149, 169; as evidence of racial heterogeneity, 104–5, 200n.72; homelessness of, 169; immobility of, 111–13, 214n.30; in *Kingsblood Royal*, 18, 72–73; spiritual and cultural deficiencies of, 18, 72–73, 149, 169
Blake, Casey, 49
Blakely, Edward J., and Mary Gail Snyder, 229n.26
Bledstein, Burton J., 175n.9
Blumin, Stuart, 175n.9
Bone, Robert, 211n.14
Boorstin, Daniel, 61
Boris, Eileen, 187n.38
Brantlinger, Patrick, 182–83n.3
Bremer, Sidney, 104, 179n.21
Breward, Christopher, 181n.28
Brodhead, Richard, 173n.2
Brooks, Van Wyck, 17, 48–49
Brown, Gillian, 7, 9, 88, 178n.19, 179n.24
Buchanan v. Warley, 36, 188–89n.51, 189n.62
Bunner, Henry Cuyler, *The Suburban Sage*, 28–29
Burgess, Ernest W., 109–12, 113, 118, 120, 212n.26, 213n.29. *See also* Chicago school of sociology